MARY MAGDALENE
AND MANY OTHERS

Carla Ricci

MARY MAGDALENE AND MANY OTHERS

Women who followed Jesus

Translated from the Italian by
Paul Burns

BURNS & OATES

First published in this translation 1994
BURNS & OATES,
Wellwood, North Farm Road,
Tunbridge Wells, Kent TN2 3DR

Published in the United States of America by
Fortress Press, Minneapolis, MN

Originally published in Italy 1991 by
M. D'Auria Editore, Naples
under the title *Maria di Magdala e le molte altre:
Donne sul cammino di Gesù*

Original edition © copyright 1991 M. D'Auria Editore
This translation © copyright 1994 Burns & Oates/Search Press Limited

ISBN 0 86012 208 5

Scripture quotations are from the *New Revised Standard Version Bible*,
copyright 1989, Division of Christian Education of the National Council
of Churches in the United States of America, with some variants
required by the author.

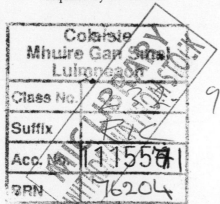
Composition by Genesis Typesetting, Laser Quay, Rochester, Kent
Printed and bound in Great Britain by
Biddles Ltd, Guildford and King's Lynn

"Mary!" ...
"Master!" ...
(John 20:16)

ABBREVIATIONS

AGSU	Arbeiten zur Geschichte des Spätjudentums und Urchristentums
ANRW	Aufsteig und Niedergang der Römischer Welt
BBIBQ	Bible Bashyam: An Indian Biblical Quarterly
BFchTh	Beiträge zur Förderung chr. Theologie
Bib	Biblica
BThB	Biblical Theology Bulletin
BToday	The Bible Today
BZ	Biblische Zeitschrift
ComLtg	Communautés et Liturgies
CSCO	Corpus Scriptorum Christianorum Orientalium
CSEL	Corpus Scriptorum Ecclesiasticorum Latinorum
DCBNT	Dizionario dei Concetti Biblici del Nuovo Testamento
DSp	Dictionnaire de Spiritualité
EC	Enciclopedia Cattolica
En Bi	Enciclopedia della Bibbia
En Ju	Enciclopedia Judaica
ESR	Encyclopédie des sciences religieuses
EvTh	Evangelische Theologie
GCB	Grande Commentario Biblico
GCS	Die Griechischen Christlichen Schriftsteller
GLNT	Grande Lessico del Nuovo Testamento
JB	Jerusalem Bible
JBC	Jerome Biblical Commentary
MO	Missione Oggi
NEB	New English Bible
New Test. Stud.	New Testament Studies
NRSV	New Revised Standard Version Bible
ParVi	Parole di Vita
PL	Patrologia Latina
RaTe	Rassegna di Teologia
RE	Real-Encyclopädie der classichen Altertumswissenschaft
RiBi	Rivista Biblica
RThL	Revue théologique de Louvain
RTM	Rivista di teologia morale
TDNT	Theological Dictionary of the New Testament
ThHandkAT	Theologisches Handwörterbuch zum Alten Testament
TWNT	Theologisches Wörterbuch zum Neuen Testament
Ve Chr	Vetera Christianorum
ZKTh	Zeitschrift für Katholische Theologie
ZNW	Zeitschrift für die Neuetestamentliche Wissenschaft
ZThK	Zeitschrift für Theologie und Kirche

CONTENTS

INTRODUCTION

It is a late September afternoon. The rays of the sun are still catching the tops of the trees. The leaves fluttering in a light breeze throw back diminishing shades of colour. Here I am with the typescript of this book in my hand, trying to work out what I am thinking. I have so long been aware of a host of deep inner feelings, but it is not easy to bring them clearly to the surface of consciousness. It involves a long, steady, silent wait, weighed down with fatigue, nourished by patience. I intended to write this introductory note in the morning, but now I know that only at this stage of the day, when I feel somehow in sympathy with my surroundings, will I be able to express in words the unease I feel when someone who knows about the book asks if it is finished. My instinct is No, it is not *finished*. Perhaps I will be able to say that it is published, but not that it is *finished*. And yet unless I find a way to accept *this end*, it will not be published either. The course of life is also the course of death. A noise makes me raise my head toward the sky, which is now tinged by the sunset: a flock of birds, migrating to warmer lands, crosses the blue vault; their wings beat in gentle harmony as they depart.

I too must *depart, let go, die* . . . and find a way to do so in harmony, with a flutter of light wings. The leaves letting go of the branches find it, so does the day as the light gently fades. Yes, perhaps this is the right moment, at the end of the day and the end of summer. Autumn is a time for harvesting fruits, and also a time for sowing. It is time for me, too, to do what my father and mother did; all through their lives they entrusted seeds to the ground at this season. The time has also come for me somehow to live the words of the gospel: "unless a grain of wheat dies . . ." (John 12:24), and entrust myself to this death-life.

All these reactions in an attempt to communicate what I am feeling may seem excessive, but the process of this research has been with me for a long time: ten years, during which the interaction between life and study has branched out and become interwoven with a deep reality, ever broadening and becoming more articulate.

The inner need of someone looking for her own deep identity as a woman provided the motivation that set this process in motion. The search for a way into the demands of those who, as women, were originally called to a way of holding to a deeper and fuller sense of life, led me to seek to discover if Jesus' message of liberation had a *word* to say to me as a woman.

This work has been and still is for me a *living* study, soaked in quest, fatigue, joy, rage, even suffering, and tears.

It is the quest for a deep authenticity as a woman that can respond to the good news.

It is the fatigue of trying to seek out and reach those voices, of digging in history, in literature, in the documents and also the conditioned thought of men, of all men and all women, including my own.

It is the fatigue of patiently acquiring working tools and methods to make this quest possible.

It is the minor fatigue of forcing myself to consult indexes, to do bibliographic research, to become acquainted with other languages.

It is the fatigue of trying to free myself from acquired structures and commonplaces so as to risk taking my own way and trying to offer my own original contribution.

Then it is the joy of experiencing how, time after time, if you risk accepting the waiting that is full of silence but also of hidden ferment, when faced with a text or problem, suddenly the obscure word gives up its meaning, the apparently casual sequence shows a logic and the unsolvable problem finds a place in an interpretative hypothesis.[1]

---

[1] On the subject of acquiring the capacity to observe, R. Assagioli, in his *The Act of Will* (New York: Viking, 1973), on pages 25–6 recounts an interesting anecdote, which he says "is told by Ramacharaka in his book *Raja Yoga*. He speaks of the famous naturalist Agassiz and his method of training pupils:

"The tale runs that a new student presented himself to Agassiz one day asking to be set to work. The naturalist took a fish from a jar in which it had been preserved, and laying it before the young student, bade him observe it carefully, and be ready to report on what he had observed

So it seems possible to apply the Gospel words: "Ask, and it will be given to you; search, and you will find; knock and the door will be opened to you" (Luke 11:10), to the reality of study and research, with their need for application and patience.

Then it is the joy of meeting other women at a deep level, of experiences of communicating and *sisterhood*.

And it is the pleasant rage felt when, having long researched and worked out a theory, you find it more or less whole in an author not previously consulted.

---

about the fish. The student was then left alone with the fish. There was nothing especially interesting about that fish – it was like many other fishes that he had seen before. he noticed that it had fins and scales, and a mouth and eyes, yes, and a tail. In a half-hour he felt certain that he had observed all about the fish that there was to be perviced. But the naturalist remained away.

"The time rolled on, and the youth, having nothing else to do, began to grow restless and weary. He started to hunt up the teacher, but he failed to find him, and so had to return and gaze again at that wearisome fish. Several hours had passed, and he knew but little more about the fish than he did in the first place.

"He went out to lunch, and when he returned it was still a case of watching the fish. He felt disgusted and discouraged, and wished he had never come to Agassiz, who, it seemed, was a stupid old man after all – one way behind the times. Then, in order to kill time, he began to count the scales. This completed, he counted the spines of the fins. Then he began to draw a picture of the fish. In drawing the picture he noticed that the fish had no eyelids. He thus made the discovery that as his teacher had expressed it often, in lectures, 'a pencil is the best of eyes.' Shortly after the teacher returned, and after ascertaining what the youth had obesrved, he left rather disappointed, telling the boy to keep on looking and maybe he would see something.

"This put the boy on his mettle, and he began to work with his pencil, putting down little details that had escaped him before, but which now seemed very plain to him. He began to catch the secret of observation. Little by little he brought to light new objects of interest about the fish. But this did not suffice his teacher, who kept him at work on the same fish for three whole days. At the end of that time the student really knew something about the fish, and, better than all, had acquired the 'knack' and habit of careful observation and perception in detail.

"Years after, the student, then attained to eminence, is reported as saying: 'That was the best zoological lesson I ever had – a lesson whose influence has extended to the details of every subsequent study; a legacy that the professor left to me, as he left to many others, of inestimable value, which we could not buy, and with which we cannot part.'"

It is suffering as a sharing in the oppression and violence experienced by those women whose story is being told.

It is the difficulty of *cutting out* what you have not been able to consult, come to terms with, develop, and have to *leave aside*, even if perhaps you intend to come back to it.

The tears are those that blurred my sight one evening in October 1986, as I was coming out of the Duomo of Milan. I was helping Joan Morris,[2] who walked with great difficulty; we were going down the steps and felt the emotions and distress caused by a refusal: we had been forbidden to say a bidding prayer in three languages during a Mass.[3]

This book, then, is the destination at the end of a journey of research undertaken in the inescapable cause of trying to capture the dialogue and relationship that Jesus had with women.[4]

In the analysis I made of the Gospels to pick out the most significant texts for my purpose, the verses Luke 8:1–3, relating the presence of women close to Jesus in his journeying, struck me as light shining through a gash in the great veil drawn over the reality of women disciples: "Now after this he made his way through towns and villages preaching, and proclaiming the Good News of the kingdom of God. With him went the Twelve, as well as certain

---

[2] Joan Morris was then vice-president of the English section of St Joan's International Alliance.

[3] The prayer consisted of a simple announcement of the presence at that Mass of women from St Joan's International Alliance, an association dedicated to achieving equality for women in society and in the church, and a prayer for their week's assembly.

[4] It might be useful to pick out some stages along this journey. My desire to undertake this line of research was focussed in 1980, when I decided to change the course of my university studies and decide on a subject for a thesis. Re-reading the four Gospels and Acts, and making a file showing the presence of women or references to them, led me to Luke's Gospel as it contains, by a wide margin, the greatest number of references to their presence. Analysis of the third Gospel led me to pick out the passage 8:1–3, dealing with the presence of women close to Jesus in his itinerant activity, a particularly valuable text that despite its brevity allows us entry, through such a seemingly narrow passage, to the vast subject of Jesus's relationship with women. In the course of the academic year 1982–3, in a seminar led by Prof. Mauro Pesce, whose presence was extremely rewarding for me in those years, I produced a first (unpublished) text with the title "Women who followed Jesus according to Luke 8:1–3".

women who had been cured of evil spirits and ailments: Mary surnamed the Magdalene, from whom seven demons had gone out, Joanna the wife of Herod's steward Chuza, Susanna, and several others who provided for him out of their own resources." This short text allowed me to open a largely closed, hidden dimension. This almost laconic bit of chronicling provided an immensely valuable key for opening the door on the reality of Jesus's dialogue with women. So it was to this text from Luke's Gospel that I devoted my doctoral thesis: *Le donne al seguito di Gesù in Lc. 8:1–3*.[5]

The next step in this specific area of research was to find texts in the other Gospels dealing with the women who followed Jesus. This wider perspective opened new avenues and, without straying from the original objective, brought possible comparisons, new questions, fresh methodological requirements, new problems ... and so new hypotheses, new attempts at answers and new reading keys with which to verify, re-elaborate and expand the research already undertaken.

The book that has grown out of this sets out first a hypothesis that, on the methodological level of exegetic analysis, seeks to bring out new instruments rendered necessary by making new demands of the texts. Discovering the silence concerning the women who can be found in the Gospels, and particularly the deep shadow in which the women disciples who accompanied Jesus lie hidden, led me to attempt *an exegesis of this silence*.

An initial overall view of the biblical texts relating to the women who followed Jesus leads me, through the dynamics of comparing the Synoptics, to put forward the hypothesis that the pericope Luke 8:1–3 is a special sign put on the road, a sign that I here try to decipher and to draw out from the surrounding silence. Then, taking a later form of the silence regarding women – that of commentary on and study of the texts concerning them – and finding, through bibliographical research, Luke 8:1–3 to be a text *forgotten by exegesis*, I try to build up an overall view of the existing literature on the subject and to draw out its basic tendencies.

My study of Luke 8:1–3 began by identifying the thematic

---

[5] Doctoral thesis in the History of Christianity, after an honours course in Philosophy, examined by Prof. Mauro Pesce of the University of Bologna, acandemic year 1985–6.

elements of each of the three verses in order then to correlate these elements with the immediate and the broader context of the text.

My research, limited to the time of Jesus's activity in Galilee (Luke 4:14–9:50), then concentrated on the two main subjects that emerged: the element of the *group* accompanying Jesus and that of the *women*. Analyzing the latter, then any general mention of Luke's Gospel and women, and any brief references to comparison between the Synoptics and John on this point, produced a scheme including all the women, or references to them, present at the time described in the accounts of Jesus' Galilean activity.

This thematic type of approach is followed by an analysis of the literary structure of Luke, taking 8:1–3 as a *revealing trace*. I then approach the specific context of the pericope, examining the women and the expressions used in relation to them. My attention then focuses on an overall view of Gospel texts dealing with the women who followed Jesus, and by comparing the Synoptics tries to give a face and an identity to the "many" women disciples.

The need to find out as much as possible about the conditions of women in Palestine at that time, in order to build a historical and cultural backgound against which to situate Jesus' attitude, has produced references, spread throughout the text, to juridical-normative and social conditions. I did not want to devote a separate chapter to a description of these, since there is adequate literature on the subject, and because it seemed more convincing to make short references to them, or to insert an *excursus*, in the course of developing an analysis and in the context of an argument.

The interest that the figure of Mary Magdalene aroused in me, as the first woman of the travelling group to have had a special relationship and dialogue with Jesus, and the attention I consequently paid to her in subsequent research, led me to wonder if I should devote a book to her alone. My decision to examine all the women together stems from the consideration that the first priority was to show the context of the group of women in a dynamic of connection and exchange that, shifting from Mary Magdalene to the other women disciples and back again, sheds light on both her and them. More generally, by choosing to research texts *forgotten by exegesis*, by trying new methods of recovering a specific memory concerning women for exegesis, another memory was suddenly and unavoidably forced on my attention. Realizing the way commentary had forgotten texts relating to women led me to discover that, where it was impossible to hide the importance and significance that one woman, Mary Magdalene, had in Jesus' earthly and post-Easter life, another phenomenon came into play: *exegetical distortion*, making Mary Magdalene into a prostitute, even though this could not be deduced from the Gospel texts. The general conclusion to be drawn from this shows the need for women (but not just women) to re-read the history of exegesis with a critical eye; the particular need in the case of Mary Magdalene – a specific choice in which I felt deeply involved – is to give back a face and a voice to the woman who was the first person to whom the Risen Christ appeared, to whom he turned with the words: "Go and find the brothers, and tell them . . ." (John 20:17), sending her to bring the news of the resurrection to the apostles.

The desire to rediscover in Mary Magdalene the woman to whom the Gospel message was entrusted also led me to look for a different tradition in her iconography, which generally shows her as a repentant sinner. I experienced a particularly intense moment in this quest when in the cathedral of Marseilles, the Vieille Major, I discovered a bas-relief showing Mary Magdalene preaching the gospel.[6]

These introductory notes need to be brought to a close, even if there is no way of *completing* them, of *communicating everything*.

Beyond the immediate and real reference point provided by images showing Mary Magdalene preaching, they awaken suggestive echoes in me as a woman. A woman expresses the *word*. Where the word has been denied to women in various ways in the texts and in exegesis, she takes the responsibility of claiming it back for herself and uttering it. Expressing her own word as a woman, a word that is also *other* within the man-woman reality, is a restitution that women make truly for themselves, but also to men in a creative dialectic in which *difference* is taken on consciously as an enrichment and in which women seek to experience and grasp their own *otherness* and to communicate it.

> "These things he said in words.
> But much in his heart remained unsaid.
> For he himself could not speak his deeper secret."
> – Kahlil Gibran, *The Prophet* (London: Penguin, 1992, p. 8).

---

[6] Reproduced on p.18.

MARY MAGDALENE
AND MANY OTHERS

MARY MAGDALENE PREACHING THE GOSPEL TO THE PRINCES OF MARSEILLE
(*Bas relief in cathedral of Vieille Major, Marseille. Photo sent by B. Laluque at my request after I personally identified the bas relief (see pp. 15 and 151–4)*

Chapter 1

HYPOTHESIS FOR AN EXEGESIS OF THE SILENCE

Silence on the Subject of Women

The first major problem encountered on undertaking research into the presence of women accompanying Jesus on his itinerant preaching ministry is the remarkable scarcity of sources from which to obtain information. This, of course, is a problem common to many areas of research. But if, in general, sources are a primary problem for the researcher, historian or exegete, it has to be said that there are degrees in the size of the problem. The difficulty varies in relation to the content, the object of one's research. If the subject one wishes to investigate today was also considered important in the past and so aroused interest among earlier historians or writers, the sources available will be more numerous than in the case of subjects previously seen as being of little or no importance.

This explains why, in general, it is so difficult to find sources concerned with women and their condition. This was a marginal, minor subject, apt to arouse little interest in historians, *literati*, philosophers, men in short, who not only dominated as protagonists in the course of human life and history, but also worked out their own interpretation of reality and handed this down through their works.[1] So when one's focus for research is limited to a specific

---

[1] According to E. Cantarella: ". . . writing the history of women is not easy. A historiography that always pays attention to politics, to events, to dates and to great personages, has cancelled out their passage through history, keeping at most the memory of certain persons whose lives were as exceptional as is their inclusion in history" (E. Cantarella, *L'ambiguo malanno. Condizione e immagine della donna nell'antichità*. Rome, 1981, p. 15). E. J. Morris, in *The Lady was a Bishop* (New York, 1973; London, Against Nature and God, 1973), states: "History may be hidden in many ways: it may be due to lack of care in the recording of events or to the loss

subject such as that of the presence of a group of women accompanying Jesus, the dimension of the problem of *scarcity of sources* is correspondingly greater. In general it is true to say that the relevant texts of the four Gospels show a poverty of references that demonstrates the little interest their compilers felt in the presence of women.

The critical analysis that can be made of the texts to reveal their patriarchal and androcentric language-structure-conception shows, then, as a prime element, the *absence* of women and the *silence* applied, generally if not completely, to them. This is a silence that is sometimes explicitly declared, thereby providing clear proof of the denial to which women were subjected.

Matthew's Gospel twice contains an expression that, seeking to relate the number of people present at one of Jesus' miracles, shows the consideration given – or rather not given – to the presence of women: "[there] were about five thousand men, not counting women and children" (14:21); "[there] were four thousand men, not counting women and children" (15:38).

Mentioning women, even if only to say that their presence was not taken into account, is in any case better than relegating them to total silence. There is a specific *silence* we need to look into: that surrounding the really normal,[2] though at the same time made truly exceptional, occasion of the last supper with Jesus. Here, silence about the presence of women is something that needs investigating,

---

of the records; to a language barrier or to the specialist's inability to see the forest for the trees. Unfortunately it may also be due to evasion of facts through prejudice. Worse, it may be due to a purposeful malicious hiding of events. Pliny the Elder tells us in his book *Natural History* that information was intentionally hidden regarding the work of women doctors, for according to the opinion of his day women should be quiet and as inconspicuous as possible so that after they were dead no one would know that they had lived. No wonder that evidence of the activities of women is not always easy to come by." Cf. A. Valerio, "Women in the History of the Church," *Concilium* 182 (1985) *Women – Invisible in Church and Theology*, ed. E. Schüssler Fiorenza and M. Collins.

[2] This innate normality of eating a meal is important in the light of an observation made by E. Schüssler Fiorenza: androcentric language mentions women only when their presence is exceptional or causes a problem, not in normal situations. See *In Memory of Her. A Feminist Theological Reconstruction of Christian Origins* (New York, 1983), p. 45.

interpreting, listening to. The expression "listen to silence" may seem illogical to the dynamics of one kind of rationalism, but the poverty of data provided by the sources becomes paradoxically an enrichment in the stimulus it provides to look for new tools of analysis in the context of an inescapable desire and need to rediscover, as a woman, the voices and the forgotten, buried reality of the women who knew and lived with Jesus. Once we can verify that silence is not always and simply absence of communication but can also be a revelation of such rich and complex significance, we need to investigate it: the women *not counted and forgotten* can still have voices in conveying the fullness of the message.

The explicit declaration in Matthew's version that the presence of women has not been taken into account also gives us a tool, a line of research. It can be considered exceptional and providential that the author of the Gospel of Matthew should on these two occasions demonstrate his own silence with regard to women. That this is exceptional is shown by Mark's version, where no reference to women appears and we read simply: "Those who had eaten the loaves numbered five thousand men" (16:44), and "now there were about four thousand people" (8:9).

That Matthew's addition to his text is also providential is shown by the methodological pointer that can legitimately be deduced: on any occasion when the texts are silent about women and do not mention their presence, to deduce their absence is unfounded and we can, on the contrary, interrogate this silence, what is unsaid, unwritten, unrecorded, not handed down.

If this demand made of the texts is new in its quality or in its modality or in the person of the interlocutor (a woman) or in the object of its enquiry, this is because the reply cannot be elicited by using only accustomed means.

If the question is addressed not to what is present but to what is absent, not to what emerges but to what lies hidden, not to what appears but to what has disappeared, not to what is full but to what is empty, not to what is there but to what is not there, the answer has to arise from new instruments. It has to do so because, in general if not exclusively, history and culture, like exegesis, have concerned themselves, and are concerned, with what is emergent, visible, not with what is submerged, invisible.

How does one reach out to what is invisible, to silence?

How does one look at what is hidden from sight?

How does one listen to what is kept from hearing?
How does one project a ray of light into the shadows?
I shall try what might be called an *exegesis of this silence*.[3] This has
to be thought out, worked out theoretically and then put to the test
when applied specifically to interpreting the texts, either in the light
of exegetical instruments and methods already acquired, or in the
light of the creative prospects that a problem or new question can
bring out.

The *silence*[4] of the texts on the subject of women is a reflection of
the wider *silence* and more extensive *denial* that forms part of
history and culture. This *silence* and denial have their counterpoint
in a *presence* of women that, even if often shut within certain
limitations and generally *hidden*, has nevertheless existed. Both the
element of *silence-denial* and that of *hidden presence* need to be
brought out today.

---

[3] The hypothesis of an exegesis of silence was explicitly presented by
me at a conference on "From Adam's Rib ... Reflections on Difference,"
held in Milan on 5 Nov. 1988, in a lecture entitled "Pensare la differenza
nell'essegesi," published in the review *Progetto donna* 2–3 (1989), pp. 41–5.
It was also the subject of a contribution to the colloquy on "Woman and
Ministry: an Ecumenical Problem," held in Palermo from 17–19 Nov. 1989,
entitled "Esegesi del silenzio: dall'assenza delle donne nei testi alla presenza
delle donne accanto a Gesù," published in C. Militello (ed.), *Donna e
Ministero. Un dibattito ecumenico* (Rome, 1991), pp. 486–96.

[4] On this cf. Schüssler-Fiorenza, *In Memory of Her*, p. 59; O. Genest,
"Evangiles et femmes," *Science et Esprit* 37 (1985), pp. 275–95, esp. "La
méthode d'analyse," pp. 283–7. As far as I have been able to discover, there
is no specific theoretical and methodological elaboration of the subject of
silence relative to women, though the fact that silence is the problem that
forms the presupposition common to all researches into women and into
women's historiography in particular makes it an element that is present
explicitly or implicitly in all works produced on this subject. Cf. M. C.
Marcuzzo and A. Rossi Doria (eds), *La ricerca delle donne* (Turin, 1987),
with bibliography; J. W. Scott, "Il 'genere': un'utile categoria di analisi
storica," *Rivista di storia contemporanea* 4 (1987), pp. 560–86; "Le genre de
l'histoire," *Les Cahiers du Grif* 37–8 (1988); L. Accati, V. Maher and G.
Pomata (eds), "Parto e maternità: momenti dell'autobiografia femminile,"
Quaderni storici 44 (1980) (though in the context of treating a specific
subject, the volume deals with general methodological and historiographic
reflections; see in particular pp. 333–45); A. Valerio, *Cristianesimo al
femminile. Donne protagoniste nella storia delle Chiese* (Naples, 1991).

Silence and denial are apparent above all in two aspects. Women in Palestine at the time of Jesus were subject to numerous denials.[5] Let me just pick out a few: denial of physical presence (women were not counted as making up the minimum number of ten required for a service to take place in a synagogue); denial of the word (women's witness had no validity in law courts);[6] denial of knowledge (in the Palestinian Talmud we read: "The words of the Torah will be destroyed in the fire sooner than be taught to women").[7] The second aspect relates to the absence of women apparent from a reading of the Gospels, which makes an *exegesis of the silence* necessary, designed to retrieve the memory of the presence of women. This is not intended to deny the value of those accounts concerning women that do appear in the texts;[8] it is on the basis of these as its starting point that this research can move forward. I am trying, as it were, to map out a path going backwards and to dig in the texts I have found to uncover the traces of a significant women's presence and examine *indicative and revealing pieces* of a far wider reality that lies hidden and, like an underground stream, from time to time trickles out of the written texts, then comes up to the surface and so reveals its permanent presence. Finding these traces and these *indicative and revealing pieces* is as much as I shall try to do through my search for the significant elements of the biblical texts in which it may be possible to find these virtually unexpected characteristics, this unlikely capacity to shift the barriers of silence farther down the line.[9]

---

[5] Some references are given belonging to rabbinic literature later than the time of Jesus, on the understanding that these texts are often "mirrors of a much earlier state of affairs and religious and social order, by reason of the conservatism and respect accorded to Tradition characteristic of late Judaism." J. M. Aubert, *La femme: antiféminisme et christianisme* (Paris, 1975).

6 *Shebu'ot* IV, 1.

7 *Sotah*, 19a.

8 The progress of this research will give ample space to the texts relating to women: these are also set out separately in the table in the appendix and form the basic support for the hypotheses put forward.

[9] At an already advanced stage of this study, I discovered that some of the concepts and terms I use are close, almost identical, to those in an essay by C. Ginzburg, "Spie. Radici di un paradigma indiziario," A. Gargani (ed.), *Crisi della ragione* (Turin, 1979), pp. 57–106. Ginzburg makes an

The Hidden Presence

The Gospels have five passages referring to the women who followed Jesus.

In Mark, in the account of Jesus' passion, we read: "There were also women looking on from a distance; among them were Mary Magdalene, and Mary the mother of James the younger and of Joses, and Salome. They used to follow him and provided for him when he was in Galilee; and there were many other women who had come up with him to Jerusalem" (Mark 15:40–41). Equally, in Matthew's account of the crucifixion, we find: "Many women were also there, looking on from a distance; they had followed Jesus from Galilee and had provided for him. Among them were Mary Magdalene, and Mary the mother of James and Joseph, and the mother of the sons of Zebedee" (Matt. 27:55–6). In Luke's narrative dealing with Jesus' activity in Galilee, we find: "Soon aferwards he went on through cities and villages, proclaiming and bringing the good news of the kingdom of God. The twelve were with him, as well as some women who had been cured of evil spirits and infirmities: Mary, called Magdalene, from whom seven demons had gone out, and Joanna, the wife of Herod's steward Chuza, and Susanna, and many others, who provided for him out of their resources" (Luke 8:1–3). Luke has two further references to the women followers, clarified by a

---

interesting inquiry into the silent appearance of an epistemological model toward the end of the last century. Among his discoveries: in the field of art G. Morelli put forward an "indicative method" of attributing works of art through examining the most negligible details; in the field of crime, Sherlock Holmes sought the author of a crime in details imperceptible to most people; at the outset of psychoanalysis Sigmund Freud himself (who had read Morelli) wrote: "I believe his method to be closely related to the technique of medical psychoanalysis. This too is dedicated to penetrating secret and hidden matters by using little appreciated or hidden elements, the left-overs or 'rejects' of our observation," (Ginzburg, p. 62). Ginzburg sums up: "In all these cases, virtually infinitesimal traces led to the understanding of a deeper reality, which could not otherwise have been attained. Traces: more precisely symptoms (in the case of Freud), indications (in the case of Sherlock Holmes), pictorial signs (in the case of Morelli)," *Ibid.*, pp. 65–6.

10. This does not diminish the value of the presence of the women who appear in John's Gospel. Cf. R. E. Brown, *The Community of the Beloved Disciple* (New York: Paulist Press, 1979), esp. the chapter on "The Role of Women in the Fourth Gospel."

third passage which, in his account of the passion, provides a list of the names not given in the two preceding passages: "But all his acquaintances, including the women who had followed him from Galilee, stood at a distance, watching these things" (23:49); "The women who had come with him from Galilee followed, and they saw the tomb and how his body was laid" (23:55); "Now it was Mary Magdalene, Joanna, Mary the mother of James, and the other women with them who told this to the apostles" (24:10).

In John's Gospel, on the other hand, there is no explicit reference to the women who followed Jesus, even if in his account of the passion he mentions the presence of the women near the cross: "Meanwhile, standing near the cross of Jesus were his mother, and his mother's sister, Mary the wife of Clopas, and Mary Magdalene" (John 19:25).[10]

From this, we see that news of the women who followed Jesus is given by Matthew, Mark and Luke, but not by John. A quick examination of the way the compilers of the three Synoptic Gospels treat the matter shows that Mark and Matthew speak of women following Jesus from Galilee only in the closing stages of their narratives, describing the events of the passion. Luke on the other hand tells of the presence of the women relatively early, when describing the first phase of Jesus' activity in Galilee; he also refers to them and their following Jesus on two further occasions, at the time of his death and of his burial. Luke's Gospel is therefore the only one in which this information is given at two different stages and in two different contexts, taking the two mentions in the final context of the passion as one. This variation among the Synoptics offers possibilities for further consideration.

What motivations underlie the differing versions? One exegetical formulation that could be called androcentric has interpreted the placing of the information in Luke 8:1–3 as bringing it forward compared to the other compilers, done with the aim of preparing his readers for the important part the women were to play later during the events of the passion. But if one considers the tendency not to register the presence of women except in exceptional circumstances, an exegetical approach from a woman's point of view immediately suggests a first question: Why do all three Synoptics note the presence of women at the passion, and, in their notice of this, give the information that these women had followed Jesus from Galilee?

The texts themselves provide the answer. Mark, after describing Jesus' arrest, says: "All of them deserted him and fled" (14:50); Matthew confirms this: "Then all the disciples deserted him and fled" (26:56).

The redactors, being unable to cite the witness of the male disciples because they had fled, are then forced to refer to the women who stayed. At this point they state who these are: women welcomed by Jesus and who had been with him since the time in Galilee; they also thereby provide a testimony to their fidelity at this serious and dramatic time when the male disciples abandoned him.

We are at the epilogue of Jesus' earthly existence. The women have been present, close to him, since the first phase of his public activity, which took place in Galilee, and only now, at the end, when their accounts are virtually finished, do Mark and Matthew say, now that they cannot avoid saying so, that the women are there, and indeed that now they are the only ones there. But they had been there first, from the beginning.

What Mark and Matthew give us, then, is a *great silence*.

A great silence from which they emerge perforce and by chance, constrained by the flight of the male disciples, which thereby reveals a paradoxically providential aspect. Perhaps if the evangelists had been able to refer to the presence of the apostles at the foot of Jesus' cross, they would have omitted to mention that the women were there and we should never have known of their presence. We should instead have had another silence to question. And in passing, but deliberately, let me note the silence surrounding the presence of women at the Last Supper: the apostles were there, and they could be quoted . . . so no need. . . .

The Fourth Gospel, unlike the other three, tells of the presence at the foot of the cross of "the disciple whom he (Jesus) loved" (John 19:26). This one male figure comes in the text straight after the list of the four women. John, the only disciple present, is thus also a personal witness to the presence of the women and attests to this in his Gospel.

Now, turning to Mark and Matthew, and approaching them exegetically as a woman, one can see that the various questions one can ask of the texts lead to a first important rediscovery of a trace, an indicative and revealing fragment within the exegesis of silence that is my hypothesis. The verses Mark 15:40–41 and Matthew

27:55–6 emit signals to indicate and reveal a reality that has been wiped out; they are a footprint left on the path, by chance not erased, showing us where this reality went, the direction it took, and indicating a possible way for us to follow it. This prospect leads us to put a second question concerning the different judgments of Mark and Matthew on the one hand and Luke on the other: why do the former speak of the women following Jesus only so late? If we look at the texts in themselves, leaving aside the problem of sources for the moment and not prematurely assuming that Luke depends on Mark, an *exegesis of the silence* is called for since Mark and Matthew hold this information back for so long. Current exegesis, however, viewing Mark as the earlier and determinant source, but also being done in a predominantly androcentric environment and therefore with little interest in the presence of women, asks why Luke has brought forward the information about the women who followed Jesus (8:1–3) with respect to Mark.

If we think of the event about which sooner or later the accounts by Luke, Mark and Matthew tell us, which is more logical: to describe it set at the time it happened or to relate it saying that it had happened long before? With regard to sources, then, the hypothesis put forward here concerning Luke 8:1–3 will emerge in the course of my analysis; here suffice it to say that one cannot uphold Mark as the source of Luke's information in 8:1–3 when the former (Mark 15:40–41) mentions, besides Mary Magdalene, two women (Mary the mother of James the lesser and Joses, and Salome) who do not feature in Luke 8:1–3, while Joanna, the wife of Herod's steward Chuza, and Susanna, are named. Luke furthermore speaks in general terms of women who had been cured, specifying in the case of Mary Magdalene that "seven demons" had gone out of her, and goes on to say that these women provided for Jesus and the disciples out of their resources. None of all this appears in Mark. Luke must therefore have used a different source. The same viewpoint suggests another question: why do Mark and Matthew mention the women following Jesus only so late and when, as we have seen, they could not avoid doing so? The answer we have to give is that of a silence concerning women and their doings, preventing news of them from appearing in the text except in exceptional circumstances. This realization suggests a course of reading that it would be interesting to put to the test in the case of each and every one of the women who appear in the four gospel texts.

We can therefore conclude that Mark and Matthew's texts have a strong capacity for disclosure: women have recovered a place and a significant role in Jesus' existence and had a close link with him, given that in the final and dramatic phase of his life they occupied the place the gospel authors themselves finally tell us of. The absence of women from the texts comes to an end at the point where the absence of the disciples from the events begins; where men are present, this acts as an obstacle to women being taken into account.

On this point comparison between the texts of Mark, Matthew and Luke appears in a new light, since the latter is the only one who tells us of the presence of women in the travelling group following Jesus in the context of the events related concerning the first phase of his activity in Galilee.

Luke, providing the information in unity of time and place with the events, gives it with a note of great interest for the line of inquiry followed here. The final conclusion these first considerations are leading to is the centrality of these three verses for my subject. The hypothesis emerging is that we can regard this pericope as a special trace, as a *footprint of memory* pointing out and unveiling a path to follow. It is therefore minimalizing to speak of Luke bringing forward information about the presence of women and to do so is to follow the line of denial and silencing.

My purpose now, therefore, is to try to follow this *footprint* and to interrogate exegetically the pervasive silence concerning the reality of the women who followed Jesus, since Luke too, between 8:1–3 and his passion narrative, makes no further explicit references to the women who travelled with Jesus and the twelve. Yet the women were there over this whole span of time.

The undertaking I propose is, then, to challenge this silence running from Luke 8:1–3 in order to discover what words one might seize on, what voices can make themselves heard and what other *footprints* we can find to enable us to reconstruct the dialogues consigned to silence and to bring a hidden reality back out into the light.

Chapter 2
A TEXT THE EXEGETES FORGOT

The first outcome of choosing Luke 8:1–3 as a starting point for this inquiry is of a disturbing and surprising nature. Bibliographic research immediately made me aware of a further dimension to the silence on the subject of women: the silence already established in the biblical texts is matched by silence from the exegetes, who have also devoted little attention to women. Luke 8:1–3 turns out to be a *text the exegetes forgot*.

The only author to have written specifically about this text in some depth comments: "Luke 8:1–3 has the dubious honour of being a New Testament pericope that has not been studied in any of the specialist reviews for the last hundred years."[1] This fact has not prevented me from tracking down a considerable amount of material to research, counting commentaries on Luke's Gospel, exegetical-theological works and monographs dealing mainly with *women's questions*. I propose to make a synthesis of the works examined, generally following a chronological course, but, where this seems a more appropriate criterion, grouping them by subject.

The literature of the second half of the nineteenth century brought out several key matters on which later studies have either agreed or disagreed. Besides commentaries, there are works specifically on female figures present in the Gospels from this period.[2] In these works a descriptive style prevails, very often

---

[1] B. Witherington III, "On the Road with Mary Magdalene, Joanna, Susanna and Other Disciples - Luke 8:1–3," *ZNW* 70 (1979), pp. 243–8, here 243.

[2] E.g. H.-D. Lacordaire, *Sainte Marie Madeleine*, 2 vols (Paris, 1860).

drawing on imagination and edifying and exhortational rather than strictly scientific in purpose.

The "Three Marys"

The subjects dealt with in these works generally revolve around "the question of the three Marys," which is of sufficient importance to merit the treatment given it here in the form of a thematic *excursus* cutting across the chronological order generally used. The expression "the question of the three Marys" in biblical criticism refers to the problem of the identity of the three women who appear in the gospel texts: Mary Magdalene, Mary of Bethany and the unnamed woman in Luke 7:36–50.[3]

Mary Magdalene as a Prostitute: an Exegetical Distortion

The verses Luke 8:1–3, where Mary Magdalene is named as a woman cured by Jesus, "ἀφ᾽ ἧς δαιμόνια ἑπτὰ ἐξεληλύθει," "from whom seven demons had gone out," appear in Luke's narrative immediately after the episode of the unnamed woman (7:36–50) who, going into the house of Simon the Pharisee, approaches Jesus and anoints his feet with perfumed ointment. This is the only reference in his Gospel to Jesus being anointed by a woman; Luke does not reveal her identity, but says of her only that she was a "ἁμαρτωλός," a "sinner."

The anointing episode is also found in Mark 14:3–9 and Matthew 26:6–13. The accounts concur in placing the episode in Bethany, in the house of Simon the leper, and in recounting the anointing without giving the woman's name. Finally, John 12:1–8 recounts an anointing, still set in Bethany though without saying in whose house, but naming Martha and Lazarus among those present and identifying the woman who anoints Jesus as Mary.

Now these two fragments are generally taken to be parallels and to relate to the same episode. In the Fourth Gospel the preceding chapter, however, also gives the following reference: "Mary was the one who anointed the Lord with perfume and wiped his feet with her hair; her brother Lazarus was ill" (John 11:2). Briefly, the main problems raised by these texts are these:

---

[3] The expression "question of the Magdalenes" is used by J. Schmid, *Das Evangelium nach Markus* (Regensburg, 1955).

1. Does John 11:2 refer to the anointing later described in 12:1–8 or to that described in Luke 7:36–50?
2. Should we reckon there to have have been two episodes of anointing or only one?
3. Who is the unnamed woman in Luke 7:36–50?
4. How should we interpret the phrase used of Mary Magdalene, "seven demons had gone out"?

The different possible answers to these questions have major consequences for the identities of the women involved. If one answers the first two by saying that John 11:2 refers to the same episode as Luke 7:36–50, which would mean that John knew Luke's account, then Mary of Bethany becomes the same person as the sinner in Luke. The same conclusion also follows from holding that Jesus was anointed on one occasion only: that recounted in John 12:1–8 and Luke 7:36–50.

The answer to the other two problems can lead, through the connotation of demons as the cause of sin, to identifying Mary Magdalene, from whom, according to Luke 8:2, "seven demons had gone out," with the sinful woman of Luke 7:36–50.

Investigation of the problem of the anointing(s) and inter-pretation of the expression "seven demons," which of themselves are two separate and independent things, come together because the figure of the sinner is common to both accounts. This produces a synthesis identifying Mary Magdalene with Mary of Bethany and making the three women one.

Finally, it is worth noting that little attention has been paid to the expression "ἁμαρτωλός," "sinner" applied by Luke to the unnamed woman (7:37) and generally taken to mean prostitute, whereas such an attribution would have required the term "πόρνη," which Luke uses elsewhere (15:30).[4] So if we come to the conclusion that the three women were in fact one and the same, we are also obliged to see this woman as a prostitute.

As for Mary Magdalene, the first woman mentioned as following Jesus, the identification of her with the sinner has led to her being regarded as a prostitute and as such she has been treated for

---

[4] Cf J. Pirot, *Trois amies de Jésus de Nazareth* (Paris, 1986), p. 16.

centuries in the liturgy, in literature and in art.[5] So we need to note, besides the silence about women shown in the texts, plus the absence of comment on this, the additional phenomenon of the *exegetical distortion*, noticeable here specifically applied to women, and in this case to Mary Magdalene.

A minute reconstruction of the history of exegesis, which developed along different lines in East and West, would perhaps reveal which authors, and at what periods, using which passages, were responsible for producing this phenomenon.[6] This being beyond the scope of the present inquiry, I am confining myself here to the most significant points that emerge from more recent writings.[7] Among the issues debated, we should include the

---

[5] Cf M. Mosco (ed.) *La Maddalena tra sacro e profano* (Milan-Florence, 1986); G. Testori and G. Ravasi, Maddalena (Milan, 1989). On the subject of the repentant sinner and the Magdalene as a legendary symbol used in the attempt to convert prostitutes, see M. Pilosu, *La donna, la lussuria e la chiesa nel medioevo* (Genoa, 1989), esp. pp. 126–44.

[6] In this area of research it would be interesting to establish the influence that the need to harmonize texts following the definition of the canon exercised on this question. Cf H. Conzelman, *Geschichte des Urchristentums* (Göttingen, 1969); M. Pesce, "The Transformation of a Religious Document from Early Christian Writings to New Testament Canon," J. Neusner, E. S. Fredrichs, N. M. Sarna (eds), *From Ancient Israel to Modern Judaism. Intellect in Quest of Understanding. Essays in Honor of Marvin Fox*, vol. 1 (Atlanta, 1989), pp. 133–48. In the East, the distinction between the three women has been maintained, as is shown in the three separate feast days: the unnmaed sinner of Luke 7:36–50 on 31 March, Mary of Bethany on 18 March and Mary Magdalene on 22 July. Further insights can be derived from apocryphal and gnostic literature, which need a whole course of research in themselves.

[7] The period under review is from the second half of the nineteenth century to the present. On the question of the three Marys, I should like to mention some significant works dating from earlier times: J. Da Varagine, *Legenda Aurea*, 3 vols (ed. A. Levasti, Florence, 1924–6); J. Lefèvre d'Etaples, *De Maria Magdalena et triduo Christi disceptatio* (Paris,[2] 1518): his thesis upholding the differentiation of the three women was condemned by the Theology Faculty of the University of Paris in 1521 – *Cesura Sorbonica de tribus Magdalenis, Acta Sanctorum* 5 (1868), pp. 196–225; his teaching was declared dangerous and he avoided being condemned as a heretic only through the intervention of King François Ier: cf V. Saxer, "Le culte de Marie-Madeleine en Occident des origines à la fin du Moyen Age," *Cahiers d'archéologie et d'histoire* 3 (1959), 5); P. de Bérulle, *Elévation à Jésus-Christ Notre-Seigneur sur la conduite de son esprit et de sa grâce vers*

questions of the cult and traditions so widespread in southern France, where Mary Magdalene is supposed to have landed on the coast together with Lazarus, Martha and others to evangelize the West.[8] Defending the authenticity of this Provençal tradition usually means upholding the unicity of the three women, since legend and this tradition have celebrated and re-imaged Mary Magdalene as the sister of Martha and Lazarus and the sinner who poured perfumed oil over Jesus' feet in Simon's house.[9]

A two-volume work by E. M. Faillon dating from 1848 sets out to uphold the authenticity of this tradition.[10] Equally, though on a different level, Henri-Dominique Lacordaire's monograph on Mary Magdalene, also upholding the unicity of the three women, is not free of elements deriving from the cult, which filter out even in a context of examining the gospel accounts.[11]

Sainte Madeleine (Paris, 1627, in J.P. Migne [ed.], *Oeuvres complètes,* Paris, 1856),. 531–96: he decides in favour of the three being one; A. Calmet, "Dissertation sur les trois Maries," *Commentaire de l'Evangile de S. Luc* (Paris, 1726), pp. 403–10: examining the arguments for both the unicity and the plurality of Marys, he concludes that the gospel texts favour the opinion that there were two or three, rather than one only.

[8] This tradition is examined in greater detail below (pp. 151–4).

[9] One of the most significant testimonies to this tradition is to be found in the Vieille Major cathedral of Marseilles. I will come back to this on the section devoted to the cult of Mary Magdalene.

[10] E. M. Faillon, *Monuments inédits sur l'apostolat de sainte Marie Madeleine en Provence,* 2 vols (Paris, 1848). F. Prat, dealing with the thesis of the unicity of the three and referring to Faillon, wrote: "A Sulpician has vigorously defended it in the name of tradition," *Jésus Christ, sa vie, sa doctrine, son oeuvre* (Paris, 1933).

[11] Examining the two episodes of anointing in Luke 7:36–50 and Mark 14:3–9, Lacordaire maintains that these are two separate events, both of which took place in the house of Simon, who lived near Lazarus' family in Bethany; the unnamed sinner in Luke would be Mary of Bethany. Lacordaire holds that there were only two Marys besides the mother of Jesus: Mary Magdalene and Mary the sister of the Virgin, called either Mary of Cleophas after her husband or Mary of James and Joseph after her sons. In Matthew 27:61 they are called "Mary Magdalene and the other Mary." Lacordaire maintains that "It is therefore necessary that Mary of Bethany should be one of the two, either Mary Magdalene or Mary of Cleophas. But she was not Mary of Cleophas, sister of the Blessed Virgin; so she was Mary Magdalene." And he immediately adds to this conclusion: "This is also what tradition, the liturgy of the Church and the oldest monuments raised

In 1872, Frédéric Godet, declaring that the identification of Mary Magdalene with the sinner in Luke "is without the slightest basis," picked out one of the reasons for it as confusing demonic possession, which is an illness, with a state of moral corruption.[12] While other authors opt for the distinction between the three,[13] there are those who still hold to the tradition that they are one and the same, perhaps not even being aware of the problem or in any case not alluding to it.[14] Marie-Joseph Lagrange, in his monumental 1920 commentary on Luke's Gospel, identifies Jerome as the author who, associating the concept of possession with that of sin, was perhaps responsible for the first step on the road of subsuming the three in one.[15] In a letter to Marcella, Jerome writes: "*Maria Magdalena ipsa est, a qua septem daemonia expulerat; ut ubi*

---

to Mary Magdalene uphold. Their language shows us in the unity of a same glory the sinner who wept at the feet of Jesus and anointed his hair, the sister of Lazarus present at the raising of her brother from the dead, the faithful friend present at the passion and death of her good friend, who followed him to the tomb and deserved to be the first to see the splendours of his resurrection. Any division of this glory is chimerical, contrary to Scripture, to the memory of ages, to the piety of the saints, to that universal cult that everywhere offers, to our eyes and in our souls, the image of one sole woman in whom are united the most touching mysteries of penitence and friendship." Lacordaire, *Sainte Marie-Madeleine*, pp. 96–7. Cf P. M. Guillaume, "Marie Madeleine," *DSp* 10 (1980), 559–75, in which he observes that Lacordaire's work was published "in order to re-launch the pilgrimages to Saint-Maximin and Sainte-Baume" (574).

[12] F. Godet, *Commentaire sur l'évangile de S. Luc*, 2 vols (Paris, 1872). "It is without the slightest basis that tradition identifies Mary Magdalene with the penitent sinner of chapter VII. Possession, which is a sickness, has been wrongly confused with a state of moral corruption. The surname 'of Magdala' is intended to distinguish this Mary from all the others, from Mary of Bethany in particular" (p. 456).

[13] Such as: A. Monod, "Marie de Magdala," ESR 8 (188), 714–6; M. F. Sadler, *The Gospel according to St Luke* (London, 1889[2]); A. Plummer, *Gospel according to St Luke. The International Critical Commentary*, 4 (Edinburgh, 1896[5]).

[14] Among these, cf: R. P. Badet, *Jésus et les femmes dans l'évangile* (Paris-Lyons, 1893); E. de Trémaudan, *Jésus Christ et la femme* (Tournai, 1897); see also M.-M. Sicard, *Sainte Marie-Madeleine*, 3 vols (Paris, 1921).

[15] J.-M. Lagrange, *Evangile selon Saint Luc* (Paris, 1920).

abundaverat peccatum, superabundaret gratia."[16] Lagrange maintains that the texts cannot support the identification of the sinner with Mary Magdalene, confirms that no early exegete before Jerome made this identification and shows how exegetes came to support the unicity of Mary of Bethany and the sinner because of the fact that the Fathers had allowed only one anointing, and how they came to identify Mary Magdalene with the sinner through the confusion in the references to each of them and demonic possession.[17] The identification of Mary Magdalene with Mary of Bethany stemmed from this, aided by the coincidence of the name Mary.

Fernand Prat, in a well-documented appendix to his book on Jesus Christ, sets out the nature of the problem, examines the Gospel texts and concludes that the three were different women.[18] After such an ample and reasoned analysis of the facts, however, the final sentences of his section on liturgy and tradition strike a false note. After a reference to J. Sickenberger, whom he calls "a Catholic scholar (who) has studied the question in depth, clearly opting for plurality," he quotes his verdict: "In the interests of historical truth, it would be desirable for the Latin liturgy for the feast of the Magdalene to be altered and for preachers and writers of pious books to conform to this."[19] Prat comments: "This is running too fast. The confusion – if we must speak of confusion – is harmless."[20]

The statement that this confusion is "harmless" merits some thought. At least one question comes to mind: is it really of no consequence that through this "confusion" Mary Magdalene has been turned from a woman cured into a prostitute? That she should

---

[16] "Mary Magdalene is that same from whom seven demons had been expelled; so that where sin had abounded grace superabounded" (Jerome, ep., 59, 4, CSEL 54, 545).

[17] Lagrange had devoted an article to this aspect of the problem in 1912: "Jésus a-t-il été oint plusieurs fois et par plusieurs femmes?" *RB* 9 (1912), 504–32. This gives a most valuable reconstruction of the views of early Alexandrian, Latin, Syriac and Asia Minor exegetes. Cf also U. Holmeister, "Die Magdalenenfrage in der kirchlichen Uberlieferung," *ZthK* 46 (1922), 402–22, 556–84.

[18] Prat, *Jésus Christ*, pp. 499–504.

[19] J. Sickenberger, "Ist die Magdalenen-Frage wircklich unlösbar?" BZ 16 (1925), 63–74. Prat, *op. cit.*, p. 503.

[20] *Ibid.*

have been thought of, painted, sculpted, remembered as a woman who sinned through lust? That she should have been spoken of and preached about so much while being turned, in the eyes of the men and women to whom she is put forward as the most important woman in the Gospels after the mother of Jesus, into a prostitute?[21] Or rather has not this confusion been itself confused with another "confusion" concerning "woman" in general and the conception generally held of her and the projections men generally placed on her through her prevailing identification with sensuality? And then can this exegetical "confusion," added to the other, have been "harmless," or would it not perhaps have generated yet another, contributing to confirming the woman-sensuality binomial and, by association, the perception of sensuality as negative and, here, as positively sinful? But Prat himself seems to be convinced and ends his note with the view that, "despite the objections of exegetes, the identification thesis is, and will long remain, the most popular in the West. And, when all is said and done, I see no harm in it, if only for the sake of mystics and preachers who are not under a categorical obligation to keep to the literal sense."[22]

I would agree with Prat that in the West the tradition of running the three women together into one has not changed and will not change in the near future, but I cannot share his assertion that "there is no harm" in this. How can there be no harm, of any sort, in an "interpretation counter to the truth"?[23]

Peter Ketter declared himself in support of the differentiation of the three women and affirms that "the great majority of exegetes" of his time are of the same opinion.[24] This same opinion is shared by

---

[21] P. M. Guillaume writes: "For Pietro di Celle (d.1183) Mary Magdalene is an example for all sinful women." And again: "In Jean Michel's *Mystère de la Passion* (1486) five episodes out of the 666 verses are devoted to the worldly life of Mary Magdalene. " Guillaume, *Marie-Madeleine*, pp. 571–2.

[22] Prat, *Jésus Christ*, p. 504.

[23] The words are by J. Pirot, who with reference to Prat's sentence wrote: "Let us not dramatize. But why give a free pass to an interpretation counter to the truth?" *Trois amies de Jésus*, p. 134.

[24] P Ketter, *Jesus und die Frauen* (Düsseldorf, 1933). He sums up the different views on the subject and provides biblical references to show that "the Gospels do not identify the two women more explicitly," p. 139. Cf also B. Kipper, "Maria Maddalena," *Enciclopedia de la Biblia* 4 (1964), pp. 1315–8.

the majority of more recent writers, though expressed in works of varying value.[25] In 1955 Josef Schmid, in his commentary on the Gospel of Mark, provided a welcome note of exegetical analysis in showing the lack of basis for the unicity theory.[26] Victor Saxer's 1966 study, part of the *Bibliotheca Sanctorum*, presents a broad panorama organized around four points: Gospel, liturgy, legend, iconography.[27] Saxer, who favours the differentiation of the three women, states that the figure of Mary Magdalene has been distorted by exegetes and hagiographers.

In his full 1969 commentary on the Gospel of Luke, Heinz Schürmann declares decisively in favour of differentiation.[28] This can be seen in his long analysis of Luke 7:36–50, which he does not consider a variant of the anointing recorded in the other Gospels (Mark 14:3–9; par. Matt. 26:6–13; John 12:1–8), and in his comment on Luke 8:1–3, where he writes explicitly about Mary Magdalene: "The new introduction of this 'Magdalene' prevents one from seeing in her, as the old tradition did, the 'sinner' of 7:36–50, the

---

[25] As a dissonant voice, see R. L. Bruckberger, *Marie Madeleine* (Paris, 1952), a work more on the level of romance than of serious exegetical enquiry.

[26] Schmid, *Das Evangelium nach Markus*.

[27] V. Saxer, *Maria Maddalena*, Bibliotheca Sanctorum 8 (1966), pp. 1081–104. Since the 1950s Saxer has produced numerous essays on the cult of Mary Magdalene, among which: "Les saintes Marie Madeleine et Marie de Béthanie dans la tradition liturgique et homilétique d'orient," *Revue des sciences religieuses* 32 (1958), pp. 1–37; a basic work is *Le culte de Marie-Madeleine en Occident des origines à la fin du Moyen Age* (1959). See also: *Le dossier vézelien de Marie Madeleine* (Brussels, 1975); "Marie Madeleine," *Catholicisme* 8 (1979), pp. 632–8; "Anselme et la Madeleine: l'Oration LXXIV, ses sources, son style et son influence," *Les mutations socio-culturelles au tournant des XI-XII siècles* (Paris, 1984), pp. 365–82; "Le culte et la tradition de Sainte Marie Madeleine en Provence," *Mémoires de l'Académie de Vaucluse* 6 (1985), pp. 41–55; "Santa Maria Maddalena dalla storia evangelica alla legenda e all'arte," M. Mosco (ed.) *La Maddalena tra sacro e profano*, pp. 24–8; "Le culte de la Madeleine à Vézelay et de Lazare à Autun: un problème d'antériorité d'origine," *Bulletin da la Société des Fouilles Archéologiques et des Monuments Historiques de l'Yonne* 3 (1986), pp. 1–18; "Les origines du culte de Sainte Marie Madeleine en Occident," E. Duperray (ed.), *Marie Madeleine dans la mystique, les arts et les lettres* (Paris, 1989), pp. 33–47.

[28] H. Schürmann, *Das Lukasevangelium, I Teil* (Freiburg, 1969).

more so since 'sin' and 'diabolical possession' in the New Testament are not the same thing."[29]

The unicity thesis is still upheld by André Feuillet, who, even taking account of the reasons put forward by exegetes who maintain the opposite thesis, states that "the basic argument in support of the identification is the Johannine account of the anointing in Bethany (John 12:1–8)," arguing that this is a different anointing to that recorded in Luke 7:36–50 and a re-telling, in his view, of John 11:2.[30] Ten years later, Feuillet devoted another article to John's account of the anointing.[31] So today most exegetes opt for the three separate women, and recent years have shown, if not an actual live debate, at least extensive reference to the problem in theological and exegetical circles.[32]

In the field of art, two recent exhibitions, dealing with the figure of Mary Magdalene in painting and sculpture, are worth noting. They have provided proof of how deep the identification of the three women has gone in artistic expression, and are further evidence of the the way this sphere is inclined to prolong the tradition of the three being one and the same.[33] Even taking account

---

[29] *Ibid.*, p. 710, n. 19.

[30] A. Feuillet, "Des deux onctions faites sur Jésus, et Marie-Madeleine," *Revue Thomiste* 75 (1975), pp. 357–94.

[31] "Le récit johannique de l'onction de Béthanie (Jn. 12:1–8)," *Esprit et Vie* 14 (1985), pp. 193–203.

[32] The *Jerusalem Bible* comments on Luke 7:36–50: "An episode peculiar to Luke, different from the anointing at Bethany (Matt. 26:6–13 par.). The sinner of this episode should not be indentified either with Mary of Bethany, the sister of Martha (10:39; cf Johnn 11:1ff; 12:2ff), or with Mary of Magdala (8:2)." Cf. E. Moltmann-Wendel, *Freiheit-Gleichheit-Schwesterlichkeit. Zur Emanzipation der Frau in Kirche und Gesellschaft* (Munich, 1977); *Idem, The Women around Jesus* (New York, 1982); P. Benoît and M. E. Boismard, *Synopse des quatre évangiles en français. Vol 3, L'évangile de Jean* (Paris, 1977), p. 304, upholding the identity of the sinner in Luke 7:36–50 with Mary of Bethany; this is opposed by Pirot, *Trois amics.* Cf also Saxer, "Marie Madeleine"; M. Adinolfi, *Il femminismo della Bibbia* (Rome, 1981); Ph.-I. André-Vincent, *Marie Madeleine et la Sainte-Baume* (Paris, 1980, 1st ed. 1950); *Idem, Marie Madeleine et le mystère pascal* (Paris, 1983); Guillaume, *Marie Madeleine.*

[33] The identification of the three women and above all the characterization of Mary Magdalene as a prostitute have been so widely diffused and popular that they will certainly last a long time yet, and indeed not only in less enlightened circles.

of the fact that the aim of these ventures is not exegetical and that therefore the identity of the three women is not really among the prime considerations, it is nevertheless interesting to see how the subject was tackled.

The first venture, a major exhibition entitled "The Magdalene between Sacred and Profane,"[34] even though not uncritically accepting the thesis of the three as one, as indeed is shown by one of the articles in the catalogue, "The Magdalene: an Identity Veiled and Violated,"[35] in general echoes the artistic and poetic climate and the subjects that the theory of three as one has caused to prevail over the centuries. Mary of Magdalene is contrasted with the Virgin[36] as *"vas peccatorum* ... full of all the sins of femininity, first of all that of sensual beauty, disturbing and dangerous for the temptation she continually poses for men."[37] Furthermore, the exhibition was subdivided into seven sections, "seven like the (seven deadly) sins of the Magdalene."[38]

The more recent venture, "Marie-Madeleine. Figure inspiratrice dans la Mystique, les Arts et les Lettres," produced an interesting catalogue,[39] but this did not show any clear awareness of the problem. Instead, with lyrical and suggestive expressions, it spoke of the beauty, the seductiveness, the penitence of Mary Magdalene, who was called "an examination on love, sin, femininity and the sacred."[40] If in this sentence the fact that "femininity" is placed just after "sin" is the result of a purely fortuitous juxtaposition, so much of the view of woman projected over the centuries through the figure of Mary Magdalene is certainly not a matter of casual juxtaposition. This view is hardly surprising in view of the process that has led to her being identified with the sinner in Luke. To quote

---

[34] Held at the Florence Exhibition Centre in 1986 and organized by M. Mosco. The catalogue is cited in note 5.

[35] Mosco, "La Maddalena: un'identità velata e violata," pp. 17–23.

[36] For an analysis of the way Mary Magdalene has been compared to Mary the mother of Jesus, see C. Ricci, "Maria: dimenticare per ricordare. Frammenti di pensieri per un tentativo di incontro," *Se a parlare di Maria sono le donne* (Milan, 1988), pp. 5–21.

[37] Mosco, "La Maddalena, un identità," p. 17.

[38] *Ibid.*, p. 18.

[39] E. Duperray and C. Loury (eds), *Marie-Madeleine* (Fontaine-de-Vaucluse, 1988). The exhibition was organized by the Petrarch Museum at Fontaine-de-Vaucluse.

[40] *Ibid.*, p. 13.

the catalogue once more: "She (Mary Magdalene) is still dangerous – a temptress – an object of desire ... in her woman's body she affirms the power of her femininity. This has the corrupting power of temptation ... Magdalene of sin, red with the blood of shame, the antithesis of White Mary the mother of God."[41]

To end this *excursus*[42] I should like to mention three of the more significant recent works relative to the problem. In 1980 Elizabeth Moltmann-Wendel devoted a chapter of her book *The Women around Jesus*[43] to Mary Magdalene, analyzing both the confusion with the figure of the sinner and the consequences stemming from this, and the reality as derived from the biblical texts. Jean Pirot, in his 1986 work *Trois amies de Jésus de Nazareth*,[44] sets out a survey of the problem and the arguments for both sides, coming down on the side of differentiation. Gianfranco Ravasi, in a 1989 article on "Mary of Magdala, a slandered and glorified saint,"[45] gives an incisive account of the ambivalence of the way this woman has been viewed, as suggested by the title.

The Course of Research from 1860 to the Present

"Serving" Women

After this long but necessary discussion of the "question of the three Marys," let us return to examining the literature relating to Luke 8:1–3. Another important matter for the object of this inquiry is the role played by the women who made up part of the close group of Jesus' followers. In the second half of the nineteenth

---

[41] *Ibid.*, pp. 13–14.

[42] Among the works published in the 1980s are: J. Kelen, *Un amour infini. Marie Madeleine, prostituée sacrée* (Paris, 1982). This work, which alternates chapters of literary fictions attributed to Mary Magdalene with chapters setting biblical, gnostic and other texts side by side, opts for the unicity theory, considering that "the privilege of the Madeleine – and her immortality – is to have a legend and not a history" (p. 14). E. Parvez, "Mary Magdalene: Saint or Sinner?" *BToday* 23 (1985), pp. 122–4, opts firmly for the differentiation thesis. C. and J. Grassi, *Mary Magdalene and the Women in Jesus' Life* (Kansas City, 1986) makes many interesting points, but falls back on the image of the sinner on the identity question.

[43] See note 32.

[44] See note 4.

[45] G. Ravasi, "Maria di Magdala, Santa calunniata e glorificata," G. Testori and G. Ravasi, *Maddalena*, pp. 15–24.

century this was always referred to simply as "serving," sometimes followed by noting the continuity of the women's travelling with Jesus and the apostles.[46] There is little discussion of the nature of this "service" and so it is usually severely limited. M. F. Sadler, writing in 1889, states: "It is not implied, *naturally*,[47] that these (women) were followers in the strict sense like the Apostles. It would after all have been inconvenient to say that a mixed group of perhaps more than twenty persons were at his service. It is probable that these women provided in turn for His basic material needs and those of the Apostles."[48] Other elements of the same cultural climate are to be found in R. P. Badet, who, to define the role of the women, observes that while the Lord "did not want women to preach his doctrine ... (since) the fragility of their nature and the modesty of their sex" would not allow this, he nevertheless left them to take care of the men's material needs in order to leave them free to proclaim the good news.[49]

The "service" aspect and material support are therefore the two elements usually considered as accounting for the presence of women. Alfred Plummer stresses the importance of this passage in showing the accuracy of Luke's sources, the authenticity of which is proved by such attention to detail.[50] This aspect is often brought

---

[46] In the Apostolic Letter *Mulieris Dignitatem*, Pope John Paul II says: "*At times* (my italics) women whom Jesus met and who received so many graces from him, kept him company as he journeyed with the apostles through towns and countryside proclaiming the Good News of the Kingdom of God; and they 'provided for them out of their resources' (see Luke 8:1–3)." On this see S. Tunc, "Un changement d'anthropologie, D'Inter Insigniores' à 'Mulieris Dignitatem,' la fin de l''infériorité' de la femme," *La Croix. L'événement* (Paris) 14 Oct. 1983, p. 13. See also C. Ricci, *Mulieris dignitatem. Esperienze a confronto* (Acts of the Congress held in Milan 17 Feb. 1989: Milan, 1990), pp. 39–51.

[47] My italics.

[48] Sadler, *The Gospel According to Luke*, pp. 199–200. Godet also characterizes the women who followed Jesus as "serving," as providing pecuniary assistance and rendering the personal services to be expected from a mother or sisters: *Commentaire*, p. 456.

[49] Badet, *Jésus et les femmes*, p. 248: "... he did not want women to preach his doctrine; this was given only to the apostles: the fragility of their nature and the modesty of their sex prevented them from exercising any difficult or important ministry."

[50] Plummer, *Gospel according to St Luke*, p. 216.

out in nineteenth-century writings: M.-J. Lagrange, in his commentary on the Gospel of Luke, considers Luke 8:1–3 a valuable piece of information, and sees the fact that he gives the women's names as proof of the accuracy of the evangelist's information.[51]

The predominant type of writing up to the 1950s was the commentary,[52] but relevant information can also be found in encyclopedias or collective works.[53] It is worth noting that in such works interest in Luke 8:1–3 is not because of anything they say that would advance the argument; they are analyzed not because of any specific interest they might have, but rather as though this work has to be done owing to what they reveal about the nature of literary composition, which makes commenting on them necessary.

Women Disciples

Albrecht Oepke and Hermann Wolfgang Beyer, examining respectively the words γυνή and διακονέω, develop aspects already examined and suggest new ones: the former paints a broad picture of the situation of women at the time of Jesus, while the latter

---

[51] Lagrange, *Evangile selon Saint Luc,* pp. 234–6. His recognition of the value of 8:1–3 contrasts with his ongoing conception of women, which makes him write: "There were also certain women, but they undoubtedly did not form a regular group like the twelve. It is in the nature of things that some would have been more and some less assiduous in following the Saviour" (p. 235).

[52] Examples of these are: B. S. Easton, *The Gospel According to St Luke: A Critical and Exegetical Commentary* (Edinburgh, 1926). He considers that 8:1–3 is suggested by the preceding pericope (the penitent sinner) and at the same time forms an introduction to the parable of the sower. At the end of the work he makes the noteworthy remark that women are named by Luke because they became pre-eminent in the church in Palestine. A. Schattler, *Das Evangelium des Lukas aus seinen Quellen erklärt* (Stuttgart, 1931): pp. 267–8 stress the function of Luke 8:1–3 in proving the autonomy of the author of this Gospel, as shown by the new names (Joanna and Susanna) but above all by the information that the women who had been cured stayed with Jesus out of gratitude and to serve him. Schmid, *Das Evangelium nach Lukas,* sees 8:1–3 as a valuable passage in that it tells how Jesus and the disciples were provided for, "and, also, that he had women too among his disciples" (p. 203).

[53] The best of these is the *Theologisches Wörterbuch zum Neuen Testament* (TWNT), ed. G. Kittel and G. Friedrich (Stuttgart, 1933–78).

develops an understanding of the concept of "diaconate" that shows it to mean really belonging to the circle of Jesus' disciples. Oepke, in relation to Luke 8:1–3, speaks of women being "among the disciples," without further clarification; Beyer identifies a "table service" in these verses.[54]

Ketter's *Christus und die Frauen*, published in 1933, is a sign that the climate was changing, that new concerns and questions were arising, with efforts being made to try out hypotheses and responses that were to be the prelude to a true theological renewal. The term "disciple" is clearly applied to women and the problem of their role in general is tackled with a wealth of detail. He asks what type of service can be meant, examines whether or not they were involved in proclaiming the gospel, and also asks whether or not they had been called by Jesus or had decided to follow him out of their own deep intuition.[55]

A "Women's Tradition" and the Emergence of "Feminist Theology"

In 1963 Martin Hengel published an article that marks an important development in the relevant literature, in both its content and its genre. Even though it continues the prevalence of commentary, it shows significant new elements, being the first, while not devoted exclusively to Luke 8:1–3, to examine these verses in such analytical detail and breadth that it has become a necessary point of reference for any later study of them.[56] The article opens with a methodological exposition that, using the the results obtained, mainly in

---

[54] A. Oepke, "γυνή," TWNT 1 (1935), 775–90; H. W. Beyer, "διακονέω," TWNT 2 (1935), 81–94.

[55] See note 24. Cf akso W. Grundmann, *Das Evangelium nach Lukas* (Berlin, 1963). He shows that among the Jews women were placed on the same level as slaves and children, could not be admitted to service in the synagogue and were exempt from a whole series of religious obligations. He then concludes that the fact Jesus admitted them into his circle implies his recognition of their full human dignity before God and man.

[56] M. Hengel, "Maria Madgdalena und die frauen als Zeugen," *Abraham unser Vater. Festschrift O. Michel* (Leyden-Cologne, 1963), pp. 243–56. Among later works cf: K. H. Rengstorf, *Das Evangelium nach Lukas* (Göttingen, 1969); C. Stuhlmüller, *The Gospel according to Luke*. JBC II (1968), pp. 115–64; B. Corsani, *Introduzione al Nuovo Testamento. Vangeli e Atti* (Turin, 1972), pp. 231–53.

Germany, from research into the "historical Jesus,"[57] applies one of the criteria of historicity, that of dissimilarity or discontinuity, to uphold the historicity and importance of those passages (Luke 8:1–3 and Mark 15:40–41) that make the women stand out as an autonomous group within the circle of the apostles.[58] He puts forward an analysis of the literary structure, picks out possible sources and reflects on the identity of the women named and their role in the group, paying particular attention to Mary Magdalene who was to be the first to carry the message of the Risen Christ.

The question of a "women's tradition," identified with Luke's own sources, was posed in 1967 by Thorlief Boman, using an earlier hypothesis put forward by Schlatter.[59] The particular singularity of Luke's source is explained with the hypothesis of a single account (covering the birth of the Baptist to the ascension) of which women would have been witnesses-hearers-custodians. Who these women were is indicated in Luke 8:1–3 and Mark 15:40–41 and their circle forms the *Sitz im Leben* of this source.

In 1969 Heinz Schürmann, drawing on the analysis made by Hengel, opened up new and wider perspectives in a commentary that differs qualitatively from all earlier ones. He starts by advancing the hypothesis that this passage could be a re-working, based on an older tradition, of elements relating to women and the part they played, thus coming back to the question of the possible existence of a "women's tradition," traces of which are to be found above all through Luke's Gospel. Of interest too is the precision with which he writes, in contrast to the earlier works examined above, of the presence of the women: "they had constantly

---

[57] Cf E. Käsemann, "Das Problem des historischen Jesus," ZThK 51 (1954), pp. 125–53; J. Dupont, "A que punto è la ricerca sul Gesù storico?" *Conoscenza storica di Gesù* (Brescia, 1978), pp. 7–31; V. Fusco, "Tre approcci storici a Gesù," *RaTe* 4 (1982), pp. 311–28.

[58] "The criterion of dissimilarity invites us to attribute to Jesus what cannot be found expressed in the contemporary Jewish world, either in language, thought or the practice of the early church." Dupont, *art. cit.*, p. 14.

[59] T. Boman, *Die Jesus Uberlieferung im Lichte der neueren Volkskunde* (Göttingen, 19670, esp. pp. 123–7. Cf also E. Schillebeeckx, *Jesus: an Experiment in Christology* (London & New York, 1979); A. Schlatter, "Die beiden Schwerter, Lk 22: 35–38," BFchTh 20 (1916), pp. 487ff.

accompanied Jesus."[60] Still on this subject, Leonard Swidler wrote in 1973: "a certain number of women, married or not, were regularly among those who followed Jesus"; seeking to ascertain what Jesus' attitude to women was, he identifies as a basic fact what can deduced from Luke 8:1–3: ". . . some women became disciples of Jesus immediately, not only in the sense that they learned his teaching, but also in that they followed him on his travels and attended to his everyday needs."[61]

Looking at theological development during this period, even though limiting ourselves to writings dealing with Luke 8:1–3, we must make at least a brief reference to the Second Vatican Council, an event of decisive importance for the general church and theological climate of the time and in the future. Announced in 1959 and held from 1962 to 1965, itself the product of various types of ferment, it in turn multiplied these ferments and gave rise to new ones in the church community and even in the world beyond. Almost as though to complete the prophetic proclamation that Gertrud Heinzelmann had sent the Council fathers in a manifesto-book entitled "We shall not stay silent any longer,"[62] what is now called "feminist theology" developed in the years following the Council.

---

[60] See note 28. Here p. 711. Schürmann writes: "There are many reasons for believing that the two stories about women in 7:11–17, 36–50 were once followed, as a generalizing final piece of information, by something like 8:2ff," and that Luke had found this complex narrative. "The community 'context' of this little composition would have been the question of women": a particularly acute problem in the culture of Palestine because of Jesus' innovative approach in welcoming women as his companions and allowing them to serve him (p. 712).

[61] L. Swidler, "Il Gesù degli Evangeli era femminista," F.-V. Joannes (ed.) Crisi dell'antifemminismo (Milan, 1973), pp. 135–58. See also idem, Biblical Affirmations of Women (Philadelphia, 1979).

[62] G. Heinzelmann, Wir schweigen nicht länger! (Bonstetten-Zurich, 1964). Cf also M. T. van Lunen Chenu, "Feminism and the Church," Concilium 111 (1976); M. Daly, The Church and the Second Sex (New York, 1968); R. Goldie, "Donne: studio, ricerca, insegnamento della teologia," C. Militello (ed.), Teologia al femminile (Palermo, 1985). G. Heinzelmann, Die geheiligte Diskriminierung: Beiträge zum kirchlichen Feminismus (Bonstetten-Zurich, 1986) contains a translation of the text addressed to the Council fathers. The German and U. S. theologians and jurists Josefa Theresia Münch, Iris Müller, Ida Raming, Rosemary Lauer and Mary Daly were part of the group that formed around Gertrud Heinzelmann.

In 1968 Mary Daly published *The Church and the Second Sex*, the "first worked-out Catholic response – as the title itself suggests – to Simone de Beauvoir's *The Second Sex* (1949), which, along with Betty Friedan's *The Mystique of Femininity* (1963) and Kate Millet's *Sexual Politics* (1969), form the basic texts of contemporary feminism."[63] These were the first signs of a new type of theological reflection that Christian women, increasingly better-educated, were beginning to develop, first in the United States and then in Europe. In this context, it is worth noting that the St Joan's International Alliance, as early as its 1963 General Assembly, had approved the resolution: "The competent authorities will allow women to attend theology courses at all levels, to take the relevant examinations and gain the honours and diplomas currently reserved only to men."[64]

---

[63] R. Gibellini, "Femminismo e teologia," *RTM* 64 (1984), p. 474. Cf. also M. T. van Lunen Chenu, R. Gibellini and A. Valerio, *Donna e teologia* (Brescia, 1988).

[64] The St Joan's International Alliance was the first, and for sixty years the only, Catholic feminist association, founded in England in 1911 as the Catholic Women's Suffrage Society in the context of the Suffragette Movement. It built up solid international contacts and now has members in twenty-four countries spread over the five continents. Its journal *The Catholic Citizen* has been published without a break since 1915. Since 1973 it has appeared in two editions, English and French, and an Italian edition has recently been added. The association is recognized as a non-governmental body with consultative status by the U. N. Socio-Economic Council and permanently registered as a Catholic organization by the Pontifical Commission for the Laity. Its aim is and always has been the achievement of equal rights for women with men in society. At the 1963 session of the Vatican Council, the Alliance asked for the ministry of deacon to be opened to lay men and women, that lay people should be invited to become members of the Conciliar Commissions, and expressed its conviction that "whenever the Church in its wisdom and at the opportune moment decides to grant access to the priesthood to women, they will be ready and willing to respond." Then in 1964 it was the Alliance that asked for qualified women to take part in the Council as auditrices (Cardinal Suenens had made the same suggestion in 1963). The first women entered St Peter's at the third session of the Council, in late 1964. One of the Council documents, *Gaudium et Spes*, finally said: "Where they have not yet won it, women claim for themselves an equity with men before the law and in fact (9c).... Every type of discrimination, whether social or cultural, whether based on sex, race, color, social condition, language, or religion, is to be overcome and eradicated as contrary to God's intent" (29b).

Opening New Horizons

The second half of the 1970s was characterized by the appearance of numerous monographs on the condition of women and on biblical and theological subjects, in the context of which the verses under examination took on an increasing significance. The greater variety of literary forms was matched by a corresponding variety of subject matter. It was Jean-Marie Aubert who, in 1975, tried to identify the responsibility of Christianity for current anti-feminism and developed an analysis on the basis of the condition of Jewish women at the time of Jesus and of "gospel liberation." He sought, through a detailed and deep assessment of the mechanisms and conditionings involved, to characterize the specifically "Christian form" of anti-feminism, ending with a consideration of the question of women's ministry.[65]

Ben Witherington's 1979 article deserves special mention as being the only essay devoted exclusively and specifically to Luke's pericope.[66] The main purpose of Luke's text, he claims, is to show that these women had been witnesses since Jesus' time in Galilee; he holds, however, that this does not mean women's traditional roles being abandoned, but that they are seen not only in the family context but in that of the community of faith.

In general, the writings of this period are distinguished by both breadth of subject matter and careful attention to detail.[67] The definition of women as disciples is placed in a context of historical-

---

[65] J. M. Aubert, *La femme: anti-féminisme et christianisme* (Paris, 1975). Cf C. Buzzetti, "Gesù e le donne," *ParVi* 20 (1975), pp. 433–50.

[66] See note 1. From the analysis made of the literary and historical context of these verses, their content and aim, he concludes that while on the one hand Jesus, who allowed women to travel with him, rejected much of the rabbinal teaching on the inferiority of women, on the other hand he reaffirmed the pre-eminence of men when he chose the twelve.

[67] Cf. J. Ernst, *Das evangelium nach Lukas* (Regensburg, 1977); N. M. Flanagan, "The Position of Women in the Writings of St Luke," *Marianum* 40 (1978), pp. 288–304; J. M. Guillaume, *Luc interprète des anciennes traditions sur la résurrection de Jésus* (Paris, 1979); G. Rouiller and C. Varone, *Evangile selon Saint Luc* (Fribourg, 1980); J. A. Fitzmeyer, *The Gospel According to Luke. Anchor Bible 28* (Garden City, N.Y., 1981); J. Radermakers and P. Bossuyt, *Jésus. Parole de la Grâce selon Saint Luc* (Brussels, 1981).

cultural analysis from which the break that Jesus made with his times emerges clearly. Against this background and with the evidence of how Jesus confronted it, it is becoming more possible to deepen our examination of Jesus' motives and the significance of his attitude to women. Questions are being raised about the problem of women not belonging to the group of the twelve. The mere fact that such questions are being asked is evidence of a changed socio-cultural climate.

The gospel texts are being examined with a new sensitivity, born of the increasingly emergent "question of women," and developing and spreading from this environment to lay new foundations for the profound changes taking place today. Could such work have been done in earlier times, and, furthermore, could such a sensitivity have shown itself in the Palestine Jesus knew? One has to be conscious of the risks inherent in projecting demands and questions backwards from our age to that in which the Gospels took shape, demands and questions that arise from the nature of this inquiry, but which in any event should be referred to the general historical-social-moral-cultural climate of the time – something very difficult to reconstruct. Now the subjects tackled are interconnecting: women are seen as apostles for having carried the message of the Risen Christ and this leads to the question of women's ordination to the ministry.[68] New approaches are being tried: psychoanalytical and one that could be called "from the woman's point of view."[69]

---

[68] On attributing the title of apostle, see Moltmann-Wendel, *Freiheit-Gleichheit-Schwesterlichkeit*, pp. 34–48, and the earlier work by L. Russell, *Human Liberation in a Feminist Perspective. A Theology* (Philadelphia, 1974), with a chapter on the ordination of women to the ministry; L. Legrand, "Women's Ministries in the New Testament," *BBIBQ* 2 (1976), 286–99; M. Alcalá, *La mujer y los ministerios en la iglesia* (Madrid, 1979); E. M. Tetlow, *Women and Ministry in the N.T.* (Lauham, N.Y., 1980); C. F. Parvey, *Ordination of Women in Ecumenical Perspective. Workbook for the Church's Future* (Geneva, 1980); C. Militello (ed.), *Donna e Ministero. Un dibattito ecumenico* (Rome, 1991).

[69] Among such see: F. Dolto and G. Séverin, *L'évangile au risque de la psychanalyse,* 2 vols (Paris, 1977–8); H. Wolff, *Jesus der Mann: die Gestalt Jesu in tiefenpsychologischer Sicht* (Stuttgart, 1975).

Elisabeth Moltmann-Wendel's book on the women Jesus met is certainly among the most important of the studies by women.[70] Having identified the need for a new way of studying the Bible, one that women can undertake, she herself opens the way to the new "theological imagination" needed in tackling the analysis of certain passages from the New Testament concerning women. Her book can be said to initiate a whole series of works, of a variety of forms, which might be generally titled "Jesus and women."[71] The amplification of the subject matter and increase in the number of questions needing investigation has been confirmed in the writings of the last few years. Themes connected with women's liberation have been to the fore in posing new problems and asking new questions of scripture: were the women in Luke 8:1–3 present at the Last Supper?[72]

---

[70] E. Moltmann-Wendel, *The Women around Jesus* (New York, 1982); of basic importance too is E. Schüssler Fiorenza, *In Memory of Her. A Feminist Theological Reconstruction of Christian Origins* (New York, 1983). For a Latin American viewpoint, see I. Gebara and M. C. Bingemer, *A Mulher faz Teologia* (Petrópolis, 1986).

[71] Cf L. Boff, *O rostro materno de Deus* (Petrópolis, 1979), Eng. trans. *The Maternal Face of God* (San Francisco, 1988). Looking for an answer to questions such as "How can the feminine . . . reveal God? How is God . . . revealed in the feminine? . . . how does the feminine we know become a way of knowing God?", and embarking on "a reflection of a theological nature on the feminine in man, in woman, in Mary and in God," Boff makes a brief but significant reference to Luke 8:1–3 in the section on "Jesus and the Liberation of Woman." He shows here how women have understood that "the central message of the historical Jesus is addressed primarily to the poor, the marginalized and the oppressed" and that it is therefore, addressed to women, who "more than anyone else" are included in these categories. And they, "against all the rules of the time . . . followed him (Luke 8:1–3; 23:49; 24:6–10)." Cf also R. Laurentin, "Jesus and Women: an Underestimated Revolution," *Concilium* 134 (1980), pp. 80–92; B. Witherington III, *Women in the Ministry of Jesus* (Cambridge, 1984); F. Quéré, *Les femmes de l'évangile* (Paris, 1982); M. Evans, *Woman in the Bible* (Exeter, 1983).

[72] Cf. Q. Quesnell, "The Women at Luke's Supper," C. Scharper (ed.), *Political Issues in Luke-Acts* (Maryknoll, N.Y., 1983), pp. 59–79; M. C. Jacobelli, *Sacerdozio-donna-celibato. Alcune considerazioni antropologiche* (Rome, 1981), pp. 98–107; S. Tunc, *Brève histoire des femmes chrétiennes* (Paris, 1989), pp. 49–51.

New questions are also emerging through theology's growing recognition of the human sciences. Anthropology is looking deep into the archaic roots of oppression of women and linking the problem of their exclusion from the priesthood to that of obligatory celibacy for the Catholic clergy.[73]

If there is a gap in the writings examined above, this is the sparse definition given to the term "disciple," though this has to a certain extent been filled lately. It is not alway fully possible to be sure of the exact value and meaning of the term as applied by the various authors to women.

The final conclusion to be drawn from this survey is that in general and over the span of time considered here, little has been written, specifically and purposively, on Luke 8:1-3. Going through the indexes to whole stacks of exegetical and theological writings held in the Pontifical Biblical Institute showed me that these verses were almost left out. With the two exceptions of Ketter (1933) and Hengel (1963), this started to change only towards the end of the 1970s. Seen from another angle, this coincides with a growing amount of research and analysis done by women, virtually non-existent before. Women are not the only ones interested in the question of women in the Gospels, but in general one can say that the questions raised by the broader women's movement that has been gaining strength over recent years have produced openings on to new horizons, new subjects and new techniques.

---

[73] On this see particularly Jacobelli, *Sacerdozio-donna-celibato.*

Chapter 3

WOMEN AND JESUS IN THE LAND OF GALILEE

Luke 8:1–3 shows the Women's Discipleship

> Soon afterwards he went on through cities and villages, proclaiming and bringing the goods news of the kingdom of God. The twelve were with him, as well as some women who had been cured of evil spirits and infirmities: Mary, called Magdalene, from whom seven demons had gone out, and Joanna, the wife of Herod's steward Chuza, and Susanna, and many others, who provided for him out of their resources (Luke 8:1–3).

A first glance at this passage will show the main elements it contains. This will make it easier to examine the links between the pieces of information the pericope provides as well as the immediate and remote contexts preceding and following it.

Luke 8:1–3	*Synthesis of Elements*	
Καὶ ἐγένετο ἐν τῷ καθεξῆς καὶ αὐτὸς διώδευεν κατὰ πόλιν καὶ κώμην		
Soon afterwards he went on through cities and villages	TRAVELLING	
κηρύσσων καὶ εὐαγγελιζόμενος τὴν βασιλείαν τοῦ θεοῦ		
proclaiming and bringing the good news of the kingdom of God	EVANGELIZING	
καὶ οἱ δώδεκα σὺν αὐτῷ, καὶ γυναῖκές τινες		
The twelve (were) with him as well as some women	COMPOSITION OF THE GROUP	Twelve Jesus Women

αἳ ἦσαν τεθεραπευμέναι ἀπὸ πνευμάτων
πονηρῶν καὶ ἀσθενειῶν,

who had been cured of   HEALING AND FREEING
evil spirits and infirmities   OF THOSE POSSESSED

Μαρία ἡ καλουμένη Μαγδαληνή

                            WOMEN OF THE GROUP

Mary, called Magdalene

ἀφ᾽ ἧς δαιμόνια ἑπτὰ ἐξεληλύθει,   THREE GIVEN NAME

from whom seven demons had gone out   MANY OTHERS

καὶ Ἰωάννα γυνὴ Χουζᾶ
ἐπιτρόπου Ἡρῴδου

Joanna, the wife of Herod's   REFERRED TO BY HUSBAND
steward Chuza   AND HEROD

καὶ Σουσάννα

and Susanna

καὶ ἕτεραι πολλαί

and many others

αἵτινες διηκόνουν αὐτῷ κ τῶν
ὑπαρχόντων αὐταῖς.

who provided for him
out of their resources.   SERVICE

It is clear straightaway that more than one phrase goes with a single
theme: so there are two referring to Jesus' healing activity – "who
had been cured of evil spirits and infirmities"; "from whom seven
demons had gone out" – as well as those detailing the composition
of the group and picking out the women present in it. Strictly
speaking, then, these last two elements, *group and women*, form a
single theme, where the second element is no more than part of the
specification of the first. Does this make the theme of the *group
around Jesus* the main centre of interest? Let us see how the other
elements identified relate to this.

The first two, *travelling and evangelizing*, making up verse 8:1,
have Jesus as their subject and contain a link to the *group* theme in
that they are placed in a context of shared resources and in that the
circle around Jesus were the first to hear the good news.

The *healing and freeing from evil spirits* has a direct dependence on the *group* theme, or rather on the *women* component of it. It conveys information about members of the group. Equally, the *reference to the husband and to Herod* provides a direct specification relative to one of the women in the group. Finally, *providing* is a direct indication of the relationship between the women, as subjects, and Jesus as the object of the action.

So there is a connection of clear dependence on the *group* element for all the individual elements, with the exception of the first two, *travelling* and *evangelizing*, which are also connected to the group, but in a different sense. Having established that the whole passage revolves around the *group* theme, we can now see that this unifying element shows the specificity of Luke's text. The group is composed of Jesus, the twelve and the women: what is the relationship between them?

Luke has already described Jesus' itinerant preaching activity (4:31; 6:17–19; 7:11), as well the presence of the twelve, the choosing of them (5:11; 6:12–17) and their following Jesus. It is not therefore these elements that he is seeking to emphasize here.

Women, however, though they have appeared as single figures, either cured or consoled by Jesus (the widow of Nain), or when they came up to him to serve him (Peter's mother-in-law) or to do him favours (the woman forgiven), have not previously had anything explicitly said about them; they have not been said to be part of the group, or to be regular followers of Jesus: this, then, is the new element Luke is bringing out here.

The particular news this little passage provides is the information that a group of women followed Jesus constantly on his travelling since the beginning of his public activity in the land of Galilee. A circle of women: Mary Magdalene, Joanna, Susanna and many others; they set out with him, leaving home, family, relations, their village, their everyday life, and stayed with him, listening, speaking, travelling, offering goods and services, living with him, in short, and in the end followed him to the cross, where they, the only faithful witnesses, were to see him die.

The great value of this Lucan text is its timely provision of this startling information. It is startling on at least two counts. First because it was revolutionary, for that time, that women should follow a master; second because this is a voice breaking through the silence on women's discipleship and appearing in the written text, if only for a moment. It is a trace that surfaces in the narrative, only to disappear again immediately, but even if the voice hardly surfaces before being stifled, it is unmistakably audible and leaves behind the incontestable certainty that Jesus wanted the restricted and privileged circle that lived with him as he went from village to village to include a group of women.

In the methodological approach used here, which is to try to draw attention not only and not so much to what the texts say, but also and above all to what they do not say, it is basic to realize that these verses of Luke's are not speaking of the disciples: the two components of the group are the twelve and the women. These, and these alone, are specifically mentioned. This is consonant with Luke 23:49, 55 and with the passages in the other two Synoptics (Matt. 27:55 and Mark 15:40) which provide indications about the women who had followed Jesus from Galilee. The disciples who appear at other times in the Gospels are a completely different group from this one, not belonging to the restricted circle of people who lived with Jesus. This would be enough to bring out the different quality of the closeness of this group of women to Jesus. Here are the twelve and here are these women; the disciples stand farther off, in a more distant relationship to Jesus. These women are, therefore, much more in relation to Jesus, who wished them to be with him, than those whom the Gospels identify with the term "disciples." The writer who compiled the text of the third Gospel has provided several opportunities for singling out those who, in 8:1–3, he calls "the twelve." He has listed them by name, has told how Jesus chose them, has given particular information about things that happened in the life of some of them, and in the course of his Gospel designates them by the term "apostles."

---

[1] The authors I have consulted agree in placing the end of the section recounting Jesus' activity in Galilee at 9:50, but vary in establishing its start. This is placed either at 3:1 or 4:14. 3:1 is supported by: R. Fabris, "Il vangelo di Luca," Various, *I vangeli* (Assisi, 1982); M. Hengel, "Maria Magdalena und die Frauen als Zeugen," Various, *Abraham unser Vater. Festschrift O. Michel*, AGSU 5 (Leiden-Cologne, 1963), p. 245. 4:14 is preferred by *The Jerusalem Bible*; C. Stuhlmüller, "The Gospel According to Luke," JBC II (1968). H. Schürmann, *Das Lukasevangelium* I (Freiburg, 1969) proposes a more detailed breakdown: first part, 3:1–4:44; section 1, 3:1–20; section 2, 3:21–4:44; second part, 5:1–19:27; section 1, 5:1–9:50; ch. 1, 5:1–6:49; ch. 2, 7:1–9:50.

And what of these women? Only three are given a proper name here; they are not gathered under a number, nor designated by a collective name. Apostles close to Jesus like the twelve? Let us leave the question open. What will emerge about their actual role will say and tell more about them than a designation and more than a conceptual scheme in which they can be included – and limited.

Going back to looking at how the thematic elements relate to one another in Luke 8:1–3, we see that, apart from the first two and the phrase "the twelve were with him," in effect all the others (*healing and freeing from evil spirits, reference to the husband and to Herod, providing*) are references to the group but with the women as their subject.

So a first look at the text shows two themes emerging as prevalent: *group* and *women*. If we then go on to a careful reading of the broad context in which the pericope is set, the section of Luke's Gospel dealing with Jesus' activity in Galilee (4:14 - 9:50),[1] we can try to find other traces that, by telling us more about the group and about women, can shed further light on the object of this research.

The Group that Formed around Jesus

The information Luke gives about Jesus travelling from one place to another, accompanied by the twelve and some women, raises certain questions. When did Luke think the group was formed? Had those he now says it included been with Jesus from the beginning? And from this time on did they stay close to Jesus all the time, sharing his day-to-day activity? What functions did the different components of the group perform?

A quick reading of the whole section covering Jesus' activity in Galilee (4:14–9:50) will show us when Jesus appeared without the disciples, when he was with them, when the disciples are not mentioned but neither are they excluded, when Jesus appears together with the women and finally when the women are not mentioned but not excluded either.

In the part of the text preceding 8:1–3 the first things set out are Jesus' teachings and the cures he worked (4:14–44). He does appear with a crowd round him, but not with any individuals linked to him in a particular way. The only passage showing Jesus in relation to other individuals is the cure of Simon's mother-in-law, who, after the fever had left her, "began to serve them" (4:39). With the calling

TABLE SHOWING THE PRESENCE OF THE DISCIPLES AND/OR
WOMEN WITH JESUS DURING HIS ACTIVITY IN GALILEE
(LUKE 4:14–9:50)

Column 1: Jesus appears without the disciples
2: Jesus is together with the disciples
3: The disciples are neither mentioned nor excluded
4: Jesus appears together with the women
5: The Women are not mentioned but not excluded either.

VERSES	DESCRIPTION	1	2	3	4	5
4: 14–15	Jesus begins teaching	X				
16–30	Jesus at Nazareth	X				
31–37	Jesus at Capernaum: he teaches and casts out a demon	X				
38–39	Cure of Simon's mother-in-law	X?			X	
40–41	Cure of many sick and possessed	X			?	
42–44	Jesus leaves Capernaum and goes through Judea preaching	X				
5: 1–11	Jesus calls the first three disciples			X		
12–15	Cure of a leper	X				
16	Jesus withdraws to pray	X				
17–26	Cure of a paralytic	X				
27–39	Call of Levi and meal with sinners		X			
6: 1–5	Plucking heads of grain and the sabbath		X			
6–11	Cure of the man with a withered hand	X		X?		
12	Jesus spends the night in prayer	X				
13–16	Jesus chooses the twelve		X			
17–49	Jesus, followed by many disciples and a great multitude, heals many and teaches		X			X
7: 1–10	Jesus at Capernaum heals the centurion's slave			X?		
11–17	Raising of the widow of Nain's son		X			
18–35	Jesus replies to a delegation from John the Baptist after curing many sick and possessed, then speaks of him to the crowd and passes judgment on his generation			X?		X
36–50	Jesus in a Pharisee's house: the woman forgiven	X?			X	
8: 1–3	Jesus travels followed by the twelve and many women		X		X	

VERSES	DESCRIPTION	1	2	3	4	5
4–18	Jesus speaks to the crowd: parable of the sower and other teachings		X			X
19–21	Who are Jesus' true family?[2]			X?		X
22–25	The storm calmed		X			X
26–39	Cure of the Gerasene demoniac		X			X
40–56	Raising of Jairus' daughter and cure of the woman with a hemorrhage		X		X	
9:-6	Jesus sends the twelve to preach and heal		X			X
7–9	Herod tries to see Jesus					
10–17	Jesus at Bethsaida: many cured, multiplication of loaves and fishes[3]		X			X
18–27	Peter's profession of faith and first announcement of the passion		X		X?	
28–36	Jesus is transfigured		X			
37–50	Cure of the possessed epileptic. Second announcement of the passion and other teachings		X		X?	

of the first three disciples, the concept of following makes its first appearance: "... they left everything and followed him" (5:11). Then two cures are worked (5:12–15; 17–26), at which the disciples are not mentioned but reappear immediately afterwards (5:27–39) in the call to Levi and the meal at his house. They are still present at the episode of the heads of grain plucked on the sabbath (6:1–5) and again are not mentioned when another cure is described immediately after this (6:6–11). From 6:12–16, the choosing of the twelve, they are present to 6:49. In 6:17–19 Luke gives details of those who were with Jesus: "a great crowd of his disciples and a great

---

[2] In the parallel text Matt. 12:46–50 explicit reference is made to the disciples.
[3] This episode has its parallel in Matt. 14:13–21, where we find: "And those who ate were about five thousand men, not counting women and children." [For an elaboration of the implications of this, see M. McKenna, *Not Counting Women and Children* (Maryknoll, N.Y. and Tunbridge Wells, 1994) – Trans.]

multitude of people from all Judea ... (who) had come to hear him and to be healed of their diseases." So there are two separate entities: disciples and multitude. The presence of women is neither mentioned nor excluded. The specification of the motives for the crowd following him is useful for the later completion of the picture. The disciples are still not obviously present at a cure (7:1–10), where there is specific mention of "the crowd that followed him" (7:9). The episode that comes next, the raising of the son of the widow of Nain (7:11–17), again mentions two groups, as in 6:17–19: "Soon afterwards he went to a town called Nain, and his disciples and a large crowd went with him" (7:11). So the disciples were with Jesus when, touched by this woman's suffering, he gave her back her son after becoming closely involved in her situation.

There then follows the account of the questions put by the followers of John the Baptist and the witness Jesus gives them, without any mention of the disciples being present. He also appears without the disciples in the following episode of the woman forgiven (7:36–50). The dialogue that develops between this woman and Jesus bears witness to a deep communication, helped by the element of physical contact.[4]

Bearing in mind that in 8:1–3 the twelve and the group of women are referred to, not the disciples, we can see that, from this moment on, either the twelve (9:1–6, 10–17) or a group designated by the term "disciples" are shown with Jesus. And the women? Are we to see them as always there even if they are no longer specifically mentioned?

The most likely interpretative hypothesis that it seems possible to put forward is that, within the sections that describe the activity in Galilee, Luke gradually puts together the picture of those who are the object of Jesus' preaching and of those who are called and chosen to stay with him: the crowd, the multitude of people, the disciples, the twelve and the women. From the moment when he tells of the first calling of the disciples, Luke mentions these as being with Jesus, except when narrating the episodes of healing. One might think, for

---

[4] Adriana Zarri has written profoundly and lyrically about the (non-genital) sexual dimension, the overall meaning of sexed experience shown here by Jesus in the meeting with this woman. A. Zarri, *E più facile che un cammello* ... (Turin, 1975), esp. pp. 258–60. The passage from Luke is discussed later in this chapter, where it is analyzed in detail.

what such a supposition is worth, that he does not mention the disciples in these because they had no precise part to play at this time[5]. Besides these episodes, there remain the passages dealing with the request of John the Baptist's disciples (7:18–35) and the episode of the woman forgiven (7:36–50). With respect to the first, in view of the fact that the ὄχλος, "crowd," is mentioned (7:24), one can ask if this included the disciples. With respect to the second, since it deals with an invitation to a meal, it is quite likely that Jesus would have gone alone;[6] one can in any case understand Luke concentrating attention on the two people whose moment of special relationship he wants to bring to the fore: Jesus and the woman.

In 8:1–3 we arrive at the completion of the composition. Luke seems to be showing where we have got to: Jesus, travelling through villages and towns, proclaims the good news (as he had declared it his purpose to do so in 4:43); he is accompanied by the twelve (of whom, as we have seen, he had already spoken in 6:12–16) and the group of women.

Of the three women called by name, none has appeared before. The statement "who had been cured" can be seen as a "revealing trace." The redactor has told of the healing of Simon's mother-in-law (4:38–9); of the healing of "many," without indicating whether they were men and/or women (4:40–41; 6:18–19; 7:21). Were any of the women mentioned in Luke 8:1–3 as having been cured present on these occasions? In each and every episode of many people being healed, he mentions diseases and evil spirits – both elements present in 8:1–3.

The writer arrives at 8:1–3 having already given several pieces of information about the cures worked by Jesus and after this pericope their course changes. Given his information on the composition of the group, what follows provides evidence of its becoming more compact than it was earlier. The twelve, or at any rate a group designated by the term disciples, and the women of 8:1–3 are constantly with Jesus.

All this raises various questions: can Luke's use of terms such as

---

[5] Later, Jesus gives them too the power to work cures (Luke 9:1).

[6] This would suggest, among other things, that the memory of the episode would have been kept and handed down by the woman concerned. There are, however, authors who hold that the disciples were there: cf C. M. Martini, *La donna nel suo popolo* (Milan, 1984), pp. 47–59.

ὄχλος, "crowd," and λαός, "people," be taken to include the disciples? Always or only in some cases? After signalling the presence of women, does Luke's term μαθητής, "disciples," then include them, or exclude them, or, more simply, not bother to mike thmir presence explicit since he has already made this clear? When the twelve are sent out on a mission, do they go alone? Do the women then stay with Jesus? Or do they all go, leaving Jesus alone? Are there also other disciples (not named in 8:1–3) around Jesus, less continuously and less intensely related to him?

An analysis of the terms used to describe various persons shows that within the section relating Jesus' activity in Galilee, the numbers around him grow: there is the crowd, to whom he proclaims the Kingdom and among whom he works cures, and a more defined group of men and women who are involved with him and follow him on his travels from one place to another.

8:1–3 seems to form a divide between one period in which Jesus travels (4:14, 16, 31, 44; 6:1; 7:1, 11), is only sometimes accompanied by disciples (5:1–11, 27–32), has contacts and discussions with women (4:38–9; 7:11–17, 36–50), and another period in which the same disciples now appear constantly with him. From 8:1–3 onward, human relations in general and his relationship to the disciples (among whom he has already chosen the twelve: 6:13–16) in particular become closer, more constant and intense, as is shown in the increased use of specific terms – disciples, twelve, apostles, woman, man – and proper names, with a corresponding lessening of generic terms such as all, crowd, people, many and the like.

With respect to the question as to whether the terms "crowd" or "people" include the disciples, it is noticeable that in some cases Luke uses the specific term "disciples" close to the other, but making it distinct: ". . . there was a large crowd of tax collectors and others... complaining to his disciples . . ." (5:29–30); "He came down with them and stood on a level place, with a great crowd of his disciples and a great multitude of people . . ." (6:17); ". . . his disciples and a large crowd went with him" (7:11). Elsewhere he speaks of the crowd or multitude and only later mentions the disciples, thereby revealing that they had been present, even though not previously mentioned explicitly. This is what happens immediately after 8:1–3 when he writes of the ὄχλου πολλοῦ, "great crowd" to whom Jeus told the parable of the sower (8:4). Then, in relation to the parable, he says: "his disciples asked him . . ." (8:9). And then later: "Now when Jesus returned, the crowd welcomed him, for they were all waiting for him"(8:40), immediately followed by Peter (8:45) and, still within the same space-time unity, Peter, John and James (8:51).

We still need to take account of the difference between the twelve and the disciples. Whether, after the choice of the twelve, Luke's use of the term "disciples" refers only to them, to a wider group including them or, in particular circumstances, to a group to which the twelve do not belong, is a question that goes beyond the bounds of this inquiry.

Perhaps Luke, before 8:1–3, specifies when the disciples are present, which would mean that the terms "crowd" and "people" effectively do not include them, while after 8:1–3 he considers it superfluous to mention continually that they are there, so one can conclude that they are always present, and so included in the more general terms. The same can be taken to apply to the women. What need would the evangelist have had, what purpose would it have served, to refer constantly to the presence of women, which he had already noted explicitly and in detail? The androcentric wider culture in which he wrote would have led him to seek and see his protagonists and witnesses in the male disciples.

Women and the Four Gospels

In order to obtain a more comprehensive view of the presence of women in Luke's narrative, we can use a comparative reading of the four Gospels through a synoptic table that directly brings out the salient points.[7] This has been compiled by taking all references to women, separating out references to single women and groups of women around Jesus, his discourses in which women appear, expressions relating to women used by persons other than Jesus or by the compiler of the account. All the elements singled out are given in the texts of each Gospel successively. This table, then, provides an attempt at utilizing and verifying the "reading key" described in chapter 1, according to which the silence surrounding women is broken only on special occasions.

What constitutes an exceptional occasion can be broken down into specific types of event or occasion, so that the necessary "exceptionalness" can be provided by:

---

[7] This table is given in the Appendix, pp. 197–212.

(a) a healing or other miraculous deed of which a woman is the object;
(b) the way a certain woman behaves, which can be held up as an example to others or has particular characteristics, good or bad;
(c) Jesus' attitude to a woman;
(d) a woman's attitude shown by her enthusiasm to turn to Jesus;
(e) the role and particular witness attributable solely or mainly to women.
(f) Finally, a mention may be made primarily because a woman is placed in relation to a man.

To make this examination simpler to use, I have placed, in the following table [in square brackets], after every woman (except Mary the mother of Jesus) listed, the letter or letters corresponding to the above list, showing the presumed main reason for her appearance at this point in the texts. Here I am detailing only particular women as they appear in person, not mentions of them in Jesus' discourses or those of others. The complete table is given in the Appendix: here I list the appearances of single figures or groups of women around Jesus, marking which are particular to one Gospel with the sign *P.

MARK
Simon's mother-in-law (1:29–31) [a, f]
Mary the mother of Jesus (3:31–5; 6:3)
The woman suffering from a hemorrhage (5:25–43) [a, c, d]
Jairus' daughter and her mother *P (5:22–43) [a]
Herodias (6:17–19) and her daughter (6:22–8) [b]
The Syrophoenician woman and her daughter (7:25–30) [a, d]
The widow (12:42–4) [b]
The woman at Bethany (14:3–9) [b, c]
The servant-girl (14:66–70) [b, f]
Women (15:40) [e]
Mary Magdalene (15:40, 47; 16:1, 9) [a, c, e]
Mary the mother of James the younger and of Joses (15:40, 47; 16:1) [e]
Salome (15:40; 16:1) [e]

MATTHEW
Mary the mother of Jesus (1:16, 18, 24; 2:11, 13, 14; 2:20, 21; 12:46–50)
Peter's mother-in-law (8:14–15) [a, f]
The daughter of a leader of the synagogue (9:18–26) [a]
The woman suffering from a hemorrhage (9:18–26) [a, c, d]
Herodias (14:3–4) [b]
Herodias' daughter (14:6–11) [b]
The Canaanite woman and her daughter (15:22–8) [d, a]
Mary the mother of the sons of Zebedee *P (20:20–23; 27:56) [d, f]
The woman of Bethany (26:6–13) [b, c]A servant-girl (26:69) [b, f]
Another servant-girl (26:71) [b, f]
Pilate's wife *P (27:19) [b, f]
Many women (27:55) [e]
Mary Magdalene (27:56, 61; 28:1) [e, c]
Mary the mother of James and Joseph (27:56) [e]
The other Mary (27:61; 28:1) [e, c] [8]

---

[8] The "other Mary" could be either the Mary the mother of James and Joseph or the mother of the sons of Zebedee or perhaps a third woman.

LUKE
Elizabeth *P (1:5–25, 40–45, 57–66) [e]
Mary the mother of Jesus (1:26–38.
39–45, 46–56; 2:5–7, 16–19, 21–35,
41–51; 8:19–21)
Anna the prophet *P (2:36–8) [e]
Herodias (3:19–20) [b]
Peter's mother-in-law (4:38–9) [a, f]
The widow of Nain *P (7:12–15) [a]
The woman forgiven *P (7:36–50)
[c, d]
Some women (8:2) [a]
Mary Magdalene (8:2; 24:10) [a, b, e]
Joanna *P (8:3; 24:10) [a, b, e]
Susanna *P (8:3) [a, b]
Many others *P (8:3) [b]
The woman suffering from a hemor-
rhage (8:43–8) [a, c, d]
Jairus' daughter (8:41–56) [a]
Martha (10:38–42) [b, c]
Mary (10:38–42) [b, c]
The woman who says "Blessed is the
womb..." *P (11:27–8) [d]
The woman who was bent over *P
(13:11–13) [a]
The widow (21:2–4) [b]
The servant-girl (22:56–7) [b, f]
The women who beat their breasts and
wail for Jesus *P (23:27–31) [b]
Mary the mother of James (24:10) [e]

JOHN
Mary the mother of Jesus (2:1–11;
19:25)
The Samaritan woman *P (4:7–42)
[c, e]
The woman caught in adultery *P
(8:3–11) [b, c]
Mary of Bethany (11:1–45; 12:1–8)
[b, c]
Martha of Bethany (11:1–45) [b, c]
The woman who guarded the gate
(18:16–17) [b, f]
Jesus' mother's sister *P (19:25) [e].[9]
Mary the wife of Clopas (19:25) [e]
Mary Magdalene (19:25; 20:1, 11, 16, 18)
[b, c, e]

From this comparison it is obvious that Luke makes most references to the presence of women, either singly or as a group: twenty-two as against seventeen in Matthew, sixteen in Mark and nine in John. Even more significant is the number of figures particular to Luke: eleven (eight single women and three groups) compared to four in John, two in Matthew and one in Mark. The other elements (brought out in the table in the Appendix) give the following result: of Jesus' discourses in which women are mentioned, Luke has twenty-one mentions, of which eight are particular to his account; Matthew has eighteen, of which five are particular to him; Mark seven, of which none particular; John just one, particular to him. As for passages relating to women in discourses by persons other than Jesus: Matthew has seven, of which six are his alone; John three, of which two are his alone; Mark one, with a parallel in Matthew; Luke just one, his alone.

[9] The sister of Jesus' mother and Mary the wife of Clopas could be two different persons or one and the same.

Luke is the Gospel with most references in all the categories considered except this last. The significant aspect of this is that it is just in accounts where the intervention of the author can most clearly be supposed that Luke comes last, equal with Mark. Of course the whole Gospel should be seen as having been compiled by Luke, but one would expect to see the compiler's hand intervening more specifically in expressions relating to women not attributable to Jesus or others.

Commentators on Luke are in fairly general agreement about the extent of the attention he pays to the presence of women. It is a more complex matter, however, to try to disentangle what might have produced this attention or to understand whether this is actually a tendency on Luke's part or whether we should look for some other explanation.

Comparing the four Gospels in this way gives a better idea of the tendency proper to each compiler with respect to subjects involving women. This would be a most interesting analysis, but one that is beyond my scope here: any hint is however useful in deciding what weight to attribute to the mentality of whoever composed the material both in its process of transmission and in the work of selecting and modifying without conscious deliberation. We would need to know what attitude Jesus' own disciples had to women. They must have been strongly conditioned by the culture of their time, so that, despite the filters introduced by the compilers, we can find traces of this in the texts that have come down to us.

In John 4:27 we read: "Just then his disciples came. They were astonished that he was speaking with a woman, but no one said, 'What do you want?' or, 'Why are you speaking with her?'"[10] The disciples' amazement at seeing Jesus talking to a Samaritan woman is an implicit indication that this was behaviour totally out of the ordinary for them and for the climate in which they lived.

Rabbinic literature contains indications of the way men were expected to behave toward women. So the Abòth treatise says of the moral code of the Hebrew fathers: "Jōçê son of Jochanan, of

---

[10] Cf. R. Schnackenburg, *The Gospel according to St John*, vol. 1 (London and New York, 1968), pp. 419–60.

Jerusalem, used to say: '... Do not have much speech with women; and if this applies to your own wife, so much the more to the wives of others.' On account of this the Doctors have said that anyone who speaks much with women does himself harm, because, turning away from study, he ends by acquiring hell."[11]

In Matthew 19:3 some Pharisees ask Jesus if it is lawful for a man to divorce his wife for any reason, and I should like to make a brief comment of the precarious state in which the possibility of being divorced left wives. Deuteronomy says: "Suppose a man enters into marriage with a woman, but she does not please him because he finds something objectionable about her, and so he writes her a certificate of divorce, puts it into her hand, and sends her out of his house ..." (Deut. 24:1). This is the text that allowed a husband to repudiate his wife by giving her a written document, countersigned by two witnesses, on which he had written the sentence: "You are free to every man."[12]

A woman had to have this document if she was to be able to contract another marriage. What could constitute valid motives for repudiating a wife and what could be understood by "something shameful" were subjects of debate in Jesus' time in the two rabbibical schools: the more rigorous one of Shammai held that adultery was the only valid ground for divorce; the more permissive one of Hillel allowed trifling grounds such as having broken a dish, not to mention the husband having found a more beautiful woman. Women, however, did not have the same right to divorce. There were extremely rare cases in which a woman, while not being able to divorce her husband, could force him to give her the certificate of divorce: when the man was impotent, had contracted a disgusting disease, and the like. So only the man was allowed to initiate divorce proceedings, and even if her husband had abandoned her, a woman was not free without a certificate declaring him to be dead. Furthermore, it seems that when a wife had been repudiated, the children always stayed with

---

[11] Y. Colombo, *Pirgê Abôth. Morale dei maestri ebrei* (Assisi-Rome, 1977), p. 3.

[12] Cf W. Dommershausen, *Die Umwelt Jesu: Politik und Kultur in Neuetestamentlicher Zeit* (Freiburg-Basle-Vienna, 1977).

the husband and so the further suffering of losing the children was always inflicted on the woman.[13]

In Matthew 19:10, after Jesus has answered the disciples' question about the legitimacy of divorce saying that it was not allowed, "His disciples said to him, 'If such is the case of a man with his wife, it is better not to marry'." Their reaction shows the disciples' conception of marriage and relations with women bound into the framework where men's power and rights over women prevailed. "A woman was under the tutelage of her father till her wedding, then passed to that of her husband, who became his wife's 'owner' or *ba'al*." In the Decalogue (Exod. 20:17), a wife is listed along with other possessions: male or female slave, ox, donkey.... And the Hebrew verb "to marry" comes from the same root as "to become owner of."[14] The Book of Ruth tells how Boaz, who was to become Ruth's husband, asks, when he first sees her gleaning in the field, "To whom does this young woman belong?" (Ruth 2:5). The complete lack of autonomy for women and their subjection to men's will, first their father's and then their husband's, are confirmed by many rules: anything a woman found belonged to her father, or, if she was married, to her husband; a woman could not make a vow without her father's approval; her husband could reverse a vow made by her or even make one binding on her; in the courts she was represented first by her father (who was entitled to receive damages if his daughter was mutilated or raped), and then by her husband, who was very probably also entitled to receive any damages awarded (see Num. 30:2–17). If on her wedding night she was found not to be a virgin, she was condemned to be stoned (Deut. 22:20–21). Her parents and relations waited outside the nuptial chamber and, once sexual intercourse had taken place, displayed the blood-stained sheet, which they then kept as a proof

---

[13] Cf E. S. Gerstenberger and W. Schrage, *Frau und Mann* (Stuttgart, 1980); A. Tosato, *Il matrimonio nel giudaismo antico e nel Nuovo Testamento* (Rome, 1976), p. 29, n. 10; J. Jeremias, *Jerusalem zur Zeit Jesu. Eine Kulturgeschichtliche Unterschung zur neuetestamentlichen Zeitgeschichte* (Göttingen, 1962): Eng. trans. *Jerusalem in the Time of Jesus* (London and New York, 1973); Adinolfi, *Il femminismo della Biblia*, p. 110; B.-Z. Schereschewscky, "Divorce," *En Ju* 6, 122–37.

[14] R. de Vaux, *Les institutions de l'Ancien Testament* (Paris, 1958): It. trans. *Le istitutzione dell'Antico Testamento* (Turin, 1964), p. 36.

to bring out if the husband later accused his wife unjustly. If a husband slandered his wife in this way, he was no longer permitted to divorce her (Deut. 22:13–19), and had to pay a fine to the girl's father. Here too the person to be recompensed is not the woman but her father, since he is the one to have suffered through goods "belonging" to him being damaged.[15]

Men's power over women is clearly shown in the rules governing cases of rape. If an engaged girl is raped by someone other than her fiancé she is to be stoned to death along with the man if the rape was committed in a town, because she should have called for help; if the rape takes place in the open country, only the man is to be stoned to death, because she might have called for help and not been heard (Deut. 22:23–7). The reason for this is explicitly given as, "because he dishonoured the future wife of a neighbour": the person who has been harmed is not the girl but a man. So if the girl is not engaged when she is raped, the man is not condemned, but has to give her father fifty shekels of silver, marry the girl and not be allowed to divorce her. Cases of adultery are judged in the same way, as a very serious crime, counted among those that harm one's neighbour. If a man commits adultery with an engaged or married woman, both are to be stoned to death. The woman belongs to her fiancé or husband, and it his rights that have been damaged. This becomes even clearer from the different treatment reserved to husbands: they are considered adulterers only if they sleep with a woman who is engaged or married to another man; women are always adulterers whether the man they sleep with is married or single. A husband is not bound to be faithful, nor does the law consider a woman's rights; it establishes and looks after those of men only.[16]

This, then, is the background to the disciples' reaction, both so spontaneous and ingenuous. It strikes us now as a childish protest

---

[15] Cf Gerstenberger and Schrage, *Frau und Mann*; J. Romney Wegner, *Chattel or Person? The Status of Women in the Mishnah* (Oxford and New York, 1988).

[16] Cf J. Pirenne, "La statut de la femme dans l'empire romain," *La femme* (Brussels, 1959), p. 113; Adinolfi, *Il femminismo della Bibbia*, p. 104; on the whole subject of the condition of women under Judaism at the time of Jesus, see Jeremias, "The Social Situation of Women," appendix to *Jerusalem in the Time of Jesus*.

at a game whose rules have been changed and are no longer acceptable.

Equally revealing is their attitude to children. Luke 18:15–16 relates: "People were bringing even infants to him that he might touch them; and when the disciples saw it, they sternly ordered them not to do it. But Jesus called for them and said, 'Let the little children come to me . . .'."[17]. Luke, like the other Synoptics who relate the episode, does not make clear, since he probably thought it obvious, that it would have been women who brought their children to Jesus for him to touch and caress, while their presence annoyed the disciples.

As a final example of the disciples' mentality, let us look at the relevant expressions variously applied to women by Matthew, Mark and Luke in their accounts of Jesus' death and resurrection. Mark, unable to claim that the disciples were present as they had abandoned Jesus, stresses that the women present were "looking on from a distance" (15:40: the same expression is found in Matt. 27:55); then the women after their visit to the empty tomb are described as fleeing from the tomb, "for terror and amazement had seized them; and they said nothing to anyone, for they were afraid" (16:8). And finally, when Mary Magdalene tells the disciples about the resurrection, "they would not believe it" (16:11).[18] Luke, having established that the women at the tomb "were perplexed" (24:4) and that at the sight of the angels they "were terrified and bowed their faces to the ground" (24:5), also relates that the news they gave the apostles was not believed: "But these words seemed to them an idle tale and they did not believe them" (24:11).

Turning now to the question of how to explain the fact that female figures and imagery play a greater part in Luke's Gospel than in the others, there are two hypotheses to consider: one that Luke was more sensitive to women, the other that he used a source that was rich in these references to women and that may have derived from a tradition kept and handed on mainly by women.

---

[17] There are parallel passages in Matt. 19:13–14 and Mark 10:13–16.

[18] This text forms part of the so-called "longer ending of Mark"; on the question of the two endings, see J. Hug, *La finale de l'Evangile de Marc (Marc 19:9–20)* (Paris, 1978).

For the first hypothesis, perhaps Luke's own personality, temperament, social background and culture can be considered as playing an important part. The fact that he probably came from the upper-middle level of society, a class that would have been exposed to Greek culture, and the likelihood that he trained as a doctor, might have given him an intellectual sensitivity and a specific set of memories that inevitably came out in his work. He gives very precise information about his approach in his prologue: "Since many have undertaken to set down an orderly account of the events that have been fulfilled among us, just as they were handed on to us by those who from the beginning were eye-witnesses and servants of the word, I too decided, after investigating everything carefully from the very first, to write an orderly account for you, most excellent Theophilus, so that you may know the truth concerning the things about which you have been instructed" (Luke 1:1–4). The evangelist in his "careful" research into "everything" to do with "the events that have been fulfilled," handed on by those who were "eye-witnesses ... from the beginning" may well have met some women among these and held rewarding conversations with them. Perhaps one of these was "Joanna, the wife of Herod's steward Chusa," named in both 8:1–3 and at the crucifixion (24:10), who could have been the source of the information about Herod provided by Luke in his work.[19]

The reference to Joanna, a woman with a position at court, in the verses under examination, can be taken as evidence that Luke came from the upper-middle "class."[20] In the same way, also in 8:1–3, the expressions, "Had been cured of evil spirits and infirmities" and "from whom seven demons had gone out," said of Mary Magdalene, can be seen as the sort of details a doctor would notice, so giving credence to the theory that Luke is the person mentioned in the Letter to the Colossians as Paul's companion, "the beloved physician" (4:14). (These considerations would also apply if Luke took his information from another source: he still noticed and

---

[19] For the references to Herod, see ch. 5, n. 58 below.

[20] Other references to persons of relatively high social standing can be found in Luke 1:3; Acts 1:1; 6:7; 8:13, 26–40; 10:1–48; 18:8; 19:31. Cf. H. Schürmann, *Il vangelo di Luca* (Brescia, 1977), p. 710: It. trans of *Das Lukasevangelium* (Freiburg, 1971).

retained these details.) If Luke, the author of a second book, Acts, was Paul's companion, then he could have known personally some of his numerous fellow workers mentioned either in Acts or in Paul's letters.[21]

The very meaningful presence of these women in the early community itself indicates the need to consider and recognize and in a sense retrieve it in the memory of events related in the Gospels. This consideration leads us to the second hypothesis. This can be put forward on the basis of the fact that Luke in his Gospel provides a considerable amount of material proper to him alone, not found in any other account, and that this material contains a consistent presence of women.

Examination of this material tends to uphold the theory that we are dealing with a tradition kept and handed on by women.[22] This leads to the formulation of the hypothesis that Luke had come to know this particular tradition and made wide use of it in the composition of his own account, finding in it the historical validity of "those who from the beginning were eye-witnesses," as he indicates at the beginning of his narrative.

In support of this proposition one can point to twenty-two references Luke makes to female figures (listed above), of which six only have parallels in Mark and can therefore be said to derive from that source, while none is paralleled in Matthew and can be held to derive from Q. So sixteen of these texts derive from the source that

---

[21] Acts mentions as co-workers of Paul and playing a very active role: Lydia (16:14) and Priscilla (18:2); Damaris (17:34), said to have become a believer; in Philip's house, where they stayed for several days, Paul and Luke found his "four unmarried daughters, who had the gift of prophecy" (21:9). Other women active in Acts are "Mary, the mother of John whose other name was Mark" (12:12) and Tabitha (9:36). In Paul's letters the following women co-workers are named: Euodia and Synteche (Phil. 4:2), Chloe (1 Cor. 1:11), Phoebe (Rom. 16:1-2), Tryphaena, Tryphosa and Persis (Rom. 16:12), Rufus' mother (Rom. 16:13), Julia and Nereus' sister (Rom. 16:15). The sisters Martha and Mary are not included in any concept of "twelve" women followers, since the text stresses that they welcomed Jesus in their house.

[22] This analysis has been made by T. Boman based on original research by A. Schlatter: T. Boman. *Die Jesus Uberlieferung im Lichte der neueren Volkskunde* (Göttingen, 1967), esp. pp. 123-37; cf A. Schlatter, *Das Evangelium des Lukas aus seinen Quellen erklärt* (Stuttgart, 1931).

Luke alone used. Such a massive presence of women and episodes relating to them would fit well with the hypothesis of a source derived from, kept and handed on mainly by women. Furthermore, the fact that Luke's account has only one episode concerning women presented within a speeech made by someone other than Jesus (24:22–4) and no references in redactional passages, tends to support the hypothesis that the greater presence of women in his Gospel should not be attributed in the first place to his own personal preference, but rather to his contact with the women of the early community and to his knowledge of the testimonies and traditions whose memory these women kept.

Who these women were can to some extent be gleaned from this tradition itself. Who other than the women mentioned in the pericope 8:1–3 (which we have seen does not come from Mark but from the source Luke alone used), who had followed Jesus from the first phase of his public activity in Galilee right up to his passion and death, could know and remember all that had happened? The source gives the names of three of them: Mary Magdalene, listed first as in the other Synoptics; Joanna, the wife of Herod's steward Chusa, unknown to the other Gospels, but identified here in such detail as to guarantee her historicity; Susanna, who does not appear in the other Gospels either.

The large number of references to women in Luke's Gospel could therefore stem from the source he possessed and utilized. The validity he accorded to this hypothetical source would have been such that he used it even though his own approach need not have been particularly favourable to women. This would seem to be the case, since at the end of his narrative he does not mention the appearance of the risen Christ to the women (as all the other Gospels do), limiting himself to the appearance of angels and bringing in three other male figures, the two disciples on the road to Emmaus (24:13–35) and Simon Peter (24:34), in line with Paul who, speaking of the resurrection, makes no reference to women but cites Peter (1 Cor. 15:3–8).

This line of inquiry, merely hinted at here, is important and would allow us to investigate the limits of Luke's openness in his account of women and what they stand for.[23] If it were possible

---

[23] On this question see E. M. Tetlow, *Women and Ministry in the New Testament* (Lauham, N.Y., 1980).

to attempt a reconstruction of this "women's tradition" we
should then be able to pick out redactional adaptations of the
source and what they suggest, as well as being able to see Luke's
own attitude to women as shown in the remaining parts of his
work drawn from other sources. If such a course were to indicate
that Luke's attitude to women was not entirely positive, or at
least not so sensitive, this would strengthen the import of the
references that do appear in his text; these *indicative traces* of
female presence would have to be more certainly held to have
derived from a source that Luke considered trustworthy enough
to make extensive use of, and this in turn would give the news of
the women who followed and served Jesus even greater value and
firmer historical basis.

Even given the obvious lack of elaboration of the comparison
between Luke and the other evangelists here, we can reach one
starting point: Luke, with the attention he gives to women,
however motivated, surely provides a confirmation of the way the
other compilers filter them out in an androcentric sense? And on
the other hand, Luke's attention to women would not seem so
particular if the other Gospels contained the same number of
references as his to women or to female images, attitudes and
expressions.[24]

Women and Jesus on the Paths of Galilee in Luke's Narrative

Luke's references to women before 8:1–3 in the section dealing with
Jesus' activity in Galilee comprise three episodes relating to women
and one saying of Jesus'. Luke puts them in this order: the healing
of Simon's mother-in-law (4:38–9); the raising of the widow's son at
Nain (7:11–17); Jesus' words, "among those born of women" (7:28);
the woman forgiven (7:36–50).

---

[24] Reference has been made here only to Mark and Matthew;
John would require a separate approach for which there is no space here.
See E. Moltmann-Wendel, *Freiheit-Gleichheit-Schwesterlichkeit* (Munich,
1977).

(a) Simon's Mother-in-Law[25]

> After leaving the synagogue he entered Simon's house. Now Simon's mother-in-law was suffering from a high fever, and they asked him about her. Then he leant over her and rebuked the fever, and it left her. Immediately she got up and began to serve them (Luke 4:38–9).

The first woman found in the narration of Jesus' course through Galilee, Simon's mother-in-law, is a very significant figure on account of the details she allows us to glimpse. Peter was married and Jesus frequented the house where his wife and mother-in-law lived. His familiarity with these female figures is shown by the neighbourly way in which he approaches her sickbed, leaning over her and commanding the fever to leave her, then letting her "serve" him.

Luke makes this episode follow on in time from the casting out of the unclean demon in the synagogue of Capernaum, which is the first miraculous event described in his Gospel. The sequence opens in 4:31 with Jesus teaching in the synagogue and, in a succession of events common in Luke, the preaching is followed by two specific acts of liberation (the healing of the demoniac and of Simon's mother-in-law). These two successive and as it were parallel accounts are followed by a more general, as it were synthetic, account of various healings (4:40–41).

This more general context indicates that Luke is here beginning the first section of his Gospel that uses Mark as a source (1:21–38), where, brought together in a sort of model day, the main aspects of Jesus' activity are described: teaching in the synagogue, casting out demons, healing the sick, the crowd pressing, prayer in solitude.[26] Luke takes up this model, making it the third stage in his account of

---

[25] Cf X. Léon-Dufour, "La guérison de la belle-mère de Simon-Pierre," *Etude de l'évangile* (Paris, 1965), pp. 125–48; M. L. Rigato, "Tradizione e redazione in Mc. 1:29–31 (e paralleli). La guarigione della suocera di Simon Pietro," *RiBi* 17 (1969), 139–74; Schürmann, *Il vangelo di Luca*, pp. 432–4.

[26] For the concept of a "typical day," see P. Benoît and M. E. Boismard, *Synopse des quatre évangiles en français*, vol. 2, (Paris, 1965) p. 93.

the day, after the healing of Simon's mother-in-law, showing Jesus' care for a woman and his intervention on her behalf. This is the first thing the episode tells us in relation to the subject of women. Luke's text moves from a wonderful intervention by Jesus with a man directly on to a similar gesture toward a woman.

This is even more revealing since we are at the outset of Jesus' healing activity, where the rhythm is first imposed on the line of music, as it were:

- first beat   – miracle: the liberation of a demoniac   (man);
- second beat – miracle: the healing of Simon's
                          mother-in-law   (woman);
- third beat   – miracles: many cured   (synthesis, all).

To liberate the demoniac, Jesus "rebukes" the demon, using words to chase it out; to cure Simon's mother-in-law he is said to lean over her (JB) and, in this friendly position, to ἐπετίμησεν (admonish, rebuke) the fever. (Matthew and Mark make more of his physical closeness: he takes her by the hand). The use of this verb, which does not appear either in Matthew or Mark, shows Luke regarding the fever almost as though it were a demon and as it were showing the difficulty of always making a clear distinction between casting out demons and healing from illness. This is reinforced by 8:2, where he speaks of women being cured of "evil spirits and infirmities," then of "seven demons" going out from Mary Magdalene. The woman's prompt response is also brought out: παραχρῆμα δὲ ἀναστᾶσα διηκόνει αὐτοῖς, "immediately she got up and began to serve them."

The curing of many people, narrated immediately after this – "As the sun was setting, all those who had any who were sick with various kinds of diseases brought them to him; and he . . . cured them" (4:40) – seems to take place in Simon Peter's house or the immediate vicinity. Luke in fact goes on: "At daybreak he departed . . ." (4:42). So Jesus perhaps spent the night in the house, where women were also present (confirmed by Mark's parallel: 1:32–5, which mentions the door of the house). This is a detail already showing the ease and trust that characterized Jesus' relationship with women.

(b) The Widow of Nain[27]

Soon afterwards he went to a town called Nain, and his disciples and a large crowd went with him. As he approached the gate of the town, a man who had died was being carried out. He was his mother's only son, and she was a widow; and with her was a large crowd from the town. When the Lord saw her, he had compassion for her and said to her, "Do not weep." Then he came forward and touched the bier, and the bearers stood still. And he said, "Young man, I say to you, rise!" The dead man sat up and began to speak, and Jesus gave him to his mother. Fear seized all of them; and they glorified God, saying, "A great prophet has risen among us!" and "God has looked favourably on his people!" This word about him spread throughout Judea and all the surrounding country (Luke 7:11–17).

Looking at this episode in the context of the narrative, the order of events chosen by Luke stands out with surprising clarity:

– Jesus' preaching, ending with the words, "I will show you what someone is like who comes to me, hears my words, and acts on them" (6:47), a saying that Luke then works out in a manner strictly coherent with his narrative technique, setting out, after Jesus' words, some of his actual deeds:
    – the healing of the centurion's servant (7:1–10)   (man);
    – the raising of the widow of Nain's son (7:11–17)   (woman);[28]
    – the curing of many people (7:21)   (synthesis, all).

This account of the widow of Nain, which echoes in all essential points the episode of the raising of a widow's son by Elijah (1 Kings 17:17–24), is found only in Luke and well expresses what might be

---

[27] Cf. Schürmann, *Il vangelo di Luca*, pp. 641–52; J. Ernst, *Luca. Un ritratto teologico* (Brescia, 1988), pp. 199–200: It. trans. of *Lukas. Ein theologisches Portrait* (Düsseldorf, 1985).

[28] The figure of the woman is uppermost because, even though it is the son who is raised, Jesus' action is motivated by compassion for this widow's condition.

called a feminine sensitivity,[29] even if the primary purpose of the
text is to show Jesus as a "great prophet," an Elijah come back to
life, as if "God has visited his people." This is the first raising of a
dead person recounted in Luke's Gospel; it is motivated by the
compassion aroused in Jesus by the tragic situation of this woman:
"When the Lord saw her, he had compassion for her. . . ."[30] This
would be literally, "moved to his bowels by pity," an expression that
can be taken as having a feminine connotation in its indication of
powerful involvement, of a feeling that takes on a physical force.

The woman was a widow. To understand this story properly, we
need to take account of the wretched condition women found
themselves in at the time when, having been handed over from their
father's tutelage to their husband's, they were then left widows.[31]
Women, in a society which placed them juridically on the same level
as slaves and children, were, when they lost the man who looked
after them, exposed to judgments and abuses of power that often
reduced them to penury. This was aggravated by the fact that they
could not inherit from their husbands and had no legal
defenders.[32]

Their sad state is confirmed by the frequent references the Old
Testament makes to the condition of widows, either to confirm that
they were under God's protection,[33] or to show rules designed to
alleviate their distress,[34] or to deprecate the injustices of which they
were victims.[35]

---

[29] This can both relate to Schürmann's hypothesis that these verses are
the first of a group that made up an early composition dealing with women
(7:11–17; 36–50; 8:2–3), and add an element of support to the hypothesis of
a tradition conserved by women.

[30] Cf. G. Nolli, *Evangelo secondo Luca*, p. 299: "Note the dramatic
effect of the three words together . . .: mother, only, son, rendered even
more effective by the lack of a verb. . . ."

[31] See S. Solle, "Vedova," DCBNT, pp. 511–13; R. de Vaux, *Les
Institutions de l'Ancien Testament* (Paris, 1958): It. trans. (see n. 15 above),
pp. 49–50; B.-Z. Schereschewscky, "Widow," *En Ju* 16, pp. 487–96.

[32] On the death of her husband, a relative had to marry the widow
while the inheritance went to the eldest son. This institution was called the
"levirate" (from the Latin *levir* used to translate the Hebrew *jabam*,
relative).

[33] Jer. 49:11; Deut. 10:18; Pss. 68:6; 146:9; Prov.15:25: Mal. 3:5.

[34] Deut. 14:29; 16:11–14; 24:17, 19ff; 26:12ff; Lev. 22:13.

[35] Isa. 1:23; Ezek. 22:7; Mal. 3:5; Job 22:9; 24:21; Ps. 94:6; Wis. 2:10.

Jesus too inveighs against those who "devour widows' houses" and will therefore "receive the greater condemnation" (Luke 20:47); to illustrate the need not to lose heart and to keep on hoping, he also tells the parable of the judge and the widow who kept coming to him and insisting on justice being done to her (Luke 18:1–8).

Going back to the story of the widow of Nain who has lost her only son, we see Jesus comforting her directly: "He said to her, 'Do not weep.'" In these words Luke seems to be making Jesus embody the text from Sirach: "Be a father to orphans and be like a husband to their mother" (4:10). In the act of touching the bier the text shows the aspect of physical contact that often characterizes Jesus' actions, and which we shall come back to because of its link with women.

(c) Jesus' Words "Among those born of woman"

I tell you, among those born of woman, no one is greater than John (Luke 7:28).

The expression Luke puts in Jesus' mouth when he speaks of John, meaning all human beings, "among those born of woman," stands out as peculiar when contrasted with the expression "mother of the sons of," which was common in the language of the time and also appears in the Gospels. In Matthew a woman is described as "mother of the sons of Zebedee" (20:20 and 27:56). So she is not only identified in relation to her role as mother, and not just as a person, but she is defined in relation not to her sons seen as hers, but to the "sons of Zebedee," of her husband, that is. Confirmation of how widespread this way of identifying sons must have been and how long it lasted is provided by a passage in the Talmud; this, dealing with cases of particularly bad behaviour which allowed for women to be repudiated without payment of the usual indemnity, speaks of "a woman who curses the sons of her husband."[36]

The words Jesus uses emerge from this comparison as peculiar in their reference to the particular fact that all human beings are born of woman. The expression can be considered more carefully by

---

[36] A. Cohen, *Il Talmud*, p. 209.

putting it in both its Old Testament context (Job 14:1; 15:14 and 25:4) and its immediate context. The Book of Job says:

> A mortal, born of woman,
>   few of days and full of trouble,
> comes up like a flower and withers,
>   flees like a shadow and does not last.
> Do you fix your eyes on such a one?
>   Do you bring me into judgment with you?
> Who can bring a clean thing out of an unclean?
>   No one can (14:1-4).
> What are mortals, that they can be clean?
>   Or those born of woman, that they can be righteous
>   (15:14).
> How then can a mortal be righteous before God?
>   How can one born of woman be pure? (25:4)

The characteristic that emerges most forcefully from these texts is the weakness of man as "born of woman."

In Luke's account, however, this weakness has to be reset within Jesus' proclamation. He says:

> "I tell you, among those born of woman, none is greater than John; yet the least in the kingdom of God is greater than he." (And all the people who heard this, including the tax collectors, acknowledged the justice of God, because they had been baptized with John's baptism. But by refusing to be baptized by him, the Pharisees and the lawyers rejected God's purpose for themselves) (7:28-30).

This is followed by Jesus' judgment on the present generation, which ends with the words: "Nevertheless, wisdom is vindicated by all her children" (7:35).

Weakness and greatness are then brought into relationship with the reality of the Kingdom. "God's plan" is being born to God's Kingdom. Those "born of woman" must become born of wisdom. The expression "children of wisdom" with which the pericope ends suggests how the weak "born of woman" can become "children of wisdom" in the Kingdom of God. And Luke follows this immediately with an example of a woman who, by being born to the Kingdom of God, becomes a "daughter of wisdom."

(d) A Woman Forgiven[37]

One of the Pharisees asked Jesus to eat with him, and he went into the Pharisee's house and took his place at the table. And a woman in the city, who was a sinner, having learned that he was eating in the Pharisee's house, brought an alabaster jar of ointment. She stood behind him at his feet, weeping, and began to bathe his feet with her tears and to dry them with her hair, Then she continued kissing his feet and anointing them with the ointment. Now when the Pharisee who had invited him saw it, he said to himself, "If this man were a prophet, he would have known who and what kind of woman this is who is touching him - that she is a sinner." Jesus spoke up and said to him, "Simon, I have something to say to you." Teacher," he replied, "Speak." "A certain creditor had two debtors; one owed five hundred denarii, and the other fifty. When they could not pay, he cancelled the debts for both of them. Now which of them will love him more?" Simon answered, "I suppose the one for whom he cancelled the greater debt." And Jesus said to him, "You have judged rightly." Then turning to the woman, he said to Simon, "Do you see this woman? I entered your house; you gave me no water for my feet, but she has bathed my feet with her tears and dried them with her hair. You gave me no kiss, but from the time I came in she has not stopped kissing my feet. You did not anoint my head with oil, but she has anointed my feet with ointment. Therefore, I tell you, her sins, which were many, have been forgiven; hence she has shown great love. But the one to whom little is forgiven, loves little. Then he said to her, "Your sins are forgiven." But those who were at table with him began to say among themselves, "Who is this who even forgives sins?" And he said to the woman, "Your faith has saved you; go in peace" (Luke 7:36–50).

---

[37] Among the extensive works on this episode, see Schürmann, *Il vangelo di Luca*, pp. 685–705; J. Dupont, "Jésus et la pécheresse (Lc 7:36–50)," ComLtg 65 (1983), pp. 11–17; R. Penna, *Letture evangeliche. Saggi esegetici sui quattro evangeli* (Rome, 1989), pp. 177–83.

This episode is generally known as "a sinful woman forgiven" (NRSV) or "the woman who was a sinner" (JB) though Luke speaks of her more as a woman than as a sinner. It is set, like a precious jewel, between Jesus' tribute to John the Baptist, ending with his verdict on the present generation, and the verses 8:1–3 telling of the presence of women among the group that accompanied Jesus.

Luke 7:20 asks, "Are you the one who is to come . . .?". The question is put by the disciples whom John sent; Jesus does not reply at first in words, but works many cures in their sight: he gives them a way of seeing the liberative acts through which he brings the good news. Then he answers them: "Go and tell John what you have seen and heard: the blind receive their sight, the lame walk, the lepers are cleansed, the deaf hear, the dead are raised, the poor have the good news brought to them" (7:22). And he ends his message by introducing a new concept: "And blessed is anyone who takes no offence at me" (7:23). This element forms a backdrop to his verdict on the present generation (7:31–5): "For John the Baptist has come eating no bread and drinking no wine, and you say, 'He has a demon'; the Son of Man has come eating and drinking, and you say, 'Look, a glutton and a drunkard, a friend of tax collectors and sinners!'" (7:33–4).

Luke in this way prepares, with considerable skill, the scene he is about to describe, which takes place in an atmosphere of scandal and embarrassed glances. He provides a reading key first, thereby showing the acute way he sets about expounding and putting across Jesus' message. Before going into its merits, he emphasizes that Jesus' behaviour can appear awkward to superficial eyes, but we have to sharpen our sight, look more deeply, move a step farther. We must overcome commonplaces, go beyond stale and hurried judgments.

The verse that ends this section immediately preceding 7:36–50 is highly significant in this regard: "Nevertheless, wisdom is vindicated by all her children" (7:35). We must be children of wisdom. Luke must have had a clear appreciation of the difficulties posed by what he was about to relate. He is furthermore the only evangelist to recount this episode. The elements that make it up are:

(a) Jesus is invited by a Pharisee to eat in his house;
(b) a woman (Luke does not mention her name, either out of

discretion or because he does not know it), a sinner,[38] generally held to be a prostitute,[39] comes in to find Jesus;

(c) this woman takes a particular attitude in her approach to Jesus;[40]

(d) the Pharisee's mental attitude;

(e) Jesus: turns to Simon and tells the parable of the two debtors, ending with the question which one loves most; continues to talk to Simon about the woman's attitude and what she has done; addresses the woman telling her her sins are forgiven;

(f) the reaction of those who are at the table;

(g) Jesus says to the woman: "Your faith has saved you; go in peace."

The central issues revolve around three figures: the woman, Jesus and Simon, with whom the others at the table should perhaps be associated. The scene can also, on further consideration, be seen to be split into two zones, with Jesus and the woman in the first, and Simon and the other guests in the second. These two zones are not just divided by physical space, but above all by ways of being, by the essence of the people in them.

The woman. Her approach immediately makes it clear that she is looking for Jesus. Why is made clear by what follows. She comes into the house uninvited, and even if spectators were sometimes expected at such meals, it was certainly not appropriate for a

---

[38] A. Schlatter is an exception among the authors consulted; his opinion is noted by Schürmann, p. 689, n.8: "Schlatter ... holds that, according to the rabbinic tradition, this could equally mean the wife of a 'sinner.' But the whole context suggests that it is was the woman who was the sinner . . . ." See J. Pirot, Trois amies de Jésus de Nazareth (Paris, 1986), here p. 16.

[39] Cf. S. Légasse, "Jésus et les prostituées," RthL 7 (1976), pp. 137–54, esp. 145–50.

[40] Cf. C. M. Martini, *La donna nel suo popolo* (Milan, 1984), pp. 47–59, in particular: ". . . It is a difficult passage because to understand it we should have get deep into the 'woman's world': into women's reactions, into the way women express themselves, which are often unknown to us, as it was to Simon, who could not get into this world and so understood nothing" (p. 49). An interesting approach is taken by A. Paoli, *La radice dell'uomo. Meditazioni sul vangelo di Luca* (Brescia, 1972), pp. 178–94.

"ἁμαρτωλός," a woman who was a sinner.[41] Once in, she is not content to spectate; she dares to go up to the most important guest, the focus of interest for all those present, and to behave in a way that shows her love, reaching out and longing for Jesus (the woman and Jesus' zone); this provokes a scandal among the guests (Simon and the other guests' zone).

This is what she does:

(a) she must already have seen Jesus, or heard tell of him, and known that he was in the Pharisee's house; she wants to meet him personally. She wants to ask, to search, to knock, in the hope that "everyone who asks receives, and everyone who searches finds, and for everyone who knocks, the door will be opened" (Luke 11:10). The image that emerges is of someone totally immersed in her quest, totally absorbed by her thirst which is the source that gives her strength to face up to her situation. She sees her chance, she knows where Jesus is, wants to get close to him even if he is not alone; he is furthermore a guest in someone else's house, with other guests. She is not invited and knows she is not welcome.

(b) She comes in bearing a gift, a jar of ointment; this gesture is an outward expression of her inner feelings on meeting Jesus: attentiveness, haste, gratitude. (The fact that she goes to find him with a gift and with her whole behaviour expressing gratitude could perhaps indicate that she has already met him before and is coming back to get close once more to Jesus who has already given her the news of her liberation.)

(c) In her apparent impertinence (from Simon and the others' point of view) she nevertheless takes up a position expressing shyness and fear: "she waited behind him at his feet."

(d) ". . . weeping, [she] began to bathe his feet with her tears": the woman expresses herself by allowing her capacity for experiencing her own situation to find outward expression; her tears cannot be held back.[42]

---

[41] Cf. Schürmann, p. 689.

[42] Cf. G. Nolli, *Evangelo secondo Luca*, p. 323: ". . . the verb means weeping with very audible sighs."

(e) "... and to dry them with her hair":[43] for a woman to show her hair loose was considered a grave fault, bad enough to allow a husband to repudiate his wife for it.[44]

(f) "... kissing his feet": she cannot contain the emotional outpouring that moves her to Jesus and expresses this by kissing and caressing his feet. (The verb "to kiss" appears in the Gospels with a positive meaning only in Luke [7:38, 45; 15:20]. In the others it is the betraying kiss that leads to Jesus' arrest. As a noun, "a kiss" appears only in Luke 7:45. In the overall picture we are building up of how Luke's Gospel differs from the others, this is a small but meaningful indication of his particular sensibilities....)[45]

(g) "and anointing them with the ointment": a gesture that "used to be made in some places as an act of honouring."[46] Here it shows that this woman could not wait to show her feelings for Jesus: "The anointing of his feet is strange, as in any case it should not have been done during a meal."[47]

The woman's personality is first expressed in expectation and the hope that gives her the courage to face up to a difficult situation; once she has approached Jesus, in the way just examined, she is

---

[43] Cf. Cohen, *Il Talmud*, p. 209, where he shows that a woman covered her head when she married and from then on was considered immodest if she uncovered it. Going out in public with her hair uncovered was sufficient motive not only for divorce, but also for her husband to refuse payment of the usual sum due *(kethubah)*.

[44] *Tosefta Sota* V, p. 9; cf Jeremias, *Gerusalemme*, p. 540: Eng. trans. *Jerusalem at the Time of Jesus* (London & New York, 1973).

[45] Cf. Nolli, *Evangelo secondo Luca*, p. 331: "... a kiss was given on the cheeks or on the hands: the latter was a sign of great respect, empasizing more than the former (more confidential) the distance between and the homage due to those who saluted each other in this way." The fact that the woman kissed Jesus' feet could perhaps have expressed the great distance there was between her and Jesus and the spirit of humility in which she approached him. Cf also R. Petraglio, "La Bibbia latina e la morale," *RTM* 32 (1976), 543–58, in particular 561 for the usage of the kiss.

[46] Schürmann, *Il vangelo di Luca*, p. 690. See also R. Schnackenburg, *The Gospel according to St John* Vol. II (London and New York, 1980), pp. 365–70.

[47] Schnackenburg, *loc. cit.*, commenting on the anointing at Bethany (John 12:1–8); cf note 15 (p. 522), where he adds: "Anointing of the feet by a woman during a meal was definitely improper in Jewish eyes."

totally caught up in what she is doing.[48] Luke's arrangement, placing this episode after the testimony sent back by Jesus to John the Baptist, seems to suggest a sort of parallel, a sort of practical application of the words Jesus uses. This woman has finally found the "kingdom of God" (8:1), for her, "the Son of Man has come" (7:34), she is a poor person to whom "the good news [has been] brought" (7:22).

Her conversation with Jesus, this discovery that has irrupted into her life and radically changed her, absorbs her whole being: thoughts, desires, actions – all seek to express her total clinging to what she feels, to the incredible and welcoming peace Jesus has brought her. She is probably so bound up in Jesus that she does not even see anyone else, Simon or the other guests, nor does she care about them.

Jesus. Jesus responds to the woman's actions with an attitude of acceptance that scandalizes and bewilders the others present.[49] Two main elements emerge: Jesus engages in first-person dialogue with the woman for whom he is the source of the proclamation of the Kingdom, of forgiveness and of God's tenderness. He sees the whole situation objectively – while she is totally absorbed in him, he, while involved in the action, maintains the detachment needed to consider the wider implications of what is happening - and grasps the difference between his and the woman's view of the experience and the perception the others have of it; this is why he opens the dialogue with Simon to try to give him a fresh insight. The parable of the two debtors forces Simon himself to give the answer to the question of who loved the more.

Jesus leads Simon and the others to see the woman and her bold behaviour in a different light. Then he turns the tables: now it is Simon's behaviour that is at fault – "you gave me no water for my

---

[48] Cf. Martini, *La donna nel suo popolo*, pp. 47–59. In particular: "She has understood the 'beyond' of Christ, for whom nothing can ever be enough and for whom there are no rules or limits since he is the all and demands one's all" (p. 54).

[49] Cf. Schürmann, p. 691: ". . . Jesus' attitude that lets her do what she wants. The unheard-of novelty contained in the account resides in his calm. It is his leaving her be that causes the scandal. . . ."

feet,[50] but she . . . You gave me no kiss, but from the time I came in she has not stopped kissing my feet. You did not anoint my head with oil, but she has anointed my feet with ointment" (7:44–6).

Simon and the others present. It was Simon who invited Jesus and this probably made him feel the scandal most acutely, worrying not only about what the others thought of Jesus and the woman, but also about what they thought of him. The scandal he and the others felt had two main components: the behaviour of Jesus and the woman, and being forced to the conclusion that Jesus was not a prophet: "He said to himself, 'If this man were a prophet, he would have known who and what kind of woman this is who is touching him - that she is a sinner" (7:39).[51]

Certain elements emerge that link 8:1–3 with 7:36–50. We have seen how the hint of scandal in 7:23, made before 7:36–50, serves as a preparation for the pericope of the woman forgiven and forms a background echo to what happens in that. Following this line, the news Luke gives in 8:1–3 of women following Jesus along with the twelve, has been doubly prepared by what precedes it. The scandal theme can be seen there in two different aspects: (a) the fact that Jesus accepted women among his following was for his time and its historical-cultural environment both unusual and scandalous; (b) Luke comes to present this information after composing his material in such a way that his readers are prepared to accept all he writes with the least possible bewilderment and to understand it more deeply. (Luke had two reasons to fear the "scandal" his account could arouse in his readers. His profound understanding of woman's nature is still a problem for many in the church today – and outside it. To the extent that they do not know women and do

---

[50] Cf. Nolli, *Evangelo secondo Luca*, p. 330: "Feet . . . had to be the first object of hospitality, according to the Eastern tradition (cf Gen. 18:4; Judg. 19:21; 1 Sam. 25:41; John 13:15; 1 Tim. 5:10)." Cf. also J. L. McKenzie, *Dictionary of the Bible* (New York and London, 1965): "People had to wash their feet when they went into a house, since they walked barefoot or with sandals: it was the duty of the host to offer his guests this facility."

[51] Cf. Schürmann, p. 692: "In effect he reveals his own thoughts to him, but only to point out to him the truly scandalous subject on which a decision has to be made. The real point is not whether or not Jesus is a prophet, but rather – in the words of the pericope 7:11–17 – whether, despite any scandal, God's visit in the activity of Jesus is accepted with love."

not allow themselves *really to meet them*, women remain a cause of scandal, something that frightens them; they do not even examine Jesus' behaviour deeply, but distort it into a more subtle and hypocritical way of *being scandalized*, one that ignores and annuls the gospel message in its truest meaning.) He is trying to prevent his readers from shifting to the viewpoint of Simon and the others.

The fact that it was unusual for Jesus to include women among his followers at that time derives from two main factors: how and when women were allowed out in public and their educational status.

Women and public life. The segregation of women had become harsher in Jesus' time than it had been earlier.[52] They were excluded from social and public life; they lived almost entirely shut into their houses, where "often the windows that gave on to the street were closed with a grille so that they could not be seen."[53] When people were invited to a meal in their house they were forbidden to take part in it.[54] This segregation of women in their houses is also confirmed by Philo as applying in the Alexandria diaspora: "Women do not go beyond the door of the atrium. Girls stay in the women's rooms, and out of modesty avoid men's glances, even those of close relatives."[55]

The variety of witnesses to this attitude to women leads us into an atmosphere that is difficult to reconstruct, and on which opinions vary. While on the one hand we have to stress that the literature on the subject does not provide absolutely consistent evidence of women's position of inferiority and the oppression to which they were subjected, which seems to have varied from one area to another, on the other we have to recognize that texts favourable to them are submerged by the enormous weight of contrary evidence. While the condition of some women is shown in a positive light, this is exceptional compared to the vast majority of them, who were deprived of education, of any autonomy, and relegated to the home.

---

[52] See J.-M. Aubert, *La donna: antifemminismo e cristianesimo* (Assisi, 1978), p. 15: It. trans of *La femme: antiféminisme et christianisme* (Paris, 1975); Romney Weger, *Chattel or Person?*, pp. 145–67.

[53] H. Daniel-Rops, *La vie quotidienne en Palestine au temps de Jésus* (Paris, 1961), p. 157.

[54] Aubert, *La donna*, p. 17.

[55] Phil., *In Flaccum* 89, ed. A. Pelletier (Paris, 1967), p. 102.

"Even Hellenistic Jews, such as Philo, state that markets, conciliar assemblies, tribunals and any sphere of public activity were forbidden to women (*Spec. Leg.* II, p. 169). Their place was in the home, where they played the dominant role."[56] But what was this role? ". . . Directed solely to their husband, his happiness, his prosperity, and to the interests of the family."[57]

On the one hand, "there is debate about how far the segregation and domestic isolation of women had spread in Palestine";[58] on the other, it is clear enough that a life shut into their houses could be led only by women of the upper classes, since the rest, having no servants, would have to go to fetch water from the well, work in the fields and help their husbands in their business.[59]

It is worth looking at the state women found themselves in when they went out, when, veiled so as to be unrecognizable, they crossed the threshold of their house and set foot on the road. "A man should never walk behind a woman on the road, even if she is his wife. If a woman meets a man on a bridge, she lets him pass on one side; and whoever crosses a river behind a woman has no part in the World to Come. . . . Walk behind a lion sooner than behind a woman (*Ber.*, 61a)."[60] The six things the rabbis held to be unsuitable for a disciple of a wise man included "talking to a woman in the public square."[61] In "a midrash it is written: 'God has not yet ever lowered himself to speak to a woman, with the exception of that holy one (Sarah) and even then only as a result of sin' (on Gen. 3:16)."[62] "No one is to remain alone with a woman in an inn, even if she is his sister or daughter, on account of public opinion."[63]

One of the occasions that could take women out of their houses was a funeral. And here they were given the major role. A chivalrous courtesy? Not so, according to Albrecht Oepke: "The

---

[56] Gerstenberger and Schrage, *Il rapporto tra i sessi nella bibbia e oggi* (Rome, 1984), p. 131: It. trans. of *Frau und Mann*.

[57] Daniel-Rops, *La vie quotidienne*, p. 161.

[58] Gerstenberger and Schrage, loc. cit.

[59] Cf. Adinolfi, *Il femminismo della bibbia*, p. 165; Jeremias, *Gerusalemme*, pp. 543ff.

[60] Cohen, *Il Talmud*, p. 133.

[61] *Berakoth* 43b; cf Adinolfi, pp. 165–66, n. 90.

[62] Gerstenberger and Schrage, p. 130.

[63] *Aboth d'Rabbi Nathan*, 2, 2, 18a; Cf Adinolfi, p. 165, n. 87.

custom, common enough in many places, of giving women pride of place in a funeral cortège, is etiologically linked to the fact that women are responsible for death."[64] The Book of Sirach states: "From a woman sin had its beginning, and because of her we all die" (25:24).

So, to conclude this brief examination of how Jewish women were able to move about in public and make contact with men outside the narrow confines of the family: even allowing for the blurred picture presented by variations in social class and geographical area, the overall impression has to be one of women being segregated, confined mainly to their houses. The general climate of opinion was one of disapproval and condemnation of possible relationships arising from women going out into public places.

Women and education. The great importance the Jews attached to conserving and handing on their inherited religious patrimony finds confirmation in the prayer recited morning and evening: "Keep these words ... Recite them to your children ..." (Deut. 6:6–7). It was therefore a father's definite duty to bring up his sons in knowledge and practice of the Torah.

A very high value, then, was placed on religious instruction. "The aim of marriage being to bring up a family, and the ideal to educate the sons in the Torah, belief in heredity led to a strong desire to marry the daughter of a master. 'A man should sell all he possesses in order to marry the daughter of a learned man, since if he dies or is exiled, he will have the certainty that his sons will be well instructed; and do not marry the daughter of an ignorant man, since if you die or are exiled, your sons will be ignorant. A man should sell all he possesses to marry the daughter of a master, or to marry his daughter to a master. This is like adding one bunch of grapes to another, which is a good and pleasing thing. But do not marry the daughter of an ignorant man, because this would be like putting a bunch of grapes on twigs of scrub, which is an ugly and unpleasing thing' (Pes. 49a)."[65] But this heightens the contrast between this and

---

[64] A. Oepke, γυνή, p. 709. Cf. also Gerstenberger and Schrage, *Il rapporto*, pp. 129–30.

[65] Cohen, *Il Talmud*, p. 205. On the secondary role played by women in temple worship, see J. Neusner, *Judaism in the Beginning of Christianity* (Philadelphia, 1984), pp. 46–7;[?] For religious legislation relating to women, see Jeremias, *Gerusalemme*, pp. 557–61.

the treatment reserved to daughters; the more one sees the importance attached to instruction in the Torah, the only basis of all education and reserved to males, the worse appears the almost total ignorance in which daughters were kept, a revealing indication of how women were regarded at the time. (Continuing studies and taking a wife were the only objectives that authorized selling a scroll of the Torah. "Reading the biblical text led to all learning: speaking of the length of life of the patriarchs taught one to count, Israel's wars taught geography, science was learnt from a miraculous event or phenomenon. The Bible was the complete book that allowed one to face up to any argument and incorporate it: this is why the rabbis of the second century of our era stated that it was useless to look elsewhere.")[66]

Boys, and only boys, could go to school from the age of five or six. "According to a Judaic tradition, it was only toward 63 C.E. that the high priest decided to institute a free school in every village for boys of six or seven and older; others, however, place the institution of public schooling around 130 B.C.E., if only for the purpose of preparing boys to read in the synagogue."[67] For girls, however, instruction in the law was considered not only unnecessary but dangerous. The following texts, though from a later period, are nonetheless indicative of a mentality that cannot be very different, with regard to women, to that obtaining in Jesus' time: "If anyone teaches his daughter the Torah, it is as though he were teaching her obscenity"; "The words of the Torah should be destroyed by fire rather than be taught to girls"; "A girl should not be taught anything except how to use a spindle."[68]

It is possible to find sayings of a different tenor, such as that of the master who said, "A man is bound to teach his daughter the Torah."[69] But if one looks at the context of this, one sees that it comes in the middle of a discussion on the procedure to which women suspected of adultery should be subjected.[70] They were

[66] C. Saulnier and B. Rolland, *La Palestina ai tempi di Gesù*, p. 41: It. trans. of *La Palestine aux temps de Jésus* (Paris, 1978).

[67] Saulnier and Rolland, p. 41.

[68] *Sotah*, 3, 4; 19a; *Joma*, 66b.

[69] *Sotah*, 3, 4.

[70] Cf. A. Destro, *The Law of Jealousy. Anthropology of Sotah* (Atlanta, 1989).

given a certain drink which did them real damage, making them ill or even killing them. If they died, this was taken as proof of their guilt. Such effects, according to some masters, were delayed if the woman under trial had previously acquired some merits. This is why Ben Azai, the master in question, maintained a man's duty to teach his daughter the Torah, "so that, if she drinks the water, she may know that this merit is delaying her punishment."[71] What is significant for our purposes here is that the merits he refers to are those relating to a woman's actions in facilitating her son or husband's study of the Torah. It is in any case generally agreed that it was a bad idea to teach the Torah to women. (Even Cohen, who in the text quoted above is trying to argue a more mitigated situation for women, more balanced than that descibed by those he calls "hostile critics," admits that the view that it is bad to teach daughters the Torah "was generally professed and put into practice."[72]) In effect, then, the Torah, so important in Jewish life and outlook, was not something to be taught to girls. Women were furthermore seen as being a hindrance to men trying to study, as this text shows: "... Anyone who multiplies conversations with women harms himself, distracts himself from (study of) the words of the Law, and his end is to gain hell for himself."[73]

Even a female, however, should learn some things – what she is not allowed to do. The negative precepts of the Torah, those beginning with "Do not ...," are to be learned and observed by women. The positive ones, beginning with "Do ...," are not for them; these are for men only. The explanation of this distinction is

---

[71] *Sotah*, 3, 4.

[72] Cohen, Il Talmud, p. 221. It is worth noting this view, since there is no doubt that it is a forced or partial view, as Cohen himself introduces his section on women by writing: "... the Talmud ... recognizing the fundamental importance of women in family life, gives them a most exalted place.... In no way are they considered inferior to men" (p. 199).

[73] *Aboth*, 1, 5; cf J. Bonsirven, *Textes rabbiniques des deux premiers siècles chrétiens* (Rome, 1955), p. 105. And if exceptional cases came to light, such as that of Beruria, a learned woman, wife of Rabbi Meir (c. 150 C.E.), they were certainly not viewed with favour by the rabbis. Beruria's reputation was destroyed by the invention of a story that she had given in to a seducer and then committed suicide: Adinolfi, *Il femminismo*, pp. 167–8. See also Oepke, "γυνή," 710–11; K. H. Rengstorf, "μαθήτρια," TWNT 4 (1942), 465.

that women are not required to carry out those religious duties that are assigned to a particular time and place. Comparing this to a woman's role in relation to her sons, the family, the home, the explanation is understandable. Looking for underlying facets, however, one can ask: Is not all this hiding the conviction that the most one can expect of a woman is for her to avoid doing harm (negative precepts) since she cannot be expected to do any good (positive precepts)?

If girls were excluded from the first level of education, they were more definitely excluded from the higher level, which was carried out with a wise man (rabbi) surrounded by disciples. The language furthermore shows the Jewish conception of the place of women in relation to culture and religious instruction: the words for woman scholar (*mathetria*) and woman disciple (*talmida*) are virtually non-existent and, Rengstorf comments, are so "for objective reasons; that is, because women were effectively excluded from scholastic activity."[74]

So the two aspects of the condition of women in Jesus' time considered in this *excursus* (perhaps too long for its place and too short to be exhaustive) show the background against which we should view the scene of the women following Jesus, which we are studying, and help to draw it out of obscurity. The revolutionary, upsetting and scandalous elements that must have been presented at that time by women accompanying Jesus can now be seen more clearly.

To return to our examination of the elements linking 7:36–50 to 8:1–3, having considerd this first, scandalous, aspect: 7:22 already speaks of the poor to whom "the good news is brought"; 8:1 then speaks of Jesus going about "bringing the good news of the kingdom of God." And in the episode of the woman forgiven, it is the proclamation of good news to her that is at issue; it is the resulting deep and liberating disturbance produced in her that is the subject; the narrative is telling of the overwhelming affective movement awakened in her.

Luke 7:36–50 brings out the woman's personality in all its complexity: mannerisms, means of expression, ways of relating and communicating, sensibilities and feelings, tears and upset, need for

---

[74] Rengstorf, *loc. cit.*

touch and tenderness.[75] What it shows above all is Jesus accepting and understanding this deep and true dialogue with the woman, with what is different in her from him.[76] This brings us to 8:1–3: Jesus is living an itinerant life, accompanied by a group of men and women. The calm he showed in the encounter with the woman of 7:36–50 prompts us to accept the serenity, depth and richness of his relationship with the women who go with him.

Jesus accepts the gift of ointment from the forgiven woman, accepts a meal from the Pharisee, just as he accepts being provided for daily by the women out of their resources, as we are told in 8:3. Accepting gifts is an expression of the deepest and most complete acceptance of other people, and of acceptance of the manifestations that express the affection of other people: loving and letting oneself be loved also. A woman is both witness to and involved subject of Jesus' actions: this is valid for the pericope examined here and for the preceding ones.

Having brought out the elements that link the episode of the woman forgiven with 8:1–3, I should like to point out that there is nothing in the text that prompts identification of this woman with Mary Magdalene. The passage 7:36–50 is followed by 8:1–3, in which Mary Magdalene, "from whom seven demons had gone out," is mentioned among the women who have been cured. The proximity of the two texts has led to claims that the two women are one and the same. But if Luke knew the name of the woman who was forgiven and did not mention it earlier out of delicacy, why should he then try to suggest it by putting the passages one after the other?

The words concerning the demons, which I will come back to later, do not allow one to draw an inference of sinfulness, of moral guilt, and thereby relate her to "the woman in the city, who was a sinner" (7:37), where the name of the city is left unspoken, whereas Mary "called Magdalene," refers us directly to her home town of Magdala.

---

[75] E. Schweitzer, *Das Evangelium nach Lukas* (Göttingen, 1982), speaks of the scene having "even an erotic colouring," p. 91.

[76] Cf. V. Gozzini, "L'altro' dell'uomo nel cammino biblico," *La donna nell'esperienza dalla prima chiesa*, pp. 131–57, esp. 137–8.

A final brief word on the heading usually given to the pericope 7:36–50. This is usually referred to as the case of the "penitent sinner": Luke indeed describes her as "a woman in the city, who was a sinner," and then makes Simon say ". . . who and what kind of woman this is . . . a sinner"; then, when he switches to Jesus' attitude or words, she is simply "this woman," three times. So emphasizing her sinfulness means using language that corresponds to the Pharisee's viewpoint. Perhaps the expression "the woman forgiven" would accord more with Jesus' viewpoint' which goes straight to the essence of her personality, and then stresses even more the reality of conversion, of change and forgiveness.

(e) Jesus' Mother and Brothers[77]

After 8:1–3 there are two further passages that carry on the subject of "women": these are the episode usually referred to as that of Jesus' real family (8:19–21), and the raising of Jairus' daughter and the healing of the woman suffering from a hemorrhage (8:40–56).

> Then his mother and his brothers came to him, but they could not reach him because of the crowd. And he was told, "Your mother and brothers are standing outside, wanting to see you." But he said to them, "My mother and brothers are those who hear the word of God and do it (8:19–21).

At first glance this episode involving Jesus' mother and brothers would seem to have little to do with the subject of women. In reality, even though the account places how he receives the news and the close relationship hearing the word brings with Jesus in the forefront, there is another concept also being strongly stated. The crowd attributes an authority and strength of bond to Jesus' mother and close relatives, assuming therefore that they have a right to see him. But Jesus' words show that relations and dialogue with him cannot be grounded in blood relationship,[78] and in the case of

---

[77] Cf. Schürmann, *Il vangelo di Luca*, pp. 744–7; J. Ernst, *Luca. Un ritratto teologico* (Brescia, 1988), pp. 236–7: It. trans. of *Lukas. Ein theologisches Portrait* (Düsseldorf, 1985).

[78] On Jesus' declaration that blood ties are secondary, see R. Petraglio, "Maria figlia e fine del potere del sangue," *Il Tetto* 152–3 (1989), 240–60.

women, not in a mother's role, but in the relationship of creatures who "hear the word of God and do it."[79]

Jesus' words must have sounded harsh at the time, when one value accorded to women was precisely being a mother, giving a man descendants. The Old Testament and Hebrew tradition bear witness to the importance attached by Jewish men to having children, and even many children, so as to assure their descendance. Expressions such as, "I will so greatly multiply your offspring" (Gen. 16:10); "Children . . . establish one's name" (Sir. 40:19); "You multiplied their descendants like the stars of heaven" (Neh. 9:23) are frequent in the Old Testament. Elsewhere it is written: "A man without children is considered as dead" (*Gen. R.*, LXXI, 6); "Whoever does not think of reproducing himself is like someone who kills his like and the image of God" (*b. Jeb.* 63*b*). When a couple did not have children, the cause was usually attributed to the wife, who was considered barren. The situation of a woman in this condition was painful, because lack of issue after ten years of marriage gave her husband the right to divorce her and take another wife; it also removed from a woman the only significant role permitted to her: being a mother. Jesus' words, however, are a clear affirmation of the reality and dignity of women simply as persons with the ability to hear and do the word of God, not in function of their maternal role. (It may not be necessary to say this, but Jesus is not casting doubt on the value of women expressing themselves as mothers – any more than he does on men doing so as fathers. He simply stresses that women are persons in their own right, not just as mothers, and apart from their ability to produce children.)

---

[79] In Luke's account, Mark's verse 3:34: "And looking at those who sat around him, he said, 'Here are my mother and my brothers!'" has disappeared. Perhaps the text ended like this in the earliest tradition. Eduard Schweizer observes that "simply *being with* Jesus is placed in the light of grace with unheard-of fullness": *Das Evangelium nach Markus*, (Göttingen, 1967: It. trans., p. 95). Mark's text ends with: "Whoever does the will of God is my brother and sister and mother" (3:35). Schweizer continues: "The last sentence as it were attenuates the incredible scope of the preceding words." As far as women are concerned, the consideration that remains, beyond textual analysis, is that the basis of relationship with Jesus is placed beyond blood ties and roles, in "simply being with," in Schweizer's words.

This is something Jesus reaffirms. In Luke 11:27–8 a woman calls out to him: "Blessed is the womb that bore you and the breasts that nursed you!," to which he replies: "Blessed rather are those who hear the word of God and obey it!" That Jesus related to his own mother from this novel standpoint is confirmed by the words, which would have sounded most strange at the time, he uses to address her directly: "Woman, why turn to me?" (John 2:4) and "Woman, behold your son!" (John 19:26).

The episode of Jesus' actual relatives reveals the deep significance, linked to 8:1–3, of the importance Jesus must have attached to his relationship with the women who accompanied him. It was not based on accepting "roles" as something above persons: "daughter of," "wife of," "mother of," "appointed to" . . ., but on adherence to the word of God, on hearing it and doing it.

According to the parallel text in Mark which attributes the words "Whoever does the will of God is my brother, sister and mother" to Jesus (3:35) – Luke omits the term "sister" which appears twice in Mark (3:32 and 35) – Mary Magdalene and the other women who followed Jesus are sisters and mothers, in that they have a deep bond with him, made up of interchange, dialogue, expressions of affection, such as can be found in natural family ties.

(g) Jairus' Daughter and the Woman Suffering from a Hemorrhage[80]

> Now when Jesus returned, the crowds welcomed him, for they were all waiting for him. Just then there came a man named Jairus, a leader of the synagogue. He fell at Jesus' feet and begged him to come to his house, for he had an only daughter, about twelve years old, who was dying. As he went, the crowds pressed in on him. Now there was a woman who had been suffering from hemorrhages for twelve years; and though she had spent all she had on physicians, no one could cure her. She came up behind him and touched the fringe of his clothes, and immediately her hemorrhage stopped. Then Jesus asked, "Who touched me?" When all denied it, Peter said, "Master, the crowds surround you and press in on you." But Jesus said, "Someone touched me; for I noticed that power had gone out

---

[80] Cf. Schürmann, pp. 769–84 and the bibliography given there.

from me." When the woman saw that she could not remain hidden, she came trembling; and falling down before him, she declared in the presence of all the people why she had touched him, and how she had been immediately healed. He said to her, "Daughter, your faith has made you well; go in peace." While he was still speaking, someone came from the leader's house to say, "Your daughter is dead; do not trouble the teacher any longer." When Jesus heard this, he replied, "Do not fear. Only believe, and she will be saved." When he came to the house, he did not allow anyone to enter with him, except Peter, John and James, and the child's father and mother. They were all weeping and wailing for her; but he said, "Do not weep; for she is not dead but sleeping." And they laughed at him, knowing that she was dead. But he took her by the hand and called out, "Child, get up!" Her spirit returned, and she got up at once. Then he directed them to give her something to eat. Her parents were astounded; but he ordered them to tell no one what had happened (8:40–56).

The two stories are set in the same space of time and the second is contained within the first.[81] Looking at the immediately preceding and following contexts we find that, as we have seen for 8:1–3 with the cure of Simon's mother-in-law and the raising of the widow of Nain's son, the text follows a familiar pattern. (The main elements of this pattern have a basis in the older tradition: this is shown by comparison with the same passage in Mark and Matthew. I shall come back to this and also show how the sequence of events has been accentuated in Luke's version.) The teaching on hearing the word of God and on faith (parable of the sower; Jesus' actual relatives; the calming of the storm - 8:4–25) is followed by:

- the cure of the Gerasene demoniac (8:26–39)   (man);
- the raising of Jairus' daughter and the healing of the woman suffering from a hemorrhage (8:40–56)   (women).

---

[81] According to Schweizer, the insertion of the episode of the woman suffering from a hemorrhage "into the middle of the story of Jairus, daughter is probably attributable to Mark, who liked to fill intervals of time with insertions of this nature." *Op. cit.*, p. 125.

Then the context immediately following tells of the sending of the twelve with the power to cure (9:1–6).

Even without trying to force the text, one can perhaps see in this last passage a synthetic aspect reminding us of what we saw in the two preceding cases where, after the account of two miracles, relating to a man and then a woman, the cure of many people followed. Here Jesus gives the twelve "power and authority over all demons and to cure diseases, and he sent them out to proclaim the kingdom of God and to heal. . . . They departed and went through the villages, bringing the good news and curing diseases everywhere" (9:1–6).

It would be useful to go deeper into an analysis of this structure, which has emerged, gradually but with surprising ease, as the underpinning of the three accounts of miracles involving women in the broader narrative of Jesus' activity in Galilee. This would show if we could bring out other elements that shed light on the procedures and ordering of events Luke chooses and on his motives for arranging his composition in this way. However, so as not to embark on a long digression here, it will be better to turn to reflecting on the two miracles in Luke 8:40–56 and to take this subject up again later.

The two episodes are each made up of least two parts: they show two actions by Jesus toward women and both involve physical contact between Jesus and the woman. Such contact involved impurity. The concept of impurity is not easy to reconstruct in its origins and manifestations in Jesus' time. It is a complex subject and brings in other concepts: the first of these is what was meant by ·holy. The term "holy" (*hághios*) "originally meant what causes (religious) shame, the tabu."[82] Authorities agree that the concepts of pure and impure are found in the histories of all religions.[83] In the Old Testament, impurity, which gradually came to have moral connotations, was originally specifically what was an impediment to the performance of worship. Jacob Neusner, dealing with the account of the purity system as it can be deduced from the Mishnà-Tosefta, maintains that "what is impure is destructive of what is of

---

[82] H. Baltensweiler, "*haghenós*," DCBNT, p. 1481.
[83] Cf. H. G. Link and J. Schattenmann, "*katharós*," DCBNT, p. 1484.

nature and what is impure is restored to a condition of purity... through the activity of nature, which is independent of human intervention in removing the impurity," and can be obtained solely through the natural power of water collected in its original state. So a "state of impurity," which is in itself unnatural, Neusner proceeds, derives from a series of elements unnatural in themselves, of which the first is death, which disturbs the environment of life, and the second is menstrual blood. It is therefore perhaps possible to assume that on the basis of this concept men feel a deep fear of power linked to the divine and therefore of anything in life, in human nature and specifically in women that they hold to be connected to this power.[84] As for the woman suffering from a hemorrhage, see the prescriptions about menstruating women in Leviticus 15:19–30;[85] as for Jairus' daughter, see those relating to corpses in Numbers 19:11.[86]

The episode of the woman suffering from a hemorrhage is important because it shows what Jesus' attitude is in general to the concept of uncleanness and the practices connected with it, and more in particular to the particular type of uncleanness to which he could be exposed by contact with the woman. It shows us how Jesus personally rides above the rules and fears associated with contagion from uncleanness.

A woman who has been suffering a discharge of blood for twelve years touches the fringe of his garment, seeking to be healed, and when Jesus asks who has touched him, she comes forward fearful and trembling, falls to the ground in front of him and confesses what she has done. Her fear is motivated by at least two good reasons: she has herself taken an initiative, becoming the active

---

[84] J. Neusner, "Method and Meaning in Ancient Judaism," *Second Series. Brown Judaic Studies* 15 (Missoula, Mont., 1981), pp. 67–81.

[85] "If a woman has a discharge of blood for many days, not at the time of her impurity, or if she has a discharge beyond the time of her impurity, all the days of the discharge she shall continue in uncleanness; as in the days of her impurity, she shall be unclean" (15:25); see also Ezek. 36:17.

[86] The city of Tiberias, built by Herod Antipas on the site of an old necropolis, was avoided by orthodox Jews as being unclean: see W. Dommerhausen, *Die Umwelt Jesu. Politik und Kultur in Neuetestamentlicher Zeit* (Freiburg, n.d.): It. trans. *L'ambiente di Gesù* (Turin, 1980), p. 30.

subject of a daring action; furthermore, she knows that the nature of her illness condemns her to a state of impurity and that she passes this on through touch.

A woman afflicted with a continuous discharge of blood makes anything she touches unclean, as indicated in Leviticus 15:25–30 where this particular condition is dealt with explicitly: the state of uncleanness lasts for the whole duration of the discharge, and for seven days after this has stopped, at the end of which an expiatory sacrifice has to made by a priest.[87] Yet Jesus does not rebuke her, as he would have been expected to do according to the cultural environment and its rules, but reassures her and shows that he appreciates her courageous initiative, which in a certain sense he himself has almost shared. The power of faith has made the woman overcome the obstacles and fears that were standing in the way of her cure.

Her action involved a high degree of psychic energy, both to face up to transgressing the rules on uncleanness and to confront a difficult situation in itself; how to meet that Jesus whose fame had certainly reached her. This in turn leads back to the type of disturbance she was suffering from. Modern medical and psychological knowledge tells us that the cause of this type of illness can often be traced to psychic disorders. And it is not totally out of place to speculate that a personality rich in intellectual, emotive and affective energies, for which she was unable to find a full and free outlet as a woman of her time and place, could have repressed her anxieties and troubles in the face of the normal problems of

---

[87] Cf. M. C. Jacobelli, *Sacerdozio-donna-celibato* (Rome, 1981), pp. 87–93; E. J. Morris, *Storia nascosta di donne*, pp. 143, 152: It. trans. of *The Lady Was a Bishop* (see n. 1 to ch. 1 above); I. Magli, *Gesù di Nazaret. Tabù e trasgressione* (Milan, 1982), pp. 87–91; U. Rapallo, "Il sangue nel 'Levitico': la parola e il testo," F. Vattioni (ed.), *Sangue e Antropologia biblica nella Patristica.* (Conference of 23–28 Nov. 1981) (Rome, 1982). Rapallo shows that blood (*dam*) in Leviticus (17:11, 14 and elsewhere) stands for an indication of one of the two differing conceptions of life: "one that sees the seat of life in the blood, the other that places its fulcrum in the breath or breathing." Still in Leviticus we find: "If anyone ... eats any blood, I will set my face against that person ... and will cut that person off from the people" (17:10) (*ibid.*, p. 331); cf also Romney Weger, *Chattel or Person?*, pp. 155, 162–5.

everyday life to the point where they found expression in these physical symptoms.[88]

There is still something perhaps more significant in this text: Jesus wishes to make what has happened public knowledge. Only he and the woman know; the others have not noticed anything, so much so that when Jesus asks who has touched him, the disciples are surprised at the question in view of the crowd pressing round him. Jesus' decision to communicate his behaviour toward a woman in a condition they judged particularly humiliating and a source of uncleanness is doubly significant, both as an expression of his attitude toward prescriptions relating to uncleanness, and of his willingness to make his views public. (This would still remain true even if we accept the compatible suggestion made by Ida Magli, that the disciples made some "adjustments" in recounting the episode, to try and cover up the fact that Jesus had broken this tabu: ". . . the formula, 'power had gone out from me' is undoubtedly foreign to Jesus' self-understanding and actions; he always works in the first person, while the expression 'power had gone out from me' implies a 'magic' mentality, in which a power like 'mana' operates outside the will of the person who has it."[89]

The raising of Jairus' daughter also involves a contaminating touch: Jesus takes the little girl who has died by the hand. The Book of Numbers states: "Those who touch the dead body of any human being shall be unclean seven days," and "All who touch a corpse . . . and do not purify themselves, defile the tabernacle of the Lord; such persons shall be cut off from Israel" (19:11, 13).

There are two main elements that link this passage with 8:1–3:

- healing as a factor common to the woman suffering from a hemorrhage, Mary Magdalene and the other women who followed Jesus.[90] An act of liberation giving these women back

---

[88] M. Cardenal's autobiography, *Les mots pour le dire* (Paris, 1975), gives a modern account of a similar experience.

[89] I. Magli, *Gesù di Nazaret* (Milan, 1982), p. 90.

[90] For the matching of Mary Magdalene with the woman suffering from a hemorrhage and the hypothesis that they are one and the same person, see C. and J. Grassi, *Mary Magdalene and the Women in Jesus' Life* (Kansas City, 1986), pp. 58–67.

the possibility of a full sexuality, since their condition of impurity rendered them unapproachable;
- touch as the most significant factor to emerge from both episodes, and one that now needs further consideration.

Touch and Womanhood

Discussing touch in relation to womanhood may not seen immediately pertinent to the subjects under discussion; it nevertheless strikes me as a prime subject for reflection and one that is opportune here, since it relates to a primary experience in the life of every man and woman, one that deeply marks the psyche. Biologically, the characteristic proper to womanhood is the distinguishing feature of the function reserved to women in transmitting life through pregnancy, which makes physical contact the first source of communication between mother and foetus. This physical contact is the first form of communication from the point of view of the foetus, one that will be the only one for a long time, falling within an experience, that of the mother, which is all-embracing. And this experience is shared by both men and women as both go through this originary phase of life. Within what is today called sexually differentiated thinking, starting from realization of the fact that there is no such thing as a neuter human being and that we are at origin and ineluctably either men or women belonging to a dual reality, there has to be an ever wider space given, not only to what is implied in saying, "We are born women or men and both from women," but to the fact that we are born of woman in particular conditions/circumstances, which are highly significant for the themes of unity-duality, equality-difference and identity-otherness.[91]

Women, by going through the concrete experience of maternity or by being biologically adapted for it, have been conditioned by

---

[91] For the basic bibliography on this subject, see: Various, *Diotima. Il pensiero della differenza sessuale* (Milan, 1987); Various, *Diotima. Mettere al mondo il mondo. Oggetto e oggettività alla luce della differenza sessuale* (Milan, 1990); L. Irigaray, *Ethique de la différence sexuelle* (Paris, 1985); M. C. Marcuzzo and A. Rossi Doria (eds), *La ricerca delle donne* (Turin, 1987); G. Boriello and C. Fiorillo, *Il pensiero parallelo* (Naples, 1986); *Memoria* 15 (1986); C. Gilligan, *In a Different Voice. Psychological Theory and Women's Development* (Cambridge, N.Y., 1982).

the Creator to experience at the same time a situation of *unity-equality-identity* (the foetus and the woman forming one body, a physical space without discontinuity) and one of *duality-multi-plicity-difference-otherness* (the foetus is "other" than the woman).

The apparent contradiction between these two situations leads to the need to emerge from *unity*, which also means *identity*, to found a *multiplicity* and so an *otherness*, and by this founding to establish the possibility of relating to them. What there is of *equal* in *unity* establishes the possibility, the point of contact, the course of transition. of relating to the *other*, the *different*. The other is not completely hidden. As furthermore, *otherness* makes the existence of the multiple, what cannot be encapsulated in equal unity, possible. A woman then goes through, or is in any case biologically able to go through, an experience of otherness-difference within her very own physical being, in that she contains the *other*. This *other* is, though, perceived as in a closeness that completely envelops it. The foetus is a contained body and the woman who, as a mother, has now experienced *containing-within-herself*, has herself been through the cycle of being first *contained*. The two points of view, of being enveloped by another being and in turn *enveloping* another can be fully held only by a woman. A man shares only the first phase with her.

So if the words of Genesis 1:27, "God created humankind in his image, in the image of God he created them; male and female he created them," provide us with the basis of our being in the world as we are, a reality made up of man and woman, the *otherness* of one in relation to the other is not only something existing from the origin of humankind, but *is the origin* of our mode of being and living. This *otherness* is not set in the act of creation as *separation, non-communication, unbridgeable gap*; rather, since the continuance of the life of humankind is willed to depend on a state of deep communication between man and woman, what is set as central to the being of the human world is *union, communication, closeness*. The aspect of relationship in otherness is the primary-central fact in the Genesis account of creation. This realization refers us back speculatively to the nature of God. If it is in God's image that we have been created, then the central, *creative* aspect (*ad extra*) and constituent principle (*ad intra*) of God's being, must be that of relating-communicating.

Encounter and relationship are possible, almost paradoxically, from two angles: that of identity and that of otherness.

Identity, what is the same in me and another human creature, makes me approachable, understandable, opens up a channel between me and that other, signals a way of communication, a coming and going.

Otherness, the difference placed between me and another being, questions my reality and goads it, even painfully, to seek in alien darkness what confronts me and what also problematically makes me perceive the vibrations of its being.

The psychological shock generated by otherness is a great richness if it is accepted and if we can free ourselves from the fear that the darkness, the shadows of the other, arouse in us.

We can maintain that not only encounter and relationship happen on the level of both identity and otherness, but that these two components are essential conditions for a greater fullness of the reality of communication, interchange and understanding.

Turning now from these wider considerations on the subject of difference and relationship to physical contact as a feminine characteristic, it is clear that in women's motherhood the experience of a reality within them but other to them, with which they have only physical contact (though this does not of course exclude psycho-physical interactions), is protracted after the birth of their child in manifestations of reciprocal contact which for baby and mother continue to embody ways of expressing needs and feelings. One need only think of nursing, with the baby drawing milk from its mother's breast,[92] and all the ways in which a baby is physically handled during its first months of life.[93]

---

[92] Cf. E. Gianini Belotti, *Dalla parte delle bambine. L'influenza dei condizionamenti sociali nella formazione del ruolo femminile dei primi anni di vita* (Milan, 1973), pp. 30–31.

[93] In my reading on this aspect, I found the following: "The reality of woman is a sort of sphere, at once closed and open, that allows her to 'touch' the deep powers of being." P. Daco, *Les femmes* (Verviers, n.d.), p. 31; and "These women, givers of life, are naturally in connivance with the secret powers and mysteries of nature and of life. They understand not only with their mind, but also with their heart, with their skin, with their bowels. 'I am an earth woman among the torrents, an earth woman for my child. . . in whose secret womb the flowers that blossom are prolonged in caresses . . .,' they sing." M. Hebrard, *Dieu et les femmes* (Paris, 1985), p. 249.

To show the great value and importance of physical contact as a means of communication, we need only to bear in mind that human life is generated and carried forward by a deep communication of this sort. Human beings are therefore, in this sense, *children of touch* and acquiring understanding of the very flesh of another being and entering into dialogue with this and "becoming what we are" (in Pindar's words), means grasping this dimension in ourselves and in others and experiencing it.

Touch as Characteristic of Jesus' Experience

Jesus does not intervene to censure the ways in which the women who approach him choose to do so, even though these are a problem for the men who follow him and still more so for the representatives of the law and worship: he accepts the touch of the woman suffering from a hemorrhage and the woman in Luke 7:36–50, he takes Jairus' daughter by the hand in a touch designed to transmit the warmth of his tenderness and recall her to life from the cold and rigidity of death.

I have tried to bring out the theme of touch, physical contact, and Jesus' attitude to it in order to assemble elements to help us understand, beyond what is explicitly said in Luke 8:1–3, that what this passage states is consistent with Jesus' whole way of acting – living simply together with women in a daily routine made up of exchanges, dialogue and silence, work and rest, stress and moments of repose, joy and suffering, worries and peace. He made this possible by clearing the ground of false problems and harmful fears, such as we have just seen in the case of the uncleanness associated with menstruation. More generally, he did so by not showing fear of women, having embraced the reality of *the other*, of the *different* from him, in an encounter allowing him to perceive, express and experience his own deep reality in dialectic with the other.[94]

In order to gain a deeper understanding of what lies hidden behind the information given on Luke 8:1–3, let us emphasize the factors that emerge most strongly.

---

[94] Fear of women is a vast subject; on some aspects see: R. Balbi, *Madre paura* (Milan, 1984), esp. pp. 49–57; Jacobelli, *Sacerdozio-donna-celibato*, esp. pp. 47–96; Daco, *Les femmes*, pp. 88–122; K. Stern, *The Flight from Woman* (New York, n.d.).

Women enjoy Jesus' attention, are healed by him and/or made to share in the benefits derived from his healing actions, are comforted by him, relate to him by serving him, showing longing, affection and tenderness to him, and offering him gifts.

Women are present to Jesus in part as mothers, through their essential biological feature which makes them give birth to every human being (in speaking of one man, John the Baptist, he says "among those born of woman" to mean "among men"), but also as persons whose being comes in the first place, so that their reality as women is not simply something to be superimposed on the roles assigned to them, however loudly these are proclaimed. Jesus overturns the usual patterns: where women, as beings capable of giving life, are usually placed second so as to give prominence to the man, the father, and identified as "mother of the sons of . . .," Jesus emphasizes the woman's place as mother, as in the expression "born of woman." And where the full reality of women disappears in their all-embracing identification with their maternal role, Jesus then proclaims the primacy of their reality as human beings (the episode of the true family, 8:19–21) and of hearing and doing the word of God over and above family duties.

The relationship built up between Jesus and women was a source of scandal, but Jesus opened up a deep dialogue with them on the basis of his serene acceptance of their real nature, establishing relations of mutual exchange. In doing so, he acted with freedom with respect to current conceptions of uncleanness, in particular to the view that one could contract uncleanness through proximity to women, who were considered cyclically unclean on account of their menstruation.

The way Jesus acted in his approach to women is important: this took account of their actual femaleness, the nature of their perceptions, the ways they expressed themselves, the typology of their intuition, their social intercourse, their language. A comparison between the way Jesus chose to approach women and the way he dealt with men could shed further light on this aspect of our subject.

Women were involved with Jesus from the outset of his public activity (the second miracle narrated by Luke and Mark concerns a woman: Simon's mother-in-law) and were called to be witnesses to his preaching. Luke 8:1–3 first establishes the presence of two specific groups around Jesus: the twelve and the women. The women shared in and witnessed to Jesus' itinerant activity and enjoyed the special teaching he reserved for his followers: Luke himself gives us a valuable confirmation of the teaching given to women in 10:38–42, where he tells that Jesus was received in Martha and Mary's house, and that the latter "sat at the Lord's feet and listened to what he was saying" (10:39), which is the only thing necessary; "Mary has chosen the better part" (10:42).

The discovery that, in the section of Luke's Gospel dealing with Jesus' activity in Galilee, the three episodes of miracles relating to women (the healing of Simon's mother-in-law, 4:38–9; the raising of the widow of Nain's son, 7:11–16; the raising of Jairus' daughter and the cure of the woman suffering from a hemorrhage, 8:40–56) follow one another on a common plan, reproduced in the same structure in each episode, is worth setting out in tabular form - see facing page.

The central structure, made up of two miracles, the first for the benefit of a man and the second for the benefit of a woman, has in its preceding context pericopes relating to preaching and in its following context a sort of synthesis of Jesus' healing activity, provided by the account of the healing of many.

The analysis of the passage dealing with the healing of Simon's mother-in-law has already shown that the structure Luke uses is found in Mark and so belongs to the earlier tradition. The account of the raising of the widow of Nain's son is not paralleled in Mark, but Luke's sequence still remains faithful to the same structure as the preceding episode. In the third pericope under consideration, the raising of Jairus' daughter and the healing of the woman suffering from a hemorrhage, there is once again a direct dependence on Mark's sequence. (The order in which Luke places the texts leaves out two short parables which Mark [4:26–32] places after that of the sower – one is replaced later [Luke 13:18–19] and one disappears. After the text relating to the healing of the woman suffering from a discharge of blood and the raising of Jairus' daughter, Mark introduces Jesus' visit to Nazareth [6:1–6], which Luke places earlier [4:16–30]. Furthermore, Luke delays the episode of the true relatives, which Mark places before the parable of the sower, to after this and the indications of how to listen to Jesus' teaching and hand it on.)

The structure is repeated in a constant rhythm, though with the variations one would logically expect. For example, the preceding

CENTRAL EPISODE INVESTIGATED	1 Healing of Simon's mother-in-law (4:38–9)	2 Raising of the widow of Nain's son (7:11–16)	3 The raising of Jairus' daughter and the healing of the woman with a hemorrhage (8:40–56)
STRUCTURE	TEXTS		
A. PRECEDING CONTEXT			
a. Preaching	1.A.a. "...to Capernaum ... and was teaching them on the sabbath. They were astounded at his teaching, because he spoke with authority" (4:31–2)	2.A.a. "Then he looked up at his disciples and said, 'Blessed are you poor ... I will show you what someone is like who comes to me, hears my words, and acts on them'" (6:20–49)	3.A.a. "He said in a parable ... these are the ones who, when they hear the word, hold it fast ... and bear fruit with patient endurance ..." (Parable of the sower, 8:4–18) "My mother and my brothers are those who hear the word of God and do it" (true family, 8:19–21) "He said to them, 'Where is your faith?'" (calming the storm, 8:22–5)
b. Miracle in favour of a man	1.A.b. Healing of the demoniac in the synagogue at Capernaum (4:33–7)	2.A.b. Healing of the centurion's slave in Capernaum (7:1–10)	3.A.b. Healing of the Gerasene demoniac (8:26–39)
B. MIRACLE IN FAVOUR OF A WOMAN	1.B. Healing of Simon's mother-in-law (4:38–9)	2.B. Raising of the widow of Nain's son (7:11–16)	3.B. Raising of Jairus' daughter and healing of the woman suffering from a hemorrhage (8:40–56)
C. FOLLOWING CONTEXT ASPECT OF SYNTHESIS HEALING OF MANY	1.C. "... all those who had any who were sick with various kinds of disease brought them to him ... and he cured them" (4:40–41)	2.C. "This word about him spread throughout Judea and all the surrounding country ... The disciples of John reported all these things to him.... (John) sent them to the Lord to ask.... Jesus had just then cured many people of diseases, plagues and evil spirits..." (7:17–21)	3.C. "Then Jesus called the twelve together, and gave them power and authority over all demons and to cure diseases, and he sent them out to proclaim the kingdom of God and to heal.... They departed and went through the villages, bringing the good news and curing diseases everywhere" (9:1–2, 6)

references to preaching vary from the short form of the first episode (4:31–2) to the fuller one of the second (6:20–49) and finally to the three pericopes of the third (parable of the sower, 8:4–18; Jesus' true family, 8:19–21; calming of the storm, 8:22–5).

In the following context, the synthetic aspect of the healing of many takes on its own particular slant in each case: in the first, Jesus, probably in the same time and place as the healing of Simon's mother-in-law, heals many people (4:40); in the second, the miracles for the benefit of many are set in continuity with the preceding episode of the raising of the widow of Nain's son with the words, "This word about him spread. . . . The disciples of John reported all these things to him" (7:17–21), so also interwoven with a passage relating to the Baptist; in the third, Luke makes the reference to healings follow straight on, but now not as miracles performed by Jesus, but rather as the power of working miracles handed on to the twelve when he sends them out to preach, and immediately operated by them (9:1–2, 6).

Looking carefully at these differences perhaps reveals a pro-gressive evolution, seen both in the preceding and following contexts: from an initial simplicity – the details in the first episode are described in time sequence: Jesus returns to Capernaum, preaches in the synagogue, where he heals the demoniac, then "after leaving the synagogue he enters Simon's house," where he heals first the woman and then many others – the composition grows, broadens out and embraces more elements. What I have called its synthetic aspect, placed at the end of the three episodes examined here in parallel, provides both an epilogue and the reading key clearly set out once more. In few words, and hence perhaps schematically more precisely, Luke tells that Jesus sent out the twelve to preach the good news and to work cures.

In the narrative the compiler is here building up, we can see a growth and progression in the successive elements of which it is formed and which also determine the structural form he has chosen to use. Then we come to a change: it is no longer only Jesus who proclaims the good news and works miracles; the fruit of his particular preaching addressed to the disciples is the development that sees them sent out. So here there is the final synthesis of the two elements that make up the structure we have examined: preaching and working cures. The word is followed by concrete actions.

In this way, Luke describes Jesus' activity and provides his words, which can be seen as the root from which he derives the structure he utilizes in his editorial work, in that they provide a confirmation of it. The proof of the way Luke sees Jesus is found in 24:19, in the way the disciples on the road to Emmaus describe "Jesus of Nazareth, who was a prophet mighty in deed and word. . . ."[95] What this brings out is the evangelist's intention to show the coherence between Jesus' teaching and his actions. Of significance here is that Luke should seek to express this coherence by including in his sequential narrative some miracles affecting women, in order to say that Jesus' activity involved men and women equally, and to prepare the way for the news that the group around Jesus included some women who had been healed, including, in particular, Mary Magdalene, cured of a most serious illness.

In consonance with the general thrust of my inquiry, I have taken references to women and the miracles of which they were recipients as the bases for my observations. I have not sought to suggest that all the miracles described in the section under review follow this man-woman-many sequence. It would be very far from my intention to try to suggest that Jesus worked as many miracles benefitting women as he did benefitting men: it would be ridiculous even to suggest they could be counted in this way. What one can perhaps more seriously say, however, is that the analysis made above needs to be deepened by a rigorous examination of the whole of Luke's Gospel and a comparison between it and the other Synoptics where the origin of this successional structure is to be found. (Mark's narrative in particular presents events in the same sequence, both in his account of the cure of Simon's mother-in-law and in that of the raising of Jairus' daughter and the healing of the woman suffering from a hemorrhage. Even such a limited analysis as that made here suggests a basis for the sequence in tradition and in the redaction of a so-called "typical day" in Jesus' life. This gives even more force to the fact that this provided for a definite space devoted to women.)

---

[95] For further research into Luke's contribution to the word-deed binomial, it might be useful to consider the characteristic of the Hebrew word *dābār*, which is to mean at the same time "word" and "thing-done." Cf. G. Gerelman, "Dābār Parola," *ThHandkAT* 1971.

As for the numerical preponderance of accounts of men being cured – four in the section under consideration not followed by the curing of women: a leper (5:12–16); a paralytic (5:17–26); a man with a withered hand (6:6–11); a possessed epileptic (9:37–43) – suffice to recall what I have said earlier about tradition being handed on by men and worked out in a period when women shared with "slaves and children" a slight enough consideration that led to their being very largely relegated to the realm of silence.

The bipolar structure *preaching and putting into practice* is also confirmed within Luke 8:1–3, where Jesus is seen first evangelizing, then working cures, with women following him and providing for him.

Chapter 4

A REVEALING TRACE

"More than in the past we are today aware that a fraction of text . . . can be understood only by starting from an analysis of the literary context of which it forms part."[1]

In the light of this conviction I now propose to take a longer look at the whole of Luke's Gospel in order to assess the part played by the verses under consideration within the broader framework.

The previous chapter looked at the literary unit that comprises Jesus' activity in Galilee and examined its two thematic elements: the *group* that formed around Jesus and the *women*. Now, following the indications that emerged from this first examination about the nature of the forms of presence of the disciples and the women before and after 8:1–3 (more fluid before, constant after), I want to look within this broader literary unit at the two sub-units 4:14–8:3 and 8:1–9:50, including the small unit 8:1–3 in both, as the conclusion to one and beginning of the other. We shall then see if this way of taking two apparently mutually exclusive hypotheses forward can lead to any conclusion.

The preceding analysis has shown 8:1–3 to be a crucial point, and this is the direction I shall continue to pursue now from the point of view of literary structure.

The Group that travelled with Jesus

Luke gradually builds up the picture of those to whom Jesus' proclamation is addressed, and those who are called to be and accepted as his followers, finally finishing the picture, completing the composition, in 8:1–3. This completion is provided by the information, here made plain and not given earlier, that women

---

[1] M. Pesce, "La profezia cristiana come anticipazione del giudizio escatologico in 1 Cor. 14:24–25," Various, *Testimonium Christi. Scritti in onore di Jacques Dupont* (Brescia, 1986), pp. 379–438, here 381.

were present, information for which we have been prepared by two previous episodes. The fact that Luke has already shown, in the account of the raising of the widow of Nain's son (7:11–17), that the relationship Jesus established with women was one of deep understanding–sharing,[2] and, in the anointing in Simon's house (7:36–50), that his relations with women were also ones of mutual exchange and acceptance,[3] prepares the ground for showing how naturally Jesus moves among the group of women.

From all that we have seen so far, we can put forward the hypothesis that, within the broader literary unit describing Jesus' preaching in Galilee, 8:1–3 is assigned the function of clarifying in what manner, with whom and by what means Jesus proclaimed the good news on his travels. Here the element with respect to which this function is to be seen is that of *preaching*. Within the sub-unit 4:14–8:3, however, the pericope 8:1–3 takes on the function of concluding and summing up with respect to the *group* theme (which can be viewed as a sub-element of *preaching*) and also acts as an explicitation and summary of the *women* element. In 8:1–3, the particular novelty lies in its information about the presence of the group of women.

Proclamation, Listening to the Word and Discipleship

Within the sub-unit 8:1–9:50, an intermediate literary unit can be identified, beginning at 8:1 and ending at 8:21, with the unifying themes of proclamation and listening:

> Soon afterwards he went on through cities and villages, proclaiming and bringing the good news of the kingdom of God. The twelve were with him, as well as some women who had been cured of evil spirits and infirmities: Mary, called Magdalene, from who seven demons had gone out, and Joanna,

---

[2] In this case understanding and sharing a mother's sorrow. Our examination of the women element in the previous chapter has already shown that this is not the main purpose of the story, but I am concerned here with what it shows in relation to the subject of women.

[3] He forgives and accepts the physical contact and the intimacy with which the woman expresses herself. Cf. H. Schürmann, *Il vangelo di Luca* (Brescia, 1977), p. 712: It. trans. of *Das Lukasevangelium* (Freiburg, 1971).

the wife of Herod's steward Chuza, and Susanna, and many others, who provided for him out of their resources.

When a great crowd gathered and people from town after town came to him, he said in a parable: "A sower went out to sow his seed; and as he sowed, some fell on the path and was trampled on, and the birds of the air ate it up. Some fell on the rock, and as it grew up, it withered for lack of moisture. Some fell among thorns, and the thorns grew with it and choked it. Some fell into good soil, and when it grew, it produced a hundredfold." As he said this, he called out, "Let anyone with ears to hear listen!"

Then his disciples asked him what this parable meant. He said, "To you it is given to know the secrets of the kingdom of God, but to others I speak in parables, so that

'looking they may not perceive,
and listening they may not understand.'

"Now the parable is this: The seed is the word of God. The ones on the path are those who have heard; then the devil comes and takes away the word from their hearts, so that they may not believe and be saved. The ones on the rock are those who, when they hear the word, receive it with joy. But these have no root; they believe only for a while and in a time of testing fall away. As for what fell among the thorns, these are the ones who hear; but as they go on their way, they are choked by the cares and riches and pleasures of life, and their fruit does not mature. But as for that in the good soil, these are the ones who, when they hear the word, hold it fast in an honest and good heart, and bear fruit with patient endurance.

"No one after lighting a lamp hides it under a jar, ot puts it under a bed, but puts it on a lampstand, so that those who enter, may see the light. For nothing is hidden that will not be disclosed, nor is anything secret that will not become known and come to light. Then pay attention to how you listen; for to those who have, more will be given; and to those who do not have, even what they seem to have will be taken away."

Then his mother and his brothers came to him, but they could not reach him because of the crowd. And he was told, "Your mother and your brothers are standing outside, wanting to see you." But he said to them, "My mother and my brothers are those who hear the word of God and do it" (Luke 8:1–21).

A quick glance shows this unit to be broken down into three further sub-units: the make-up of the travelling group (1–3), the parable of the sower (4–18) and the episode of Jesus' mother and brothers (19–21).

Leaving aside 1–3 for the moment, we can see that 4–18 is futher sub-divided into:

(1) the parable itself, 4–8;
(2) the disciples' request and the explanation of the parable reserved for them, 9–10 and 11–15;
(3) two independent logia, 16–17 and 18, on the subject of the need for proclamation and the manner of listening.

Turning to the first verse of this whole intermediate unit (8:1), we find a reference to the proclamation theme: "proclaiming and bringing the good news of the kingdom of God." In the verse that introduces the parable of the sower (8:4), one of the means of proclamation used by Jesus is described ("He said in a parable") and who the addressees are is indicated: "a great crowd" and "people from town after town."

In verses 5–7, the seed, which refers back to the "good news of the kingdom of God" of verse 1, falls three times – the significance of three will be examined in the next chapter – in wrong places where it cannot grow: on the path (on which birds eat it), on rock (where it withers), among thorns (which choke it). Finally, some falls "into good soil" where it "produced a hundredfold." The second sentence of this verse (8) ends with the stereotypical formula, "Let anyone with ears to hear listen!," which works as a strong ending to the passage and explains, besides the images used previously of unsuitable places, the subject of listening.

The reply Jesus gives to his disciples' asking what the parable means (v. 9): "To you it has been given to know the secrets of the kingdom of God, but to others I speak in parables, so that 'looking they may not perceive, and listening they may not understand'" (v. 10) carries a double reference: to the distinction between the type of proclamation reserved to the disciples and that reserved to others, and then to the manner of listening, with which the verse ends.

The pericope 11–15 then provides the explanation of the parable.

From the passage examined so far, three themes emerge clearly: proclamation, listening, the good news of the kingdom of God, i.e. the seed. Verse 11, which introduces the explanation, adds a further clarification through its words: "The seed is the word of God (λόγος τοῦ θεοῦ)."

From the theoretical point of view too, one can see that the appearance in the text of the term "word," which then remains forcefully present to verse 21, responds to the dynamic that links the three themes proclamation–word–listening. Of these concepts, that of the word is the central one: it is the intermediary between proclamation and listening. Proclamation is projected toward listening through the word and listening is tied to proclamation only by means of the word. This is the relational intermediary between the other two themes; it is the object and the content of both, without which neither proclamation nor listening can subsist. Proclamation is the act that brings about the relationship, listening is the objective toward which the first action proceeds and the cause that motivates proclamation. The term λόγος seems to act as the conductor of the text, and it reappears in 8:12, 13 and 15.

In 8:11 and 8:21, respectively the first and last times it appears in the section under review, the expression used is λόγος τοῦ θεοῦ, "word of God," and it is with this fullness of meaning that the other expressions present in the span of text between these two verses are charged.

Verses 12–14 show how the three unsuitable places in which the seed falls are those who have heard the word in such a way that it is then either "take[n] ... away from their hearts" (v. 12) or they have "no [lasting] root" (v. 13) or they are "choked by the cares and riches and pleasures of life" (v. 14). Finally, with a structure that parallels that of the preceding passage, verse 15 concludes it with the positive indication: "But as for that in good soil, these are the ones who, when the they hear the word, hold it fast in an honest and good heart, and bear fruit with patient endurance."

The interweaving of the noun λόγος and the verb ἀκούω, "to listen," winds through the whole pericope. The following diagram shows that both appear four times and that the structure of verses 4–8 (the telling of the parable) and 11–15 (its explanation) are symmetrical.

Luke 8:4–8	*Luke 8:11–15*	
v. 4 introductive	v. 11 introductive	(λόγος)
v. 5 ⎫ three	v. 12 ⎫ three types of	(λόγος and ἀκούω)
v. 6 ⎬ unsuitable	v. 13 ⎬ inadequate	(λόγος and ἀκούω)
v. 7 ⎭ places	v. 14 ⎭ hearing	(ἀκούω)
v. 8 positive content	v. 15 positive content	(λόγος and ἀκούω)
as conclusion	as conclusion	

The two *logia* that follow (verses 16–17 and 18) refer respectively to the need for proclamation: "No one after lighting a lamp hides it under a jar, or puts it under a bed, but puts it on a lampstand, so that those who enter may see the light. For nothing is hidden that will not be disclosed, nor is anything secret that will not become known and come to light," and to the way to listen: "Then pay attention to how you listen; for to those who have, more will be given; and from those who do not have, even what they seem to have will be taken away."

The verdict contained in the second part of this last verse closes verses 16–18. This is also found in the parallel text in Mark (4:1–25), the order of which Luke follows up to this point. Then Luke 8:19–21 goes on to the episode of the true relatives, which Mark places just before the parable of the sower (3:31–5). This passage has already been examined in the preceding chapter in the analysis made of the *women* element; here we need only to underline that true parentage, meaningful relationships and discipleship are all founded on the word of God: "My mother and my brothers are those who hear the word of God and do it" (8:21).

Luke, in placing this section here, emphasizes its sharing in the *proclamation-listening to the word* theme, and uses it as a conclusion to the unit 8:1–21.

There is also an element of synthesis with respect to the terms used: in the last verse, 21, the words ἀκούω, "to listen," and λόγος τοῦ θεοῦ, "the word of God," all appear. A confirmation of the thematic emphasis in this unit is also provided by a consideration of the fact that the verb ἀκούω, which appears forty-two times in the whole of Luke's Gospel, is never used as frequently as in this passage, where it appears eight times in the space of a mere fourteen verses (8:8–21).[4] Even more significant is the specific use of λόγος in the sense of "word–good news," which appears eight times in the whole of Luke, of which four in this sub-unit 8:1–21, which could therefore well be called "proclamation–listening," or, more simply, "the word."[5]

This analysis shows that the fraction 8:1–3 which is my main concern serves as an opening and provides the elements of information neeed for the development of the theme "proclamation–listening." If we list these elements, we see that some of them have already appeared in Luke's preceding narrative, but some are new here:

(a) the subject, the one who acts: "he," that is Jesus;
(b) the action, what he does: "proclaiming and bringing the good news";
(c) the content, what is proclaimed: "the kingdom of God";
(d) the place, where this happens: "cities and villages";
(e) the way, how it happens: "he went," i.e. he travelled;
(f) the situation, with whom:
   (f_1) (part of the information already given): "The twelve were with him";
   (f_2) (part of the new information) "as well as some women";
(g) further information with respect to the subject of "listening" and added to the new information concerning the presence of women:
   (g_1) "who had been cured of evil spirits and infirmities";
   (g_2) identification and news of three of these: "Mary, called Magdalene, from whom seven demons had gone out, and Joanna, the wife of Herod's steward Chuza, and Susanna";
   (g_3) they provided means of sustenance; "who provided for him out of their resources." This last phrase is the conclusion,

---

[4] The data relating to the verb ἀκούω, in the sense of "listening to Jesus, to what particularly concerns him," are taken from J. d'Arc OP and others (eds), *Concordance de la Bible. Nouveau Testament* (Paris, Cerf, n.d.), here from It. trans. pp. 51–2.

[5] Ibid., p. 405.

bringing together the two main subjects of the section, Jesus and the women.[6]

Women are therefore fully involved in this phase of Luke's text, which focusses on all the elements that revolve around the theme of the "word" and in 8:1–3, a passage that provides the elements needed to move into the theme of *proclamation–listening*, they are the most prominent component.[7] That the "word" is a central reference-point for Luke is made clear from the outset of his narrative. In his prologue he himself states:

- what his intention is: "to set down an orderly account of the things that have been fulfilled among us" (1:1); "to write an orderly account ..." (1:3);
- how he intends to carry it out: "I too decided, after investigating everything carefully from the very first ..." (1:3);
- the sources he is consulting: "those who from the beginning were eye-witnesses and servants of the word" (1:2);
- his aim in doing so: "so that you may know the truth concerning the things about which you have been instructed" (1:4).

---

[6] The verse that follows (8:4) opens by indicating the broader context of the listeners: "a great crowd gathered and people from town after town came to him ..." and brings in the *addressees* element, allowing the *listening* theme to develop fully. The text brings back here a "great crowd" which has already been introduced in 7:11. This verse thereby serves as a coupling between the short unit 8:1–3 and the longer 8:1–21, which includes it. It also provides a glimpse of the broader context 5:1–8:21 in which themes linked to the "word" stand out as basic elements. 5:1 in effect shows at the same time the start of Jesus' audience coming together with a purpose not previously defined ("to hear the word of God") and the first calling of the disciples, the choosing of those who were to stay with him.

[7] Luke uses the term λόγος or λόγος τοῦ θεοῦ eight times in his Gospel in the sense of word–good news; other than those already indicated (1;2; 5:2; 8:11, 12, 13, 15, 21), the only usage is in 11:28. The pericope 11:27–8 parallels 8:19–21 in content. In the latter, true parentage is said to be based on the word of God and 11:27–8 shows that true blessedness is not that proposed by the woman who says, "Blessed is the womb that bore you and the breasts that nursed you!," but that, "Blessed rather are those who hear the word of God and obey it!" This is a context in which the message relating to the word is specifically connected to a woman and again the centrality of the word is proclaimed by Jesus as being beyond roles and functions.

Luke then seeks out those who are still alive, the memory of those who have seen, witnessed, heard and then proclaimed the *word*. Women therefore come into this framework.

The central elements of the literary unit 8:1–21, *proclamation-listening–word* are brought out already in the prologue and women are sharers in this reality; news of their presence in Jesus' following is given in Luke's narrative in a special way just at the point where he goes deepest into the themes dealing with proclamation of and listening to the word of God and with discipleship.

Summary as Conclusion and Introduction

The expression that opens verse 8:1, "καὶ ἐγένετο," "soon afterwards," can be seen as an introductory formula characteristic of Luke. In this form he uses it twenty-two times, against two in Mark.[8] It is a significant device which, marking Luke's narrative in continuous fashion, serves to identify the sequence of events. Here it can be seen as opening the literary unit 8:1–3, which itself is in the shape of a summary already found in Luke: 4:44 and 21:37 function as summaries by way of conclusion.[9]

A single short verse provides an introductory summary to the account of the raising of the widow of Nain's son: "Soon afterwards he went to a town called Nain, and his disciples and a large crowd went with him" (7:11); this has structural parallels with 8:1–3:

7:11	8:1–3
Καὶ ἐγενετο	Καὶ ἐγένετο
πόλιν	πόλιν
αὐτῷ οἱ μαθηταὶ	οἱ δώδεκα
αὐτοῦ	σὺν αὐτῷ
καὶ ὄχλος πολὺς	καὶ γυναῖκές τινες

---

[8] Cf. J. Radermakers and P Bossuyt, *Lettura pastorale del vangelo di Luca*: It. trans. of *Jésus: Parole de la Grâce selon saint Luc* (Brussels, 1981), p. 177, who show that in various forms this formulation appears thirty-six times in Luke.

[9] The two texts summarize: "So he continued proclaiming the message in the synagogues of Judea" (4:44), and "Every day he was teaching in the temple, and at night he would go out and spend the night on the Mount of Olives" (21:37). Cf. Schürmann, *Il vangelo di Luca*, p. 707.

Three of the four summaries mentioned have the composition of the group assembled around Jesus as their central subject. The redactional element that emerges from a comparison of 7:11 and 8:1–3 shows that Luke must have paid conscious attention to his argument. This reinforces the importance of what is said in 8:1–3, this being the synthesis, apogee, final point of arrival in defining the composition of the inner group around Jesus. The literary parallel too shows how Luke moves from the μαθηταί, "disciples," of 7:11 to the δώδεκα, "twelve," of 8:1–3 and how the ὄχλος πολύς, "large crowd," of 7:11 is replaced by the γυναῖκές τινες, "some women," of 8:1–3.

The shift from larger groups to smaller and more defined ones shows those who were closest to Jesus. His closest followers were the twelve and the women.

By way of synthesis and in an attempt to gather up the conclusions to be drawn from these two types of analysis, of thematic elements and literary units, it would seem possible to single out 8:1–3 as a special coupling-link:

(a) In the material preceding 8:1–3, the two main themes are the group and the women; of the three verses we are examining, the second and third are devoted to women, their relationship to Jesus, the way they provided for him.

This concluding function seems also to be confirmed by the fact that if one looks at 8:1–3 in the overall comparison of the Synoptics, it appears to be the final part of a section (6:12–8:3) which is particular to Luke.[10]

---

[10] Cf. J. M. Guillaume, *Luc interprète des anciennes traditions sur la résurrection de Jésus* (Paris, 1979), p. 47. J. Ernst, *Il vangelo secondo Luca:* It. trans. of *Das Evangelium nach Lukas* (Regensburg, 1977), looks at the passage 6:20–8:3, defining it as "a short insertion deriving mainly from Q," with "both long and short sections that are Luke's own (6:24–6; 7:11–17, 36–50; 8:1–3)" (p. 38). In Ernst's interpretation of Jeremias' "hypothesis of blocks," he points to a special block of Luke's in 6:12–8:3 (excepting 6:17–19 = Mark 3:7–11a) (p. 33). Schürmann, op. cit., pp. 713–4, identifies the "short insertion" as 6:12–16, 20–8:3 and holds that it is made up of a single passage from the source of the discourses: 6:12–16, 20–49; 7:1–10, 18–35; 8:1, and of special material which he sees as a pre-Lucan narrative complex: 7:11–17, 36–50; 8:2–3.

Already the broader literary unit 4:14–9:50, often identified as the section covering Jesus' preaching in Galilee, opens with a synthetic composition: "Then Jesus, filled with the power of the Spirit, returned to Galilee, and a report about him spread through all the surrounding country. He began to teach in their synagogues and was praised by everyone" (4:14–15). (Yet again, still within this broader unit, there is an overall view in 6:17–19: "He came down with them and stood on a level place, with a great crowd of his disciples and a great multitude of people from all Judea, Jerusalem, and the coast of Tyre and Sidon. They had come to hear him and to be healed of their diseases; and those who were troubled with unclean spirits were cured. And all in the crowd were trying to touch him, for power came out from him and healed them.") And on this point, Heinz Schürmann's hypothesis is interesting: that verses 7:11–17, 36–50 and 8:2–3 make up "a primitive composition . . . in which the question of women is dealt with in a particular way."[11]

(b) In relation to what follows it, 8:1–3 acts as a short literary unit introducing Jesus' discourse on proclamation, how to hear the word and how to be his disciples.

Luke, according to the hypothesis in (a) above, would have put together the traditions available to him by inserting 8:1,[12] thereby producing the effect of distancing, without separating, 8:2–3 from the preceding context and projecting it toward what follows.

8:1 has parallels in both Mark and Matthew (Mark 1:39 and Matt. 4:23; 9:35), which raises the possibility that Luke may have used Mark, even if there are traces of 8:1 in the source of the discourses, Q.[13] The joint Luke uses it to make allows him to fuse the materials and information available to him by bringing several separate objectives together: maintaining the unity of this particular composition whose unifying theme is *women*, achieving the composition of the final picture of those who constantly followed Jesus, summing up the situation at the moment when he sets out to

---

[11] Schürmann, *op. cit.*, p. 704, n. 72; see also p. 712.

[12] Cf M. Hengel, "Maria Magdalena und die Frauen als Zeugen," p. 245, n. 4: "Redactional insertions by the evangelists."

[13] This view is upheld by Schürmann, who analyzes Matthew's composition to prove it. *Op. cit.*, pp. 711–2.

describe the beginning of Jesus' most intensive period of preaching in Galilee. The immediately following context of the parable of the sower with its references to proclamation and listening confirms this.

The process of putting these two hypotheses – thematic and literary – together gives 8:1–3 a concluding-introductory function in a synthesis that is one of rounding-off some subjects and becomes one of opening out on to others. To look for other and different hypotheses, once this has proved possible using these evaluative elements, could be another choice of method opposed to limiting research to a single track, were this not decisively demonstrable.

At the beginning of this study, I proposed the view that Luke 8:1–3 had the special quality of being able to lead us, like a well-defined *footprint*, on a course of investigation recovering *indicative pieces* that would bring the reality of the women who followed Jesus out from under the veil of silence that covered them. From the analysis undertaken and the ground covered so far, which has uncovered other *revealing traces* that can be referred and assigned to the characteristics of the presence and experience of the women with Jesus, we can say that the initial hypothesis has been confirmed, even that going ever deeper along tracks hardly glimpsed, even only hoped for, at the outset, has borne fruit.

Chapter 5

MARY MAGDALENE AND THE WOMEN DISCIPLES

Turning now specifically to Luke 8:1–3, let us try to evaluate the implications of unearthing, within the literary unit relating to Jesus' activity in Galilee, the traces, scattered here and there, of the reality of Jesus' relationship with women. The light we need in order to piece together as far as possible the life and context of the women who journeyed with Jesus will perhaps be a reflected light, a glimpse in a mirror, but it will still illuminate the scene we are seeking to establish.

The course of this *exegesis of the silence* is a hard one and strewn with problems. But the strength, the intensity of women's desire to discover, in Jesus' liberative message, the *word* he proclaims to women, fears no obstacles or fatigue in uncovering and relaying that word, is not afraid of the work of digging in the past, in biblical texts and thought conditioned by men – by all men and all women, including myself. It is not afraid of the risk involved in venturing, methodologically, along new tracks that may turn out to go only part of the way and need extending.

> Soon afterwards he went on through cities and villages, proclaiming and bringing the good news of the Kingdom of God. The twelve were with him, as well as some women who had been cured of evil spirits and infirmities: Mary, called Magdalene, from whom seven demons had gone out, and Joanna, the wife of Herod's steward Chuza, and Susanna, and many others, who provided for him out of their resources.

In 8:1, Luke tells of the realization of a need already seen and partly realized when he makes Jesus proclaim in advance the necessity of travelling to carry the news of the Kingdom of God to other cities: "I must proclaim the good news of the kingdom of God to the other cities also; for I was sent for this purpose" (4:43). The opening clause, "Soon afterwards he went on through cities and villages ..." gives an indication of the change of rhythm affecting the narrative from this point on. The evangelist describes those who accompany Jesus on his travels. First he mentions the twelve, mentioned previously only when they were chosen (6:13–16).[1] Next, Luke speaks of the group of women. He does not mention disciples. He refers explicitly and only to two components of the travelling group: the twelve and the women.

The Group of Women Cured

Some women who had been cured of evil spirits and infirmities (8:2).

Jesus' work of healing is one of the characteristics traits of his activity.[2] The cures he works fall into two categories: healing from physical diseases and infirmities and freeing from evil spirits or demons.[3] These two types of intervention by Jesus, not always clearly or easily distinguishable, are also placed together: "... a great crowd of his disciples and a great multitude of people ... had

---

[1] For the problem concerning the terminology twelve–apostles–disciples and the historicity of Jesus forming a group of twelve, cf K. H. Rengstorf, "δώδεκα," *TWNT II* (1935) (It. trans. *GLNT* 2 [1966], pp. 1536–80); E. D. Schmitz, "Numero," *DCBNT*, pp. 1103–4; H. Conzelmann, *Le origini del Cristianesimo*, pp. 211–16; E. Schweizer, *Gemeinde und Gemeindeordnung in Neuen Testament* (Zurich, 2d ed., 1962); J. Dupont, "Le logion des douze trônes (Mt. 19:28; Lc 22:28–30)," Bib 45 (1964), pp. 355–92; *Idem*, "Le douzième apôtre (Actes 1:15–26): à propos d'une explication récente," W. C. Meinrich, ed., *The New Testament Age. Essays in Honour of Bo Reicke*, vol. I (Macon G.A., 1984), pp. 139–45.

[2] H. W. Beyer, "θεραπεύω," *TWNT III* (1938), pp. 128–32; F. Graber and D. Müller, "θεραπεύω" and "ἰάομαι," *DCBNT*, pp. 1644–50. The Greek word Luke uses is θεραπεύω. Both in secular Greece and Hellenized Judaism the word was used with two principal meanings, "to serve" and "to heal." In the New Testament, however, "it never occurs in the secular meaning of serving, and only once in the religious-cultic sense of serving the divinity, Acts 17:25," but "far more frequently ... it appears in the sense of healing, though not meaning medical treatment ... but in its true and proper sense of leading to a cure": Beyer, *art. cit.*

[3] Cf. G. Stählin, "ἀσθένεια," *TWNT I* (1933), pp. 488–92; H. G. Link, "ἀσθένεια" and "νόσοσ," *DCBNT*, pp. 450–6.

come to hear him and to be healed of their diseases; and those who were troubled with unclean spirits were cured" (6:17–18, see also 4:40–41 and 8:2).

It is also worth noting that the cures are placed in close relationship to preaching and proclaiming the Kingdom. In the section relating Jesus' activity in Galilee (4:14–9:50), there are six episodes of healing from diseases and infirmities: Simon's mother-in-law, 4:38–9; the leper, 5:12–14; the paralytic, 5:17–26; the man with a withered hand, 6:6–11; the centurion's servant, 7:1–10; the woman suffering from a hemorrhage, 8:43–8. There are three examples of freeing from demonic possession: the man with an unclean spirit in the synagogue of Capernaum, 4:33–7; the Gerasene demoniac, 8:26–39; the possessed epileptic, 9:37–42.

The way in which Jesus works cures is sometimes described as touching, done directly by him (5:13) or done by the person who has faith in being cured (6:19; 8:44–7), sometimes as taking by the hand (14:4) or by laying on hands (4:40; 13:13), and at other times as simply by saying a word (6:10; 9:42).[4]

The value and importance attached to Jesus' healings are shown in several ways. When Luke speaks of preaching the good news he immediately adds references to miraculous cures effected by Jesus.[5] Luke here shows his clear intention of linking proclamation and liberation from sickness, both in the episode at Nazareth (4:16–19) and when he receives the delegation from John the Baptist. John's disciples ask him: "Are you the one who is to come... ?" Luke comments: "Jesus had just then cured many people of diseases, plagues, and evil spirits, and had given sight to many who were blind. And he answered them, 'Go and tell John what you have seen and heard: *the blind receive their sight*, the lame walk, the lepers are

---

[4] Cf R. Grob, "ἅπτω," *DCBNT*, pp. 1874–6: But it is above all in the accounts of cures that *háptomai* is used frequently (30 times)," p. 1875.

[5] Cf W. Grundmann, "The Concept of Power in the NT," *TWNT* II (1935), pp. 300–19: "Jesus defeats the empire of demonic forces, meaning diseases, sin and death, and it just in this that the truest sense of New Testament prodigies consists. In effect Jesus manifests and impersonates the Kingdom of God, his miracles – and this is what distinguishes them from other prodigies, whatever the outward similarities – represent and proclaim the affirmation of the Kingdom of God over the demonic and Satanic powers, and so, like all Jesus' works, have an eschatological dimension," 1519.

cleansed, the deaf hear, the dead are raised, *the poor have good news brought to them'"* (7:20–22).

It is often made clear that a presupposition for healing is faith (6:19; 8:44–8). The centurion at Capernaum has "such faith" that his servant is cured without Jesus even seeing him (7:1–10). Matthew writes that in Nazareth Jesus "did not do many deeds of power there, because of their unbelief" (13:58). Luke is not quite so explicit, but his whole account of Jesus' dealings with the inhabitants of Nazareth (4:16–30) seems to be saying the same thing in other words.

Many cures are worked on the sabbath (Luke 6:1–11; 13:10–16; 14:1–5) because, as Jesus himself says, "The Son of Man is lord of the sabbath" (6:5). Mark's parallel puts this even more strongly: "The sabbath was made for humankind, and not humankind for the sabbath; so the Son of Man is lord even of the sabbath" (2:27–8).

Jesus makes the disciples sharers in the power of healing: "Then Jesus called the twelve together and gave them power and authority over all demons and to cure diseases, and he sent them out to proclaim the kingdom of God and to heal" (Luke 9:1–2). Here too, the connection between proclamation and healing is made. The value attached to healing actions is underlined by the analogy Jesus himself makes between physical disease and moral evil: "Those who are well have no need of a physician, but those who are sick; I have come to call not the righteous but sinners to repentance" (5:31–2). This analogy is not to be understood in the sense that would be given it by the current conception that sickness was the result of a fault, as witness the reply Jesus gives, in John's Gospel, to his disciples when they see a man blind from birth, and ask him: "Rabbi, who sinned, this man or his parents, that he was born blind?" . . . "Neither this man nor his parents sinned; he was born blind so that God's works might be revealed in him" (9:2–3, see also Luke 13:1–5).

As for the personages involved in 8:1–3, there is a reference to "some women who had been cured of evil spirits." This "some" is followed by a list of three names. The first question this raises is whether all those named had been cured by Jesus. Of the first, Mary, called Magdalene, this is clearly stated in the phrase "from whom seven demons had gone out," but nothing further is said of Joanna, the wife of Herod's steward Chuza, or Susanna. Having said "some" and followed this by the three names, it may be thought that Luke is implying that all three had been cured; otherwise he might have used not the expression "some," but the number two, as he was to do in another context (24:13), for example, in referring to the disciples on the road to Emmaus.

The "many others" that follows can give rise to two hypotheses: it refers to many others who had been healed, whose names are not given;[6] alternatively, it identifies a group of women who were with Jesus, but who had not been healed.[7] In view of the contra-distinction between the terms "some" and "many," the second hypothesis seems definitely more probable. The closing phrase, "who provided for him out of their resources," also suggests the presence of a larger group than just those who had been cured, who would not necessarily have had many resources.

There are three women named. The first is Mary Magdalene, and the place she occupies in the list cannot be considered fortuitous. Luke names her again, and again places her first: "Now it was Mary Magdalene, Joanna, Mary the mother of James, and the other women with them who told this to the apostles" (24:10). Looking at other lists of names in Luke, we find that among the disciples with Jesus on the mountain of the transfiguration, he chooses three names: "Now about eight days after these sayings Jesus took with him Peter and John and James, and went up on the mountain to pray" (9:28); the same is true of those Jesus allowed to be present at the raising of Jairus' daughter: "When he came to the house, he did not allow anyone to enter with him, except Peter, John and James, and the child's father and mother" (8:51). In both lists, Peter is placed first: the order is therefore according to the importance given to the persons involved.[8]

A comparison of these lists will show that the number of names given is always three. According to Deuteronomy 19:15, for evidence to be valid a minimum of two or three witnesses is

---

[6] Some commentators hold the view that the women followed Jesus out of gratitude, so opting for this hypothesis.

[7] Cf. H. Schürmann, *Il vangelo di Luca* (Brescia, 1973), p. 709: "Now there were also 'many' ... women among Jesus' following, some of whom ... had experienced Jesus' exorcizing and healing powers."

[8] Cf. M. Hengel, "Maria Magdalena und die Frauen als Zeugen," *Abraham unser Vater. Festschrift O. Michel* AGSU 5 (1963), pp. 243–56.

required;[9] in the Greek and Hellenistic-Roman worlds the number three also had a particular significance: "An action, if carried out three times, acquired definitive efficacity; a word, an expression, a phrase, if pronounced three times, acquired full validity and power."[10]   In the Old Testament, "in the field of human relationships, three persons formed a particularly close group. . . . In some accounts one has, then, the impression that three is a round number generically applied to a household, to a group of persons, etc. There are three champions of David, . . . three comforters of Job, . . . three just men, . . . three heavenly guests of Abraham . . .," and in the New Testament, "three sometimes has the value of a precise number," but it is also notable that "when certain actions or certain facts appear three times, this means that they are complete, finished, definitive."[11] Luke uses this device, as do the other New Testament authors: so, for example, "in Luke 20:12 . . . the sending of a third servant . . . in 23:22, Luke – alone among the Evangelists – makes Pilate ask a third time what fault Jesus has committed, thereby demonstrating his complete innocence."[12] And so in the account of the passion, the presence of women is shown three times: on Calvary, at the burial, by the empty tomb. The presentation of three names confirms the clear intention on the part of the writer to give value, importance and certainty to the facts he is relating, in episodes concerning both men and women: the transfiguration, the raising of Jairus' daughter (in both of which Peter, John and James are given the value of witnesses by Luke), the news of the women following Jesus, the events relating to the passion and resurrection (where Mary Magdalene and Joanna, with Susanna in the first case and Mary the mother of James in the second, are cited as witnesses). In his concern to set down "an orderly account of the events that have been fulfilled among us" (1:1), about which he has "investigate[d] everything carefully from the very first" (1:3), Luke, by using three names, produces the double effect of emphasizing the veracity of the episodes concerned, by giving them three witnesses,

---

[9] This is the thesis put forward by Hengel, *art. cit.*, p. 248. Deut. 19:15 states: "A single witness shall not suffice to convict a person. . . . Only on the evidence of two or three witnesses shall a charge be sustained."

[10] G. Delling, "τρεῖς," *TWNT* 8 (1969), 215–22.

[11] *Ibid.*

[12] *Ibid.*

and of stressing the importance of the persons listed, who form a salient group. So in his prologue he speaks of "the events that have been fulfilled among us, just as they were handed on to us by those who from the beginning were eye-witnesses and became servants of the word."

Has Luke not perhaps intended to draw a parallel between the group of these three women and the group of the three apostles? Martin Hengel speaks of "a tendency to groups of three" which "refers back to that group of three persons who made up the inner circle of the apostles."[13] If one takes Luke's evident tendency to use parallels into account, plus what we have seen of his succession of a miracle for the benefit of a man followed by one for the benefit of a woman, it is valid to suppose that he saw this group of three women in relation to the rest of the group as analogous to the three apostles in relation to the twelve.

Mary Magdalene

The privileged position Mary Magdalene holds in relation to Jesus, the witnessing role to which Christ calls her, the choice by the Risen Christ to send her to proclaim the glad tidings of the resurrection to the apostles, thereby making her the mediatrix of his word, all serve to make this woman a figure of exceptional importance and justify the space given to her here.

If from what we have seen so far, it is possible to see an analogy between the group of the twelve and the group of women, and between the inner group of three apostles and the inner group of three women, then the conclusion to be drawn is that the figure of Mary Magdalene should be seen in equal terms with that of Peter, who receives so much more attention in the texts.

Mary is a common name in the Bible: "in Hebrew *mirjam*, Aramaic *mârjam*, of uncertain origin; the Hebrew form derives from the Egyptian *mr'* (to be loved) or from *rà a* (to see, the seer); the Aramaic form derives perhaps from *marà* (lady)."[14]

---

[13] Hengel, "Maria Magdalena," p. 248.

[14] G. Nolli, *Evangelo secondo Luca*, p. 339. On questions relating to the name Mary, see also R. E. Brown, *The Gospel According to John*, 2 vols. (Garden City, N.Y., 1966–71).

Magdalene, however, means "of Magdala," the town from which she came, which "rose out of the plain of Genezaret, on the west bank of the Sea of Galilee, some three miles north of Tiberias."[15] In modern times it was El Mejdel, an Arab village up to 1948, when it was destroyed in the Arab-Israeli war. Since 1971 an archeological mission led by P. Corbo has been undertaking research there. Buildings of the town of the Roman period (first century) have come to light, including a tower, a villa and a synagogue, the oldest yet discovered in Palestine. Some authors hold that the name Magdala is derived from the Hebrew *Migdol* or *Migdal*, meaning a tower.[16] The town, rich in fishing and associated trades, was in Jesus' time called Tarichea, from the Greek *tarikhos*, meaning salt fish. It is found under this name in the writings of the Hebrew historian Flavius Josephus, who, probably exaggerating, gives it forty thousand inhabitants with a wealth of artisans other than fishermen and a fleet of 230 fishing boats. At the time of the first Jewish uprising (66–70 C.E.), the Jews chose it as their headquarters in their struggle against the Romans. Titus conquered it after a long resistance in 67 C.E.[17] The bad reputation the town enjoyed in rabbinic literature after the first century appears to stem from corruption brought about by excessive wealth.[18] Perhaps this element had some hand in perpetuating the confusion over attributing the character of "sinner" to Mary Magdalene.

In Luke the town is mentioned only twice, both times in the form of the "surname" given to Mary Magdalene (8:2; 24:10). In the other Synoptics (Mark 15:40, 47; 16:1, 9; Matt. 27:56, 61; 28:1) and in John (19:25; 20:1, 18), other than reference to it as the place from which

---

[15] R. Fabris, "Maria di Magdala la testimone dell'annuncio pasquale," *Rocca* 6 (1984), pp. 52–3; cf. P. de Ambroggi, "Magdala," *EC* 7, 1815–6; M. Avi-Yonah, "Magdala," *En Ju* 11, p. 685; G. Hölscher, "Magdala," *RE* 14, p. 298; J. L. McKenzie, *Dictionary of the Bible*, p. 534; J. Schmid, *Das Evangelium nach Markus* (Regensburg, 1955).

[16] Such as J. L. McKenzie, *Dictionary of the Bible*, p. 576; A. Diez Macho, "Magdala," *En Bi*, 4, pp. 832–5. [Also Y. Aharoni, *The Land of the Bible* (London and New York, 1966, p. 98 – Trans.]

[17] *Ant. Iud.* XIV, 7, 3; *Bell. Iud.*, III, 10, 1.

[18] See J. Ernst, *Das Evangelium nach Lukas* (Regensburg, 1977); Fabris, "Maria di Magdala," p. 52; Schürmann, *Il vangelo*, p. 709, n. 13: "According to Billerbeck I, 1946ff, Magdala was a town famous for its licentiousness."

this woman called Mary came (to distinguish her from the other Marys in the Gospels), it may appear in Mark 8:10, where, at the end of his description of the second multiplication of loaves, he says: "And immediately he got into the boat with his disciples and went to the district of Dalmanutha." The parallel text in Matthew (15:39) has Magadan – "a place mentioned just this once; some authorities give the name as Magdala, but this could be a later modification. But it is likely that Dalmanuta was an early alteration and that the correction to Magdala is right."[19] "The form Dalmanuta is probably a popular deformation of Magdal-Nunaya (Nunaya, meaning 'city of fish,' is the Aramaic equivalent of Tarichea."[20]

With regard to the expression used of Mary Magdalene, "from who seven demons had gone out," let us first look at the two words "seven" and "demons" separately, then at the phrase as a whole.

The number seven – like other numbers – had a special signifcance not only in the area of semitic culture and in the Bible, but also in Greece, Egypt and elsewhere. The origins of this would appear to lie in the four lunar phases of seven days each, rather than in the seven observable planets. According to Karl Rengstorf: "In Babylon, where ... attention was paid to the seven planets earlier than anywhere else, the number seven already had great importance in myth and worship before the planets were taken into consideration," and, "on the other hand, the phases of the moon could be seen earlier and for primitive man were an obvious datum for working out and dividing time."[21] Symbolically, the number seven expresses a complete period of time and the idea of totality itself.

A religious use of the term can be seen in Hebrew culture in the institution of the sabbath, the seventh day dedicated to God, and of the sabbatical year. In the New Testament writings it appears eighty-eight times.[22] While in some of these cases, the number itself may be meant (e.g. Matt. 15:34), in others the influence of the old

---

[19] Schmid, *Das Evangelium nach Lukas*: It. trans. p.197.

[20] P. Acquistapace, *Guida biblica e turistica della Terra santa* (Milan, 1980), pp. 342–4.

[21] K. H. Rengstorf, "ἑπτά," *TWNT* II (1935), pp. 623–32; see also Schmitz, "Numero," pp. 1099–104; S. Boncompagni, *Il mondo dei simboli* (Rome, 1984), pp. 89–98.

[22] The word επτά appears nine times in Matthew, nine in Mark, six in Luke, eight in Acts and fifty-five in Revelation.

conceptions is clear: "And if the same person sins against you seven times a day, and turns back to you seven times and says, 'I repent,' you must forgive" (Luke 17:4), or the parallel passage in Matthew 18:21–2: "Then Peter came and said to him, 'Lord, if my brother sins against me, how often should I forgive? As many as seven times?' Jesus said to him, 'Not seven times, but, I tell you, seventy times seven." The sense the word takes on here is that however great and complete the situation of sin, forgiveness must be as complete and more so.

The demonological concept, which "in some form has survived down to medieval and modern times," has its roots in Mesopotamia: "the evils of life that were not due to great natural catastrophes were attributed to the wicked influence of demons."[23] This conception influenced the Hebrews and spread into the Greek world, where popular belief saw demons as intermediate beings between the gods and human beings and tried to interfere in their doings through magic. The concept attached to the word "demon" underwent an evolution among the Greeks, starting from a generic divine power and moving to these intermediate personal beings, messengers between gods and humans or supervisors of humans, and, under the influence of manifestations close to animism – magic, exorcism – was drawn into cultic practices. "In many philosophical systems, demons are beings who 'possess' human beings. Certain abnormal events are attributed to the 'divinity' that inhabited the body, as we can read in Hippocrates and still more in the tragedians. . . . More diffuse, but nevertheless still recognizable, is the conviction that particular diseases were to be attributed to certain spirits . . . those that we would call 'internal diseases,' diseases, that is, whose natural

---

[23] On demonology see: W. Foerster, "δαίμων," *TWNT* II (1935), pp. 1–21; H. Bietenhard, "δαίμων," *DCBNT*, pp. 457–61; M. Limbeck, "Demonio," J. B. Bauer and C. Molari (eds), *Dizionario teologico* (Assisi, 1974), pp. 181–9; McKenzie, *Dictionary of the Bible*, pp. 191–4; J. E. Martins Terra (ed.), *Existe o diabo? Respondem os teólogos* (São Paulo, 1975); F. Bovon (ed.), *Analyse structurelle et exégèse biblique* (Neuchâtel, 1971); above all the essays by J. Starobinski, "L'indemoniato di Gerasa: analisi litteraria di Marco 5:1–20," pp. 60–88, esp. p. 88, and F. J. Leenhardt, "Saggio di esegesi: Marco 5:1–20," pp. 89–113. As a minimum of information on Mesopotamian demonology, let me add that there were also good demons, who were invoked to chase out the bad ones.

causes the ancients were unable to discover, unlike, for example, a wound."[24]

In the New Testament the word δαίμων *demon* occurs once (Matt. 8:31) and δαιμόνιον sixty-three times.[25] The elements of demonology present in the New Testament stem from Judaism and the Old Testament, though they are less obvious in the New than in the Old. Limbeck makes the interesting point that, "The problem of human motives for speaking about the devil is shown at its most acute in serious reflection on Jesus' words or silence about the devil . . . but the passages that deal with Satan generally reveal a formation by the *first* proto-Christian community or one or another Evangelist." He goes on to give three examples.[26]

Most of the cases where the Gospels touch on the problem are ones of demonic possession. This belief does not appear in the Old Testament, even though, according to J. L. McKenzie, "in Judaism psychic illnesses were considered manifestations of demonic possession." McKenzie on the one hand states that "many modern authors have explained the accounts of demonic possession in the Gospels by saying that they demonstrate the ingenuous belief of the ancients according to which evils whose cause was unknown were works of the devil: persons who were called possessed suffered from psychic disturbances that could not be identified as such. . . . These authors hold . . ." that just as Jesus' speech shows him accepting "the *earth centre* geocentric universe and a flat earth, so he also accepted the demonic explanation of psychic disturbances." But, he goes on: "The parallelism is not perfect. In the Gospels the episodes of demonic possession form part of a wider framework of thought. . . . The coming of Jesus is a challenge to the kingdom of Satan, the powers of evil. The demoniacs certainly show psychic disturbances. The question is not whether Jesus adapted his speech to popular usage, but whether the authors of the Gospel traditions had other means of describing these psychic disturbances and their cures apart from the language of possession and exorcism."[27]

---

[24] Foerster, "δαίμων," pp. 751, 757–8, 757, n. 3.

[25] Eleven in Matthew, thirteen in Mark, twenty-three in Luke, six in John, once in Acts and nine in the other writings.

[26] Limbeck, "Demonio," pp. 751–2.

[27] McKenzie, *Dictionary*, p. 193.

J. Starobinski also has an interesting observation on the interpretative aspects of possession: "The most widely held conception
among historians of science is that cases of demonic possession
provide us with a good example of how a natural phenomenon
comes to have a cultural interpretation. Demoniacs, it is said, were
individuals who presented alarming symptoms – such as we see
today in epileptics, spastics or schizophrenics. Physical disorder, an
evident fact, is given meaning through the interpretative tools
available to the language of a time (or a civilization). The object that
needs to be interpreted is violence, shaking, shrieking. The
interpretative instrument, in the first century, was the concept of
demonic possession."[28] Starobinski goes on to point to a circularity
in the interpretative process, by which what starts off as an
interpretation – demonic possession – "becomes in turn a datum
offered to the interpretation given. . . . One can in fact hold that the
'world view' in Jesus' time, and still more in the evangelists' time,
accentuated the opposition between the kingdom of God and the
kingdom of the devil to an extent that it became necessary for those
who experienced this to produce an ensemble of signs: so it was not
the morbid symptoms that were the primary fact, but the 'cultural'
concept of the devil, a concept that was explained through shaking,
shrieks and the like. The disturbed behaviour, the shrieks, the 'non-
language,' the violence, therefore become the means with which
individuals interpret and actualize the presence of the devil, about
which they have previously been informed through religious
discourse."[29]

The influence of the Judaic and other contemporary traditions is
also present in the Old Testament, but this contains no speculative
theoretical view of demons, despite its presence in these traditions.
A hermeneutic of the gospel narratives of possession would first

---

[28] Starobinski, "L'indemoniato di Gerasa," p. 86. For a characteristic
description of epilepsy, see Luke 9:37–43.
[29] *Ibid.*, pp. 86–8. Starobinski states that the circularity that can arise
between the data to be interpreted and the interpretative tool has already
been observed in relation to hysteria: "the definition and clinical picture of
which, as they have been diffused in written and oral form, have played an
often determinant role in the manifestation of most cases of this affliction.
One can speak, in this regard, of the sociogenesis or logogenesis of the
symptom" (p. 87).

have to take account of the fact that it is not the writers' intention to indicate the physical or psychic causes of suffering within a purely human framework, but to present it under a definite light: a violence brought about by a power of evil. In the demoniacs, the elements of physical suffering are manifestations of diabolical presence, which devastates spirits but also bodies.[30]

From the context in which "from whom seven demons had gone out" is set, and from what we have just analyzed, the meaning it contains can be seen from two points of view, the one accepted when Mary Magdalene lived and our own today. As perceived in her time, this woman was considered victim of a disease not easily understandable, which took her over physically and psychically, completely (shown by the use of the number seven) and which took her into the category of those possessed by demons.

The only evidence we have for trying to reconstruct the nature of the disturbances from which Mary Magdalene was suffering is the expression under examination. In the light of recent advances in medical and psychological knowledge, we can suggest hypotheses. It was perhaps something in the nature of a psychic disorder. She may have been a woman of strong sensibilities, whose equilibrium had not withstood the impact of the painful problems life can bring, particularly those special problems a woman faced in the Palestine of Jesus' time.

The unhappiness of woman's condition was foreseen, marked out, codified from the moment of birth: "The world could not exist without males and females, but happy the man whose children are male and woe to the man whose children are female."[31] The Book of Ecclesiasticus (or Sirach) gives a list of the worries a father feels on account of his daughter:

A daughter is a secret anxiety to her father
    and worry over her robs him of sleep;
when she is young, for fear she may not marry,
    or if married, for fear she may be disliked;

---

[30] H. Schlier, "Demõnios e espiritus malignos no Novo Testamento," Martins Terra (ed.), *Exista o diabo?*, pp. 103–38, esp. 110–11, 114–6.
[31] A. Cohen, *Il Talmud*, p. 213.

while a virgin, for fear she may be seduced
    and become pregnant in her father's house;
or having a husband, for fear she may go astray,
    or, though married, for fear she may be barren.
Keep strict watch over a headstrong daughter,
    or she may make you a laughingstock to your enemies,
a byword in the city and the assembly of the people,
    and put you to shame in public gatherings.
See that there is no lattice in her room,
    no spot that overlooks the approaches to the house.
Do not let her parade her beauty before any man,
    or spend her time among married women
for from garments comes the moth,
    and from a woman comes woman's wickedness.
Better is the wickedness of a man than a woman who does
      good;
    it is woman who brings shame and disgrace
(Sir. 42:9–14).

In the same vein, the Talmud's explanation of the priestly blessing, "The Lord bless you and protect you" (Num. 6:24) is, "May he bless you with male offspring and protect you from daughters who need strict surveillance." As for prescriptions relating to the uncleanness incurred by women giving birth, Leviticus lays down that, "If a woman conceives and bears a male child, she shall be ceremonially unclean seven days. . . . Her time of blood purification shall be thirty-three days. . . . If she bears a female child, she shall be unclean two weeks . . . her time of blood purification shall be sixty-six days" (Lev. 12:2–5). And when the juridical obligation to maintain children came to an end when they reached the age of six, boys could be sent away from home to learn a trade, but girls could be sold as slaves. Aspects of women's subjection to male authority in the person of father, husband, brother or owner, which allowed women neither meaningful autonomy nor space to realize and express themselves have already been discussed.

So Mary Magdalene probably felt suffocated in her lack of space to express and develop her sensitivity; her psychic energies were probably pent up for lack of constructive and creative outlets; the tension produced by a repressed life-force may well have finally upset the balance of her mind. All this, of course, is in the realm of supposition, but it would be interesting to know what in this woman's life, what episode or drama, had finally brought about her psychic disturbance. There is perhaps a trace of her hypersensitivity in Luke 8:1–3, in her leaving everything to follow Jesus, in her rush towards the one who freed her from her state, in her total giving of herself, her following of the Master to help him and share the experience of his sorrows and joys. And in her taking a decision that for women of her time was disruptive and scandalous in relation to ruling customs.

F. J. Leenhardt writes of the Gerasene demoniac in words that could equally well be applied to Mary Magdalene and her healing encounter with Jesus: "It is certainly a case of a cure, but what happens on the occasion of this cure is that Jesus meets a person dispossessed of himself by a dark power that is tyrannizing him."[32] Mary Magdalene, then, whatever suppositions we make, and whatever the actual details of her condition, was a woman "dispossessed of herself."

Her Cure

We have no record of the first time Mary Magdalene heard about Jesus or saw him. Maybe, if we accept Schmid's assertion that Magdala was the town to which Jesus withdrew after the second multiplication of loaves and fishes, we can imagine her present at this long session of preaching ("... they have been with me now for three days ..." Matt. 15:32).[33] In any case, considering how much of Jesus' activity was carried out on the shores of the lake on to which Magdala faced, there would probably have been several occasions on which she could have met him. Nor do we have any record of her actual cure; we can, however, perhaps piece together the circumstances in which it took place by taking elements common to the cures described in the Gospels.

Luke speaks of Jesus at Capernaum, a lakeside town like Magdala and not far from it, where he heals a demoniac in the synagogue and then goes into Simon's house, where he heals his mother-in-law. "As the sun was setting, all those who had any who were sick with

---

[32] F. J. Leenhardt, *Saggio di esegesi Marco 5:1–20*, p. 96.
[33] J. Schmid, *L'evangelo secondo Marco*, p. 198.

various kinds of disease brought them to him; and he laid his hands on each of them and cured them, Demons also came out of many, shouting, 'You are the Son of God!'" (4:40–41). (We have already seen how this description, placed immediately after Jesus' visit to Simon's house, where his mother-in-law, after being cured, "got up and began to serve him," suggests the likelihood that these cures also took place in the neighbourhood of Simon's house.) It is just a supposition, but Jesus could well have cured Mary on a similar occasion.[34] The manner of her cure would not have been very dissimilar to that used on other occasions and therefore, as with the others, is likely to have been through physical contact or taking her by the hand.

But beyond the unknowable specific details of her cure, Mary Magdalene, a women "dispossessed of herself," came back from Jesus as a woman restored to herself, to the depths of her own being. And perhaps rather than one central moment, there was a process, a developing relationship of discovery and growth.

From the redactional aspect too, one needs to bear in mind that things that developed gradually over time could easily not have been recorded as successive stages. When the traditions and the texts were composed, the events had all taken place and the compilers knew what they were setting down as a whole. The events were present to them all at one time. The compilers ran the risk of anticipating with regard to the actual course of events, of reading and handing on what had happened first in the light of subsequent happenings, of ironing out events that had undergone developments, progressive growth, into a single time-scale.

If one of the features that identified Mary Magdalene's experience, noticeable at the time the texts were being drawn up, was her new and changed condition, her recovery of psycho-physical

---

[34] Looking for accounts of cures beside the lake in Matthew, I find that, just before the second multiplication of loaves, he puts in the following pericope: "After Jesus had left that place, he passed along the Sea of Galilee, and he went up the mountain, where he sat down. Great crowds came to him, bringing with them the lame, the maimed, the blind, the mute, and many others. They put them at his feet, and he cured them, so that the crowd was amazed when they saw the mute speaking, the maimed whole, the lame walking and the blind seeing. And they praised the God of Israel" (Matt. 15:29–31).

liberation, tradition could have expressed this immediately it mentions her by name. Her restoration to herself by Jesus could well have been a more dynamic reality, more complex and more protracted than the texts immediately suggest; her relationship of dialogue-exchange with Jesus would have opened up a course of growth, of "healing," of "return to self," which, even if it had its crucial moments, was to extend to the resurrection ... and beyond.[35]

Her role

The Synoptic Gospels and John agree in giving Mary Magdalene a privileged place. She is placed first in the lists of women present at the events of the passion in Mark, Matthew and Luke. In John she comes after the mother of Jesus and her sister. The fact that she is named together with his close relations is a different way, compared to the Synoptics, of showing her importance. The discrepancies evident in the various accounts of the passion and resurrection are one of the problems that exegetes have been investigating for hundreds of years. Yet it is notable that all the texts agree on the presence of Mary Magdalene and on the importance of the role she played, even if they describe this in differing ways.

What significance can be attributed to the special place given to this woman? The reply can produce various elements: the special

---

[35] A lucky coincidence in my reading meant that I found the expression "return to self" in L. Ravasi Bellocchio, *Di madre in figlia. Storia di un'analisi* (Milan, 1987), where the author quotes a passage from L. Andreas-Salomé's *My Gratitude to Freud*, which had such an affinity with what I was thinking that I should like to quote it: "An analysis that has been fully efficacious thereby becomes, for the subject who has been cured, a strengthened vision of one's own creative potential. The return to self comes about for him as a return to something he effectively is, but which is also something more than himself: it is a power that rises up before him as a model so that all the experiences he had most deeply forgotten and those that have longest been familiar to him can only now become stimuli to his own personal life. Therefore what is made manifest in him is very different from a simple intention or decision, very different from the simple understanding of the causes of his illness or from simply condemning them: No, the throbbing explosion, once set free, should be transmuted into a new loving bliss. I deliberately choose this incisive expression: healing is an act of love."

place she occupied in relation to Jesus; her function within the group of women who followed him; the importance of her presence and her witness to Jesus' life and teaching, from the time in Galilee right up to the dramatic events of his crucifixion and death; her being chosen as the first person to witness his resurrection (alone by John and Mark; with another woman by Matthew and with other women by Luke, but first in the list); the major part she played in the first community.

Her special place in relation to Jesus. This is shown by what the Gospel writings say of her. Luke names Mary Magdalene in 8:2 and privileges her, both by naming her first, and by making her the only one he specifies individually as having been cured by Jesus, and of what – of "seven demons." Of the others he says generically, referring to the whole group and not distinguishing between individuals, that they "had been cured of evil spirits and infirmities." We then find her again in Luke, again placed first, when, after relating the events on Calvary, at the burial and the visit to the tomb, and referring to the women in general ("The women who had followed him from Galilee," 23:49; "The women who had come with him from Galilee," 23:55), he picks her and two others out by name: "Now it was Mary Magdalene, Joanna, Mary the mother of James, and the other women with them who told this to the apostles" (24:10). The lists in 8:2–3 and 24:10 are both made up of three names, but, whereas the third is different (Susanna in the first, Mary the mother of James in the second), Mary Magdalen comes first in both, followed by Joanna.

In Mark, on Calvary, Mary Magdalene (15:40) is first in the list of the three women singled out by name among the "women looking on from a distance," who "used to follow him and provided for him when he was in Galilee" (15:41), to which Mark adds that "there were many other women who had come up with him to Jerusalem." This description shows three levels of importance, corresponding to three different degrees of closeness to Jesus: the three women named personally – Mary Magdalene, Mary the mother of James the younger, Salome; a larger group who had followed and provided for Jesus from Galilee; the many other women, making an even larger group, who had come up to Jerusalem with Jesus. In this, which can be seen as a series of concentric circles of women, Mary Magdalene is the one nearest to the centre, to Jesus. Mark, always placing her first, names her again when, with Mary the mother of Joses, she watches Jesus being buried, (15:47), and when, with Mary the mother of James, and Salome, she goes to the tomb and receives the news of the resurrection (16:1–6). Finally, she appears alone, when Jesus appears to her and she goes and tells those who had been with him (16:9–10). Here again we find confirmation that she had been healed – "Mary Magdalene, from whom he had cast out seven demons."

Matthew, like Mark, places Mary Magdalene on Calvary (27:56), at the burial (27:61), on the visit to the tomb (28:1), at the announcement of the resurrection (28:6), at the appearance of the Risen Christ (28:9) and in charge of taking the news to the brethren (28:10). While Matthew places Mary Magdalene, on Calvary, first among the women "looking on from a distance" who had "followed Jesus from Galilee and had provided for him," followed by "Mary the mother of James and Joseph, and the mother of the sons of Zebedee," he then names only "Mary Magdalene and the other Mary" (27:61, 28:1) and finally continues his narrative without naming her further but just referring to these two.

John has: "Meanwhile, standing near the cross of Jesus were his mother, and his mother's sister, Mary the wife of Clopas, and Mary Magdalene" (19:25). John does not put Mary Magdalene first, but I have already said how significant it is to find her name together with those of Jesus' close relatives. Furthermore it is John who, with his description of Mary Magdalene going to the tomb alone (20:1, 11, 16, 18) and above all with his account of Jesus appearing to her, an account full first of fear and sorrow and then of intense joy, in fact gives us the most comprehensive witness to the special relationship between Jesus and this woman.

Mary Magdalene's sensitivity and strength of feelings are confirmed in the Synoptics and in John in their accounts of the events that ended Jesus' life on earth, which show her and the other women present on Calvary (Luke 23:49; Matt. 27:55–6; Mark 15:40–41; John 19:25), at the burial (Luke 23:55–6; Matt. 27:61; Mark 15:47). It may have been Mary Magdalene's intense feelings and rich vitality that made her capable of becoming a reference point for the other women too. The group re-forms around her and at dawn sets out for the tomb (Luke 24:1–10; Matt. 28:1; Mark 16:1–2). John on the other hand singles out her alone (20:1), and it is his account (20:1–18) that accords best with her deep feelings. Mary goes to the tomb, "early on the first day of the week, while it

was still dark": she could not wait. Finding the tomb empty, "she
ran and went to Simon Peter and the other disciple, the one whom
Jesus loved," saying to them, "They have taken the Lord out of the
tomb, and we do not know where they have laid him": she could
not contain herself. (By the repeated "could not," I do not mean
inability to choose, but intense feeling.) She ran, she had to tell
others what had happened, she could not keep it to herself and for
herself. When the two disciples, having found the tomb empty,
"returned to their homes," what could have been more reasonable
than for her to go back with them, so that they could console one
another in the sorrow they felt and together consider this new fact
of the disappearance of the body? But would they have been able to
console her? And so Peter and other disciple went away, "But Mary
stood weeping outside the tomb": she stayed, she could not go
away, and she gave herself up to tears.

John's narrative goes on with, "As she wept": this was no
momentary giving way to grief but an intense and continuing
lamentation, so that first the angels and then Jesus later ask her why
she is weeping.[36] To the angels, she replies with grief: "They have
taken away my Lord, and I do not know where they have laid him"
and then to the man she supposes to be the gardener she rushes to
say: "Sir, if you have carried him away, tell me where you have laid
him, and I will take him away": her whole being is bent on finding
him. And Jesus allows himself to be found, lets himself be
recognized. He says her name, "Mary!" and she immediately says to
him "Rabbouni," teacher. Jesus turns to her as though following the
thread of the attitude he himself described, of the shepherd who
"calls his own sheep by name . . . and the sheep follow him because

---

[36] As I find them so appropriate, I give here Adriana Zarri's words in
E più facile che un cammello . . ., p. 258, referring to Luke 7:44–7: "And
you, Lord, were glad to have her there: you were glad there were women
in the world, with their hair and their tears: women who know how to
weep better than men; and this is a richness they have in their eyes, a sign
of humble and sweet remission such as men rarely know. You knew that, as
a man, you would no longer have been able to join her in certain follies,
certain sweetnesses, in certain yearnings; you who were as a man easier,
more elementary and direct. And, just as all men are different, while the
common people despised her, you admired her as a miracle, a miracle done
by you."

they know his voice" (John 10:3–4). Jesus lets himself be recognized by the voice in which he says the name Mary.

There is in this moment a meaningful and indescribable synthesis of their existing relations and communications: in hearing herself called, the woman finds at the same time the voice she knows, the voice of the other, and now here of the Other, and finds herself, her perception and understanding of her own depths. The relationship, this contemporaneous double meeting with the other and with herself, in which otherness and identity are both present, this unity that includes duality, could be comprehensively such only in the manifestation of the Risen Christ to a woman, in harmony with the creation by God of a human being, the adam, with two visages: man and woman. (The extraordinary fullness of the encounter that takes place here is linked to the simultaneous presence of otherness and sameness, the two modalities through which communication, knowing, deep contact with the other, take place. And the greatest otherness between two beings is in the God–human being relationship; and the fullest measure of sameness is to be found in the Creator–creature meeting. The apex of communication is therefore reached in dialogue with the Absolutely Other.) Mary, like the "friend of the bridegroom, who ... rejoices greatly at the bridegroom's voice" (John 3:29), would perhaps wish to communicate all her feelings, the intensity of this experience of hers of living the drama of separation and death and then the joy that fills her at having found him again. Jesus' words are still being fulfilled: "I am the good shepherd. The good shepherd lays down his life for the sheep.... I know my own and my own know me, just as the father knows me and I know the Father. And I lay down my life for the sheep.... For this reason the Father loves me, because I lay down my life in order to take it up again. No one takes it from me, but I lay it down of my own accord. I have power to lay it down, and I have power to take it up again" (John 10:11–18). Now this is another meeting, between life and death, between losing and finding, between giving and receiving oneself (laying down one's life and taking it up again), between sorrow and joy. Mary, after the uncontainable sorrow of losing, is now completely filled with the joy of finding what she sought.

But, "Jesus said to her, 'Do not hold on to me, because I have not yet ascended to the Father. But go to my brothers and say to them: I am ascending to my Father and your Father, to my God and your

God'" (John 20:17). Mary must grow and pass from the known dimension of her relation to Jesus to a new one; she has to die to the first in order to be born to the second; the Lord has reserved a task for her: to take to the brethren the news of this extraordinary new event and to live this new dimension of distance and closeness together.[37]

Her function within the group. The fact that Mary Magdalene is constantly placed first in the list of those who make up the group shows that she is a reference point, a guide perhaps, for the others. Furthermore, her particularly intense dialogue with Jesus and the personality she probably had could well have given her some authority over the other women, even though this should not be seen as confining her position to one within the group of women alone.

Her presence and witness. Mary Magdalene, together with the other women who followed Jesus, was a witness to the Master's life and preaching from the time in Galilee down to the dramatic events of his crucifixion and death; this should be seen in the Hebrew context in which, from the juridical point of view, a woman's witness had no value.

Jesus in effect challenged this mentality, first by gathering the women around him, thereby giving a value to their presence and making them effective witnesses to his life and message. Then, having brought them into the closest and most privileged circle of those gathered around him, he made them recipients, with the other disciples, of his special proclamation. Finally, it was just the women who, drawing close to the dramatic events of his crucifixion and death, when "all the disciples deserted him and fled" (Matt. 26:56) and when Peter denied him, followed him and were present at his crucifixion, death and burial.

Chosen as first witness to the resurrection.[38] In the resurrection stories the concept of witness reappears, but this time shown in a context of non-acceptance: Mary Magdalene is not believed, and Paul in the list of appearances he gives in his first letter to the Corinthians does not mention her, nor the other women: ". . . he

---

[37] Cf. E. Moltmann-Wendel, *Le donne che Gesù incontrò*, pp. 79–81.
[38] Cf. F. Bovon, "Le privilège pascal de Marie-Madéleine," *New Test. Stud.* 30 (1984), pp. 50–62.

appeared to Cephas, then to the twelve. Then he appeared to more than five hundred brothers at one time, most of whom are still alive, though some have died. Then he appeared to James, then to all the apostles. Last of all . . . he appeared to me" (1 Cor. 15:5–8). One can ask whether Paul included women among the five hundred, those who followed Jesus in particular, but it is perhaps more realistic to assume that he does not mention them because he realizes that their witness would not be given any credit whatever. While this may just be an indication of Paul's attitude, this does not lessen the seriousness of their omission. It is a bitter confirmation, but a confirmation nonetheless, of my hypothesis of an *exegesis of the silence*. Paul's silence on the presence of women is absolute, complete, whereas this presence is incontrovertibly registered, and even stressed in various ways, in the accounts by Mark, Matthew and John, and, though to a lesser degree, in Luke's Gospel. Paul is perhaps just setting down what might have ben expected of Jesus according to the cultural and androcentric logic of the time: that he would have appeared first to Peter (though he in fact leaves the chronological primacy vague, as he does not say "first").

In John, by contrast, Mary Magdalene is invited by the Risen Christ: "Go to my brothers and say to them . . ." (20:17). She has to carry the news to the others, who are lamenting Jesus' death, as mediatrix of the proclamation that life prevails over death, light over darkness.

The major part she plays in the first community. In the Acts of the Apostles, which set out to provide a picture of the birth and life of the first Christian community, the presence of women is attested: "All these were constantly devoting themselves to prayer, together with certain women, including Mary the mother of Jesus, and his brothers" (1:14), even though no more is said about who they were. But which women, other than those who had, with Mary Magdalene in the first place, gathered round Jesus in Galilee, remained faithful to him right up to the end of his life on earth and been chosen as witnesses to his resurrection, could have gone on working together with the apostles, as they had previously done when Jesus was with them? It was therefore these women who together with the apostles made up the central nucleus of the post-Easter community.

A *trace* of the significant presence of women in the first community surfaces in one text in Acts, the main purpose of which is to describe the persecution carried out by Saul (the future Paul) against this community: "But Saul was ravaging the church by entering house after house; dragging off both men and women, he committed them to prison" (8:3). This passage, placed straight after the description of the stoning of Stephen in Jerusalem, tells us indirectly that the witness and presence of women in the post-Easter community was such that it was noted from outside the community and considered dangerous. Confirmation of this persecution can be found in Acts 9:2 and 22:4–5.

In these women persecuted for their following of Christ and of whom the tradition handed down to us says nothing more, we can see the first *shadows* of a procession of women who witnessesd and confessed their belonging in faith with suffering and to the point of laying down their lives. The names of most of these have remained in silence.

In the Acts of the martyrs of the second century this reality emerges from silence; there we find consistent evidence of what the little *revealing fragment* of Acts 8:3 pointed to. By then, some of their names are given: Blandina, Biblis, Perpetua, Felicity, Agatha. . . .[39]

The part Mary Magdalene must have played in the first community is in some way confirmed by the significant place she occupies in apocryphal and Gnostic writings. These even give strong indications of a sort of rivalry between her and Peter, and it is worth quoting one or two passages to see if they provide any evidence of what was perhaps a real problem. These texts, which need to be considered within the specific philosophical and cultural context that produced them, give expression to debates that were lively ones at the time. The whole question is extremely complex and can only be hinted at here, however interesting it would be to pursue it further.[40]

---

[39] Cf. A. Valerio, "Libertà e radicalismo nelle martiri del II secolo," *Cristianesimo al femminile. Donne protagoniste nella storia delle Chiese*, pp. 33–56.

[40] [For an account of the documents discussed here, see J. Doresse, *The Secret Books of the Egyptian Gnostics* (London, 1960, reprinted Rochester, Vermont, 1986), pp. 64–94. -Trans.]

In the second-century *Gospel of Mary* (Magdalene), we find Mary Magdalene consoling the disciples after Jesus' ascension:

They grieved greatly and said, "How shall we go to the pagans to preach the gospel of the reign of the Son of Man? If he has not been spared, how shall we be spared?" Then Mary . . . said to his brethren: "Do not weep and do not sorrow and above all do not be indecisive. His grace will be with you and will protect you. . . ."[41] Peter turns to her and says: "Sister, we know that the Saviour loved you more than other women. Tell us those words of his, which you remember and know, not us. . . ." But when she finishes speaking Andrew says he does not believe her and Peter asks himself, "Did he then talk to a woman unbeknown to us, not openly? Must we then turn round and listen to all women, as much preferred to all of us?" Mary rose to her feet and so turned to Peter: "My brother Peter, what are you thinking? Do you perhaps think that I myself have dreamt up all these things in my heart or that I would lie concerning the Saviour?" Levi, taking the word, replied to Peter: "Peter, you are always angry. Now look, you are treating this woman as you would an enemy. If the Lord has made her worthy, who are you to reject her? Certainly the Lord knows her very well. Because he loved her more than us. . . ."

Another text, the third-century *Pistis-Sophia*, provides confirmation from the mouth of Mary Magdalene of this conception of Peter's temperament and attitude. Turning to Jesus, Mary Magdalene says: "Yet I fear Peter; he often threatens me and he hates our sex."[42] And, to stress Jesus' predilection for Mary Magdalene, the second-century *Gospel of Philip* states: "There were three who walked always with the Lord: his mother Mary, her sister, and the

---

[41] M. Erbetta, *Gli apocrifi del Nuovo Testamento. Vangeli giudeo-cristiani e gnostici* (Casale Monferrato, 1975), p. 294.

[42] *Ibid.*, pp. 295, 296, 447.

Magdalene. . . ."[43] "The other disciples then said to him: 'Why do you love her more than all of us?' The saviour replied and said to them: 'Why do I not love all of you as her?'"[44]

How should one interpret this? Perhaps it can be seen as a confirmation of the difficulty that the prevailing mentality of the age in general, and the Jewish mentality in particular, found in accepting the space Jesus gave women during his lifetime, and even more in seeing them as first and privileged witnesses to the message of the Risen Christ: chosen by Jesus as the means of taking to the disciples, after the sorrow and darkness of the passion, the proclamation of the overcoming of death and the victory of life, of joy, of light; chosen as "messengers of glad tidings" who proclaim, after the prevalence of fear and weakness (the disciples had fled), courage and tranquility; after defeat and suffering, victory and exultation; after betrayal and injustice (Judas and the execution of the "Just One"), solidarity and justice; after lying and torment (Peter's denial and remorse), truth and peace; after the sorrow and dark silence of death, joy, light, the Word, life; after the wound of separation, the happiness of a new reality of union; after living through the suffering of "loss," the joy of "finding"; after hatred, love.

Who she was

The rivalry that emerges from the passages just examined, besides providing an indirect confirmation of the important part played by women in Jesus' lifetime and in the post-Easter community, also provides a clue for investigating the more buried motives that, together with the others, have fostered the phenomenon of exegetical distortion in relation to the identity of Mary Magdalene and to her connotation as a prostitute. There is perhaps a trace of this rivalry between a man and a woman, Peter and Mary

---

[43] M. Craveri, *I vangeli apocrifi* (Turin, 1969), p. 517. Cf M. Erbetta, *Gli apocrifi del N.T.*, p. 225, who translates: "Three women walked always with the Lord: Mary his mother, her sister and the Magdalene, who was said to be his companion. . . . Mary in reality, is sister, mother and wife to him."

[44] Craveri, p. 521. Cf. Erbetta, p. 229: "The other women, seeing his love for Mary, said to him: 'Why do you love her more than all of us?' The Saviour replied to them: 'How on earth do I not love you as her?'" [Cf. Doresse, pp. 222ff.]

Magdalene, already in the New Testament writings. The Gospels of John and Matthew and the "longer ending" of Mark relate the appearance of Jesus risen to Mary Magdalene as the first (to her alone or with others); Luke, who mentions the women only at the tomb, explicitly recounts only the appearance to Peter: ". . . they found the eleven and their companions gathered together. They were saying, 'The Lord has risen indeed, and he has appeared to Simon!'" (that is, Peter: 24:33–4). Then, in the list given by Paul, Cephas is named first and there is no mention of the women (1 Cor. 15:5–8). So we have two different typologies of texts: on the one hand those that mention Mary Magdalene, signalling her out as the first to whom the Risen Christ appeared; on the other, those that make a reference to Peter, even if they do not specifically say that he was the first to whom Christ appeared – thereby perhaps indirectly confirming the existence of the tradition on Mary Magdalene.

I have already referred to the interpretative dynamic that has led to the identification of Mary Magdalene with the penitent sinner of Luke 7:36–50, and with Mary of Bethany, the sister of Martha and Lazarus. What I want to concentrate on here is the occasion for asking ourselves about the exegetical motivations and procedures, even unconscious ones, that led to the building up of the prostitute Magdalene, that resulted in the woman who had a special relationship with Jesus becoming an "Eve" covered in sin, and sin of a sexual nature. Over the centuries Mary Magdalene has been the object of deep projections by generations of men, not only – generally celibate – exegetes, but writers, poets and painters; these projections furnish a really extraordinary field of research. With the use of the tools of psychoanalytic investigation, particularly the phenomena of projection on to the being of another of what really belongs to one's own personal unconscious baggage, we find at our disposal an enormous quantity of exegetical, literary, homiletic, poetic, pictorial and other artistic material describing, not the reality of Mary Magdalene, but the most hidden pyschological traits of men who have represented her in all sorts of ways.[45] One finds that in effect what has been written and portrayed of Mary Magdalene is

---

[45] Cf. V. Saxer, *Maria Maddalena, Biblioteca Sanctorum* 8 (1966), 1091–2; *idem*, "Santa Maria Maddalena dalla storia evangelica alla leggenda e all'arte," M. Mosco, (ed.), *La Maddalena tra Sacro e Profano* (Milan-Florence, 1986), p. 25.

nothing other than a kind of photographic negative, from which the real image of the author can be developed.

This phenomenon, which has largely escaped from the confines of exegetic disquisitions, cannot be fully unfurled without comparing it to a more general question concerning the conception of woman and, first, that of sexuality: two streams of thought that flow together in the all-embracing and misleading identification of women with sexuality.

Mary Magdalene has become the most commonly used exemplar in referring to sin, repentance, redemption. One might say that so great is the extent and power of this phenomenon that Mary Magdalene herself has become the personification of sinfulness. Within this dynamic, another can be seen at work: sin and evil are closely connected to sexuality, corporeality, and more specifically to that of women. One example will suffice to show that the predominant message that has come down to our time and been attached to women, after centuries of elaborations on Mary Magdalene, is that of the projection of sexual guilt on to this woman: this is so prevalent in reference to Mary Magdalene that her very name, "magdalene" with a small "m," has come to mean reformed prostitute, as current dictionaries in many languages still testify, as do "Magdalene houses" as refuges for "fallen women" in many countries.[46]

I leave this line of reflection here, in the hope that it will be taken further by someone with the necessary psychological formation.

As time moved on from Jesus' lifetime there came a change of attitude to women and a return to androcentric structures that tended to relegate them to their traditional roles, thereby fostering identification of woman solely with sexuality, understood in the most negative sense. This culture perhaps shows the first traces of those elements that produced the exegetical distortion. Another sign of it can be seen from the cultural climate in which Jesus gave space to women in general and to Mary Magdalene in particular. The bewilderment this aroused among the disciples themselves has left traces in the Gospels: we have seen this in regard to their amazement at his talking to the Samaritan woman (John 4:27).[47]

---

[46] Cf. S. Cohen, "Convertite e Malmaritate," *Memoria* 5 (1982), pp. 46–63.

[47] The more specifically exegetical aspect of the distortion has been examined in chapter 2.

Her Cult

Of all the cults that grew up around the figure of Mary Magdalene, the one that developed in southern France, mainly in the eleventh and twelve centuries, was certainly the most extensive.[48] This tradition, for which no sure historical basis has been found, has it that Mary Magdalene, with Lazarus, Mary of Bethany, Maximian and others, following a persecution in Palestine, had been turned loose in a boat without sails or oars and had eventually drifted on to the shore of Provence, to become its first evangelizers:

> The Provençal tradition tells us that the persecutors acceded to the wishes of the holy people of Bethany by putting them to sea in a boat without sails or oars; and from the shores of Palestine, thanks to the hand of their divine Friend, they were transported to the shores of Provence. Together with Lazarus, Martha and Mary were Salome and Mary the mother of James, their servant Sarah ... and St Maximian, one of the seventy-two disciples, who became the first bishop of Aix. As good missionaries of the gospel, the friends spread out: Lazarus residing in Marseilles, of which he became the first bishop, Martha going up the Rhône, Maximian staying in Aix. Mary Magdalene, responding to a solitary vocation at the feet of the Master, went to carry the light of the gospel to the heights of Sainte-Baume. . . ."[49]

Hagiography tells of Mary Magdalene preaching to the inhabitants of Marseilles from the sacred precinct of the temple of Diana, and, influenced by the Latin legend of Mary of Egypt, also has her

---

[48] Cf. the works by V. Saxer cited in ch. 2, n. 27; also E. Moltmann-Wendel, *The Women around Jesus* (New York, 1982); Ph.-I. Vincent, *Marie Madeleine et la Sainte-Baume*; P.-M. Guillaume, "Marie Madeleine," DSp 10 (1979), pp. 559–75; E. Mâle, *Les Saints compagnons du Christ* (Paris, 1958, reprinted 1968), pp. 63–86.

In this short examination of these traditions I am omitting all reference to the so-called Vézelay and Burgundian cycles. On these see the works cited above, particularly Saxer, "Santa Maria Maddalena dalla storia evangelica alla legenda e all'arte," (n. 43 above).

[49] André-Vincent, *Marie Madeleine et la Sainte-Baume*, p. 12. He continues: "Historical knowledge today accords with the legend in placing the evangelization of this part in the first century. But there are no documents from which to draw more precise conclusions."

leading a hermit's life for thirty years, clothed only in her long hair.[50] It was only in the twelfth century that Mary Magdalene's hermitage came to be identified with the grotto of Sainte-Baume in the neighbourhood of Marseilles.

In the Vieille Major cathedral of Marseilles one can find a sort of synthesis of the elements of the Provençal tradition. In the fifteenth century, on the orders of King René, the last count of Provence before this region once more became part of the kingdom of France in 1481, a chapel was built to house the relics of St Lazarus, recognized by tradition as the first bishop of Marseilles. On the altar made to contain them, three figures appear: Lazarus in the centre and on either side of him, Martha (with beneath her the legend that she freed the inhabitants of Tarascon) and Mary Magdalene with a jar of ointment. At the base of the altar, seven panels in bas relief depict scenes from the Gospels and moments from the legend: the first three are inspired by the raising of Lazarus and the anointing at Bethany; the other four show the arrival in the boat, Mary Magdalene preaching to the inhabitants of Marseilles (see p. 18), the consecration of Lazarus as bishop and his martyrdom. The work has been attributed to two Italian craftsmen, Francesco Laurana and Tommaso di Como.[51] Laurana appears to

---

[50] Cf. B. Laluque, "Quand Marseille fut évangélisé par une femme," *Marseille* 148 (1967), 50–57; *idem.*, "Marie de Nazareth et Marie de Magdala figures de l'Eglise, *Revue Carmel* 35 (1984), 228–38. The evangelization by Mary Magdalene is depicted in an anonymous painting dating from 1490, oil on canvas (Musée du Vieux Marseille coll.). This picture, which also provides the earliest representation of the port of Marseilles, has a sketch of the boat, without sails or oars, in which Mary Magdalene and her companions are supposed to have reached Provence, in the foreground. The composition is dominated by the figure of Mary Magdalene preaching from the sacred precinct of the temple of Diana. At her feet the princes of Marseilles listen, with others. On the conversion of the princes of Marseilles, see Saxer, "Santa Maria Maddalena," p. 25. On Mary of Egypt, see M. Mosco, "La Maddalena tra Sacro e Profano," *ibid.*, p. 18; Saxer, p. 24. The long hair is a constant feature of pictorial representation of Mary Magdalene.

[51] The authorship of this work was unknown till 1884, when the *Bulletin Archéologique* of the Comité de Travaux Historiques et Scientifiques published an account of its session of 16 April, at which Dr Barthélemy delivered the results of his research (p. 184). See also F. Benoît, *L'abbaye de Saint-Victor et l'Eglise de la Major à Marseille* (Paris, 1936), which contains an ample bibliography.

have lived in Marseilles from 1477 to 1483 and to have married a painter's daughter there. 1481, the date carved in the Carrara marble in which the work is executed, can be taken as the year when the altarpiece was finished.

In the last century, E. M. Faillon published a description of the seven panels, presenting them as the story of St Lazarus and, following the legend, describing each scene from the point of view of Lazarus, mentioning Mary Magdalene only once, and then in second rank: "Jesus Christ is at table with Lazarus: saint Mary Magdalene is wiping the feet of the Saviour with her hair, having anointed them with a perfume."[52] But what is worse is that, after describing the arrival in Provence as: "St Lazarus, in a boat, arrives in Provence" (there is absolutely no doubt that the bas relief shows many people in the boat, including women), he states that it is Lazarus preaching, not Mary: "He is preaching (il prêche) the Gospel before the governors of the country." So it is not Mary Magdalene preaching, but Lazarus.[53] Lack of care, an involuntary error? The bas relief is quite clear and obviously shows a woman preaching, not a man.

Jesus' prophetic saying: "I tell you, if these [disciples] were silent, the stones would shout out" (Luke 19:40),[54] is more true than ever today, in the sense that where the disciples, the compilers of the Gospels, the men who have over the generations handed on their message and the events that concerned them, have silenced or covered over in silence, it is "the stones" (literally, in this case) or the texts themselves, that sometimes succeed in shouting out, in the sense that they allow us to see beyond the limitations or even errors of those who have done the handing on and interpreting. Once again, we are faced with the *silence* of texts dealing with women, a silence from which we can sometimes escape thanks to forms provided by the texts themselves.

---

[52] E. M. Faillon, *Monuments inédits sur l'apostolat de sainte Marie-Madeleine en Provence* (Paris, 1848), c. 1170.

[53] Faillon's error in stating that it is Lazarus preaching on the bas relief and not Mary Magdalene is repeated by Benoît, *L'abbaye de Saint-Victor*, p. 96: "Lazarus preaching to the governor and people of Marseilles."

[54] E. J. Morris uses this phrase as an epigraph to ch. 2 of her book, *The Lady Was a Bishop* (see n. 1 to ch. 1 above.)

Finally, it needs to be emphasized that, leaving aside the questions raised about the historicity of the Provençal tradition, the representation of Mary Magdalene preaching has its Gospel basis in Jesus' words: "Go to my brothers and say to them . . ." (John 20:17) and the statement that Mary Magdalene "went and announced . . ." (20:18).

Joanna

Joanna, the wife of Herod's steward Chuza (Luke 8:3)

This woman is a figure who belongs to Luke alone. There is no mention of her in the other Synoptics or in John.

There is evidence of the presence of "the wife of the king's procurator" among the women who followed Jesus in a passage from the Gospel of Marcion, which has come down to us through Tertullian: "*Quod divites Christo mulieres adhaerebat, quae et de facultatibus suis ministrabant ei, inter quas et uxor regis procuratoris. . . .*"[55]

In Luke she is mentioned twice, both times placed after Mary Magdalene, in 8:3 and 24:10 (the visit to the tomb by the women who had followed the events of the passion). Who could she have been? She is the only one in the group in 8:1–3 of whom two qualities are specified: she was married and she belonged to a relatively high social class, the members of Herod's court. Knowing that Joanna was Chuza's wife clarifies her status and at the same time raises questions. In order to follow Jesus as he travelled about, would she have had to leave her husband and remove herself from his tutelage, or was she perhaps a widow? Even supposing that the regime in Herod's court was not particularly strict in observing the laws of tutelage, it is still hard to imagine that this woman, whether wife or widow, was able calmly to leave the protected and privileged state in which she lived to follow Jesus in a situation of uncertainty and precariousness.[56] We therefore have to suppose that it must

---

[55] "The fact that there were rich women attached to Christ, who also provided for him out of their goods, among whom was the wife of the king's procurator. . . ," Tertullian, *Adv. Marc.* 19, 1.

[56] Cf. S. B. Pomeroy, *Goddesses, Whores, Wives and Slaves* (New York, 1975); J. Jeremias, *Jerusalem in the Time of Jesus* (London & New York, 1973); L. Peppe, *Posizione giuridica e ruolo sociale della donna romana in età repubblicana* (Milan, 1984).

have been a traumatic decision for her to make in her situation, one requiring a most powerful stimulus. What can have been the reason that drove her to it? From Luke, we gather that she had met Jesus and been healed.[57]

If Chuza was still alive and occupied an important post at Herod's court, the situation is even more complicated. Would he have agreed with his wife making a decision that would put his career in jeopardy? Or would Joanna, besides abandoning her position, have had to bear her husband's hostility and loss of affection? There is no mention of possible children of the marriage, so there is no point in further speculation on this point, on which there is no evidence.

The information that Joanna came from Herod's entourage is important. On one hand it accords with Luke's tendency to mention people of high social standing; on the other, it is another addition to the considerable amount of information about Herod that Luke provides in his writings.[58]

As evidence of the importance Luke attaches to Joanna, he mentions her the same number of times, twice, as he does Mary Magdalene, and in the same situations. She is therefore an important figure in indicating a line of research into Luke's sources: one of the traditions Luke made use of may stem from her. This woman is recorded by him alone and could then be the origin of his special

---

[57] Moltmann-Wendel suggests that Joanna may have been at the feast at Herod's court when Herodias' daughter, spurred on by her, obtained the head of John the Baptist as a reward for her dance: *Le donne che Gesù incontrò*, p. 149.

[58] The first mention, in Luke 1:5: "In the days of King Herod of Judea . . .," refers to Herod the Great (37–4 BCE). In 3:1 Luke gives a historical synthesis: "In the fifteenth year of the reign of Emperor Tiberius, when Pontius Pilate was governor of Judea, and Herod was ruler of Galilee, and his brother Philip ruler of the region of Ituraea and Trachonitis, and Lysanias ruler of Abilene. . . ." The Emperor Tiberius had succeeded Augustus in 14 CE, Pontius Pilate governed Judea from 26 to 36 CE. The Herod tetrarch of Galilee of whom Luke is speaking was Herod Antipas who came to power in 4 CE and held it till 39 CE, when he was exiled to Gaul. He is named twenty-seven times in all in the Gospels and Acts: twice in Matthew, twelve times in Mark, thirteen in Luke (3:1, 19; 8:3; 9:7, 9; 13:31; 23:7, 8, 11, 12, 15) and Acts (4:27; 13:1). The name Herod appears another six times in Acts, but the person referred to is Herod Agrippa I, tetrarch from 38 CE and king in 40–41 (Acts 12:1, 6, 11, 19, 20, 21). Another Herod, Agrippa II, is also mentioned in Acts (25:13, 22, 23, 24, 26; 26:1, 2, 19, 27, 28, 32).

source; furthermore she came from Herod's entourage and this would explain the amount of information Luke provides about his court. This would also fit in with the characteristic of historical reconstruction that Luke seeks to give his work.

Susanna

Susanna is the third woman named in Luke 8:1–3. She belongs to the group of "women who had been cured of evil spirits and infirmities," though her trouble is not specified. Other than her name, in fact, nothing is said about her, unlike Mary Magdalene and Joanna who come before her. Luke perhaps has no other information about her, or, more likely, considers her known in the circles to which his account is addressed, to an extent that made further details unnecessary. As there is no other mention of her in the New Testament, nothing more is known of her.

The Group of "Many Other" Women

and many others, who provided for him out of their resources (Luke 8:3)

This phrase closes the passage 8:1–3. The expression "and many others," while not numerically precise, tells us that the women who had made the decision to follow Jesus were not a small group, limited and therefore easily identifiable, but a considerable number.

Is it possible to draw conclusions about the identity of any of these women whom Luke records here as an overall group? There is only one other woman, Mary the mother of James, who is named, along with Mary Magdalene and Joanna, in the passion narrative (24:10). But if we want to enquire further into the nature of the group, we need to use Matthew, Mark and John's narratives as well; this will be seen more clearly shortly.

The text "who provided for him out of their resources" has a variant reading which it is important to mention: they provided for αὐτῷ, "him," or αὐτοῖς, "them."[59] Within 8:1–3, αὐτῷ stresses

---

[59] These sources give the reading αὐτῷ: אALΨf¹ 33, 565, 1241 pm it vgᵉˡ syʰ co; Marcion. The following, however, have αὐτοῖς: BDKWΘf¹³ 28, 700, 892, (1010), 1424 pm latˢ·ᶜ·ᵖ·ʰᵐᵍ sy. See E. Nestlé-Aland, *Novum Testamentum Graece et Latine* (Stuttgart, ed. XXVI: Deutsche Bibelgesellschaft, 1984), p. 180.

attention paid to Jesus. Is this in accordance with the overall dynamic of the text? From the point of view of its contents, the whole passage gives information about Jesus and the women. The twelve are mentioned as being with Jesus, but there is no qualification of them other than the words σὺν αὐτῷ, "with him." Syntactically too, the word δώδεκα, "twelve," has a lower function in the structure of the sentence, which has Jesus as its first and main subject and the women as its second. The former is referred to by the verbs διώδευεν, "went on," κηρύσσων, "proclaiming," and εὐαγγελιζόμενος, "bringing the good news." The latter are referred to by ἦσαν τεθεραπευμέναι, "had been cured," and, in the case of one of them, Mary Magdalen, δαιμόνια ἑπτὰ ἐξεληλύθει, "seven demons had gone out." Both these last two phrases also refer back to Jesus. Within this dynamic, the verb διηκόνουν, "provided," the subject of which is the women, seems to be more in harmony with what precedes it if it has αὐτῷ, "for him," as its object, referring back to the first subject, Jesus.

In his *A Textual Commentary on the Greek New Testament*, B. M. Metzger, preferring the reading αὐτοῖς, observes that "the singular seems to be a christocentric correction, stemming perhaps from Marcion."[60] This would amount to maintaining that all the texts with the singular reading are due to Marcion; the christocentric concentration here, however, is something internal to this passage. The christological question is explicitly posed in the penultimate verse of the pericope on the woman forgiven (7:36–50): "Who is this who even forgives sins?" And christological concern has already emerged in the affirmation (7:16) or doubt (7:49) that Jesus was a prophet.

So how to explain the existence of texts with the variant αὐτοῖς?

In the community context in which the tradition behind this passage took shape, Jesus was no longer present: this fact effectively changed the situation of the women who had followed him and provided for him during his public activity. With the loss of this central reference point, the community comes to the fore and the

---

[60] B. M. Metzger, *A Textual Commentary on the Greek New Testament* (Stuttgart, 3rd ed. 1971), p. 144. Marcion is one of two ancient textual sources that give the singular reading.

women have to re-arrange their own position within this new situation. It is then from the group perspective, in the understanding of the compiler, who experienced its needs, that the choice to make the women provide for the community, not just for Jesus, emerges. This could perhaps explain the replacement of the singular αὐτῷ with the plural αὐτοῖς.

The other passages in Mark and Matthew telling of the presence of women, all inserted into the context of the passion, have αὐτῷ uniformly. But of course in these only Jesus is mentioned (the twelve having fled) and the verb διακονέω, "to provide for," could not have other than a singular object. But if the tradition that the compiler had before him had referred specifically to the women providing not just for Jesus but for the twelve, the author of the text could well have mentioned this equally in the context of the passion, even though the apostles were not present.

In the composition of this final clause, the verb διακονέω is of particular importance in qualifying the presence of the women. The information about them previously provided tells us that they travelled with Jesus like the twelve and that some of them had been cured; διακονέω is the verb in the pericope that has the women fully and independently as its active subjects. The verb διηκόνουν is followed by the phrase "out of their resources" (ὑπάρχοντα).[61] The subject of worldly goods is one to which Luke gives particular attention, placing it in strict relation to the following of Jesus: "they left everything and followed him" (5:11); "And he got up, left everything, and followed him" (5:28). This is in accordance with the Lord's teaching: "none of you can become my disciple if you do not give up all your possessions" (14:33); "Sell all that you own and distribute the money to the poor, and you will have treasure in heaven; then come, follow me" (18:22). the disciples understand this requirement for following him; Peter says: "Look, we have left everything we had and followed you" (18:28).[62]

---

[61] This term appears fourteen times in the New Testament, mostly in Luke (eight times). Cf. Fr. Selter, χρῆμα, τα ὑπάρχοντα," DCBNT, 1341–3; "χρῆμα," TDNT IX (1974), 480–2; Jeanne D'Arc OP, Le concordanze del N.T., p. 69.

[62] On the subject of possessions in Luke, see R. Fabris, Il vangelo di Luca, pp. 1075–87.

In Luke 8:1–3 the women have evidently not only left behind their homes and other goods as required in order to follow Jesus, but have placed their patrimony at the disposal of the group. Luke here informs us about one of the ways in which Jesus subsisted, perhaps the only place in the New Testament where we hear about this, while the other writings tell us only about disciples: see John 12:6 and 13:29, which mentions only the common purse, held by Judas.

Supposing that before setting out on his travels, Jesus had supported himself as a carpenter-joiner,[63] the news that the women then provided for him out of their resources is certainly significant and is confirmed in the passage from the Gospel of Marcion handed down by Tertullian, *"de facultatibus suis ministrabant ei."*[64]

There is still one problem: since the condition of women in Palestine was generally one of deprivation, including in the economic sphere, how can one explain the finances that some of the women who followed Jesus were able to provide? Jewish law forbade a daughter to inherit from her father, and a wife from her husband. Not even the dowry assigned when a daughter became engaged was hers: up to the time the marriage vow was made, her father managed it and reaped the profits. Only if her husband divorced her or died did the woman come to own these goods. That women generally were not allowed to and did not own goods is indirectly confirmed by the fact that even objects found by chance belonged to their husband or father, that is to the person to whom they themselves ultimately *belonged.* When situations arose in which daughters were in fact to inherit, such as there being no male heirs when their father or husband died, then in the first place they were bound to be married (seeing that it was not women who married, but who were married) to a man belonging to the paternal clan; failing this, their husband's brother had to marry them and the first male child would inherit.[65]

---

[63] Cf. H. Hobbs Herschell, *An Exposition of the Gospel of Luke* (Grand Rapids, 1966), p. 13.

[64] Tertullian,. *Adv. Marc.*, 19, 1.

[65] Cf. R. de Vaux, *Les Institutions de l'Ancien Testament* (Paris, 1958): here It. trans., p. 41; J. Pirenne, "Le statut de la femme dans la civilization hébraïque," *La femme* (Recueils de la Société Jean Bodin) XI (1959), pp. 107–26.

Despite these rules, which gave men control over the amount and management of patrimonies, it sometimes happened that a father or husband would assign goods or delegate some degree of their management to his daughter or wife. So in derogation of the law that said "a court cannot in the first instance appoint a woman as administrator" (*T. Terumoth* I, 11), men sometimes appointed their wives to positions with economic implications. So it is written: "If anyone puts his wife to sell (as a shopkeeper) or makes her administrator, he can require an oath from her whenever he wishes" (*Kethuboth* 9, 4). This is confirmed by: "If their father has put them (wives and slaves) in charge during his lifetime, they can be appointed administrators" (*T. Terumoth* I, 11).[66] Furthermore, Greek and Roman influence was spreading in the Palestine of the time, and in those cultures, particularly on the higher social levels, women were known to own goods. The fact that Joanna came from circles close to King Herod's court could be significant in this respect.[67]

To sum up, then, the group of women who gathered around Jesus, as depicted in Luke 8:1–3, forms an entity alongside the twelve with its own autonomous character. The text we have examined speaks in effect of only two groups who followed Jesus: the twelve and the women. The disciples are not mentioned. In this context, which is his view of those set around the Master as in concentric circles, Luke places the women in the first rank alongside the twelve with particular reference to their travelling with and closeness to Jesus.

The women are witnesses to his life and preaching and, in particular, to that special teaching reserved to the inner group of his followers.

A confirmation of the significant part played by the group of women round Jesus is provided by the news of their presence in the first community (Acts 1:14).

---

[66] Cf. W. Falk Ze'ev, "Women," *Introduction to Jewish Institutions of the Second Commonwealth*, part II, 2 (Leiden, 1978), pp. 261–3.

[67] Cf. E. Cantarella, *L'ambiguo malanno. Condizione e immagine della donna nell'antichità* (Rome, 1981), p. 112; C. Préaux, "Le statut de la femme à l'époque hellénistique, principalement en Egypte," *La femme*, p. 143; Peppe, *Posizione giuridica e ruolo sociale della donna*, p. 26; S. B. Pomeroy, *Goddesses, Whores* (It. trans., pp. 171–2).

Jesus' attitude in his dealings with women and the way he takes their nature into account have their counterpart in the final phase of his life: at the moment of his death and still more so at the resurrection.

The women (or just Mary Magdalene, or perhaps more probably her predominantly among them) are interposed between Jesus and the apostles just at this crucial and culminating moment of the Christ event, when, that is, he replaces the rigid and unfathomable silence of death that *closes* with the dense, relational and unspeakable word of the resurrection, the mystery of life that *opens*.

Chapter 6

WOMEN IN THE TIME OF MEMORY

Having examined Luke 8:1–3 as a special "footprint" of the memory relating to women following Jesus on his travels, let us now turn to the other biblical passages that mention them. The texts are these:

1. Mark 15:40–41: "There were also women looking on from a distance; among them were Mary Magdalene, and Mary the mother of James the younger and Joses, and Salome. These used to follow him and provided for him when he was in Galilee; and there were many other women who had come up with him to Jerusalem."

2. Matthew 27:55–6: "Many women were also there, looking on from a distance; they had followed Jesus from Galilee and had provided for him. Among them were Mary Magdalene, and Mary the mother of James and Joseph, and the mother of the sons of Zebedee."

3. Luke 23:49; 23:55; 24:10: "But all his acquaintances, including the women who had followed him from Galilee, stood at a distance, watching these things"; "The women who had come with him from Galilee followed [Joseph of Arimathea], and they saw the tomb and how his body was laid"; "Now it was Mary Magdalene, Joanna, Mary the mother of James, and the other women with them who told this to the apostles."

The context in which the women disciples are mentioned by all three Synoptics is that of the passion-death-burial of Jesus. These passages concentrate on the fact that the women had followed him from Galilee and not on the dramatic manner in which Jesus' earthly life came to an end. I shall therefore limit my considerations to this aspect.

We have already seen that news about the women is given only very late in Mark and Matthew, practically at the close of their narratives. This, compared to the different way Luke plans his,

ELEMENTS	Mark 15:40–41	Matt. 27:55–6	Luke 8:2–3	Luke 23:49	Luke 23:55–6	Luke 24:10
1. Terms relating to women	Ἦσαν δὲ καὶ γυναῖκες *There were also women*	Ἦσαν δὲ ἐκεῖ γυναῖκες πολλαί *Many women were also there*	καὶ γυναῖκές τινες *as well as some women*	αἱ γυναῖκες *including the women*	αἱ γυναῖκες, αἵτινες *the women who*	
2. Proper names	ἐν αἷς καὶ *among them were* three proper names	ἐν αἷς ἦν *among them were* three proper names	three proper names			three proper names
3. Words used to describe the women	ἠκολούθουν αὐτῷ καὶ διηκόνουν αὐτῷ *they used to follow him and provided for him*	αἵτινες ἠκολούθησαν τῷ Ἰησοῦ διακονοῦσαι αὐτῷ *They had followed Jesus and had provided for him*	αἵτινες διηκόνουν αὐτῷ *who provided for him*	αἱ συνακολουθοῦσαι αὐτῷ *who had followed him*	ἦσαν συνεληλυθυῖαι αὐτῷ *had come with him*	
4. Reference to place	ὅτε ἦν ἐν τῇ Γαλιλαίᾳ *when he was in Galilee*	ἀπὸ τῆς Γαλιλαίας *from Galilee*		ἀπὸ τῆς Γαλιλαίας *from Galilee*	ἐκ τῆς Γαλιλαίας *from Galilee*	
5. Other terms referring to the women present	καὶ ἄλλαι πολλαὶ *and ... many other women*		καὶ ἕτεραι πολλαὶ *and many others*			καὶ αἱ λοιπαὶ σὺν αὐταῖς *and the other women with them*
6. Word relating to point 5	αἱ συναναβᾶσαι αὐτῷ *who had come up with him*					
7. Reference to Jerusalem	εἰς Ἱεροσόλυμα *to Jerusalem*					

placing the information in the context of his description of the first phase of Jesus' public travelling/preaching, has opened the way to taking Luke 8:1–3 as a pericope of prime importance, as a *revealing trace* along the course we have set out to follow, still within the prevailing *silence* in which the reality of the women whom Jesus accepted into his inner circle lies hidden.

Comparison among the Synoptics offers us significant elements that can ultimately enrich the picture of the women who followed Jesus, as the table on the facing page shows.

The Present Time of the Passion and the Time of the Memory of Galilee

This synoptic table takes as its main element the phrases used in the different accounts to designate the women. We need to bear in mind that the passages examined are underlaid by two lines of time superimposed on one another: the unit of the present time, that of the passion, and, linked to this by the women, the unit of the time remembered, the past, the first phase of Jesus' preaching and travelling. The women are the only common subject of the present time and the time remembered.[1]

---

[1] Luke 23:49 has, together with the women, "πάντες οἱ γνωστοὶ αὐτῷ" (literally, "all those known to him"). Luke seem to be showing an apologetic concern for the apostles; he makes no reference to their abandoning Jesus, predicted by him in Mark 14:27, Matthew 26:31 and John 16:31–2, and told in Mark 14:50, Matthew 26:56. It is also significant that here, in 23:49, he does not use the term disciples, let alone apostles, but "γνωστοί," which has a general meaning and is not often used in the New Testament (fifteen times in all, of which twelve in Luke's writings – two in the Gospel and ten in Acts; two in John and one in Romans). See J. Ernst, *Das Evangelium nach Lukas* (Regensburg, 1977): here It. trans. p. 34. Though in a different context from that under review here, Ernst lists, among the principles that might have led Luke to modify the model of Mark, indulgence toward the disciples (Luke 8:24–5; 18:25ff; 22:31–4, 60). An indication of this can also be seen in 24:22–3 where a reference to the women is made by disciples. Earlier in his text there are references that diminish the role of women, at least in relation to that of the male disciples. The account of the visit to the empty tomb hardly shows them in a positive light: "While they were perplexed about this . . ." (24:4), "The women were terrified and bowed their faces to the ground . . ." (24:5). Luke is also the only evangelist who does speak directly of appearances of Jesus to the women. The disciples on the road to Emmaus act as a filter to the women's

The word all the texts use is γυναῖκες, "women"; this is then immediately qualified in Matthew by the specification πολλαί, "many," a term found also in Mark and in Luke 8, but used by him at the second mention (point 5 in the table).

Luke 8:2, on the other hand, has τινες, "some," who are then described by the phrase ἦσαν τεθεραπευμέναι ἀπὸ πνευμάτων πονηρῶν καὶ ἀσθενειῶν, "had been cured of evil spirits and infirmities," followed by the indication of three names. He develops a structure that considers the group and describes it on three levels. One is that of the women who belong to the present time of the passion (clearly excluding 8:2–3); the second level is that which picks out the group of women who had followed Jesus from Galilee, in which both present time and time remembered come together; the third singles out a group of three women individually named. In Matthew's account (27:55–6) and Luke's (23:49, 55 and 24:10) the group of women who have been disciples since Galilee and the group of those present on Calvary are the same. In effect, the least structured account is that of Matthew, who gives no other relevant indications; Luke, on the other hand, reaches his chapters 23 and 24 having already provided information about the women who followed Jesus and so regarding the situation as known. He goes no further into discussion of their number (speaking neither of "some" or "many"), but only hastens to mention the three names (24:10), in order to give value to their witness and speaks of λοιπαί, "other[s]" without specifying further.

The structure of Luke 8:2–3 and Mark 15:40–41, however, is much more careful. In the latter three different spatial-temporal units converge: the present scene on Calvary, the time remembered linked to Galilee, and another, more recent time when other women had come up to Jerusalem. The group that Mark's account has present at the passion is in effect made up of two sub-groups: one

___

story: "Moreover, some women of our group astounded us. They were at the tomb early this morning, and when they did not find his body there, they came back and told us that they had indeed seen a vision of angels who said that he was alive" (24:22). Furthermore, the disciples had not believed this story: "But these words seemed to them an idle tale, and they did not believe them" (24:11).

made up of the women who have followed Jesus from Galilee (which has its own sub-group in the three women named), the other of the "many other women" who had come up to Jerusalem. Mark therefore picks out and differentiates the presence of "many other women," those who had come up to Jerusalem (though without saying where they had come from, so not excluding the possibility that among them might have been some who had come from Galilee, besides those named). This last element is specific to Mark, though Luke tells that, while Jesus was being taken to the place where they crucified him, "A great number of the people followed him, and among them were women who were beating their breasts and wailing for him. But Jesus turned to them and said, 'Daughters of Jerusalem, do not weep for me, but weep for yourselves and for your children'" (23:27–8).

The structure of Luke 8:2–3 relates wholly to the group of disciples travelling through Galilee and is confined to this spatial-temporal unity. The group is here seen from closer to, defined more clearly and with with greater internal differentiation. It is shown to be made up of two sub-groups: one formed by the women who have been cured, of whom three are identified by name, and another by the "many others, who provided for him out of their resources" (as may have done any of those who had been cured: the text does not make this clear).

If we compare the structure of Luke 8:2–3 with that of Mark 15:40–41, we can see that the information given in each about the make-up of the group cannot be superimposed, because Luke adds on his own account a series of pieces of information not given in Mark. Luke is therefore not using Mark as a source here; nor do his final chapters take up the reference to the women who had come up to Jerusalem in the same way. Luke is therefore using a different source, and as his account does not accord with Matthew either, this source cannot be taken as Q.

Luke's account in 8:2–3 gives us the greatest amount of news of the group of women who followed Jesus and this confirms my initial claim that this pericope represents a *special trace*. Mark's text, nevertheless, gives a fuller overall view of the groups of women present at the passion and death of Jesus.

We can now sum up these two texts and the facts they adduce in relation to the objective of this study, which is to draw women out as far as possible from silence and effacement. The group of women present at Jesus' passion is made up of two sub-groups: the women whom Jesus had collected round him when he was in Galilee (some of whom had been healed, including Mary Magdalene, Joanna and Susanna; others whose names are provided by Mark: Mary the mother of James the younger and Joseph, Salome, plus the "many others who provided for him out of their resources") and the group of "many other women" who have gone up to Jerusalem with Jesus. These two different groups, gathered together at the present time of the passion, make reference to two unities of past time and place, the immediate past linked to Jerusalem and the more distant past remembered from Galilee.

The time of memory of Galilee also marks the greatest continuity: it traces an arc going back to the beginning of Jesus' preaching in Galilee and reaching forward to the present of Jesus' passion and death. Seen like this, the time remembered from Galilee becomes the time of continuity, the time that links the past to the present. This time of continuity belongs specifically to the women, and is so profoundly theirs, and recognized as theirs by Jesus, that it also receives from the Risen Christ the connotation of future time, in that he entrusts the proclamation of the resurrection to the women. This time of remaining faithful belongs so clearly to the women that it receives from Christ the full and ultimate connotation of continuity: projection into the eschatological future, beyond the limits of human time. The time of continuity thereby leaps over the barriers of time and takes on connotations beyond human finiteness, in the eternal infinite.

From this time of continuity, the apostles and the male disciples are excluded. Their following suffered the break of their abandonment at the time of Jesus' arrest and passion, harshly illustrated by Peter's denial (Mark 14:66–72; Matt. 26:69–75; Luke 22:54–62) and scarcely attenuated by the presence of "the disciple whom he loved" recorded in the Fourth Gospel (John 19:26). This interrupted, broken line is re-tied after the death of Jesus the man, in relation to the Risen Christ through the mediation of the women. The life of Jesus of Nazareth ends in tragedy, without the presence and witness of the male disciples (to say no more here of the pain and mystery of those who betrayed and denied him). Jesus was abandoned by them but the women who stood by him constitute both the witness to the events that took place, and the continuous thread by which relations with the apostles were re-established and restored.

Following

The verbs used to designate what the women do are respectively:

1. ἀκολουθέω (to follow) in Mark 15:41 and Matthew 27:55;
2. συν-ακολουθέω (to accompany) in Luke 23:49;
3. συν-έρκομαι (to come with) in Luke 23:55;
4. διακονέω (to serve, provide for) in Mark 15:41, Matthew 27:55 and Luke 8:3.

In Mark and Matthew both ἀκολουθέω and διακονέω are found in the same verse, while Luke uses διακονέω, (8:3)[2] συν-ακολουθέω (to accompany) (23:49) and συν-έρχομαι (to come with) (23:55) successively.

These last two verbs are assimilable to the concept indicated by ἀκολουθέω (to follow), which appears ninety-one times in the New Testament, but are used less frequently in it.[3]

"Following" is used in the New Testament in two main senses:

1. "Calling to the definitive discipleship is characteristic of Jesus on earth."[4] "And he said to him, 'Follow me.' And he got up, left everything, and followed him" (Luke 5:27–8).
2. In the strict sense of "going with." It is said of the crowd that followed Jesus. "In this case it is not a call ... though this is not excluded."[5]

The Old Testament and rabbinic literature present a certain ambiguity in regard to the concept of following and serving. Kittel, analyzing how the disciple Elisha followed his master Elijah, notes: "This 'following' does not indicate a form of service, as the succeeding expression 'and served him' clearly does: the disciple

---

[2] "Following" is implied in 8:1–3, since Jesus is spoken of as "going on" and the twelve and the women are said to be with him.

[3] συνακολουθέω appears only three times (Mark 5:37; 14:51; Luke 23:49), συνέρχομαι appears thirty-two times, but only ten of these in the sense of "to come with, to accompany" (besides Luke 23:55, in John 11:33 and the remainder in Acts).

[4] Ch. Blendiger, "ἀκολουθέω," *DCBNT*, p. 1718.

[5] Ibid.; on the two meanings see also G. Kittel, "ἀκολουθέω," *TWNT* 1 (1933), pp. 210–16.

accompanied the master as a true and proper servant."[6] We need to bear in mind, however, that if the reality of being a disciple involved serving, the opposite was not necessarily true: that a servant had to be a disciple. The connection between following and serving is found in John 12:26: "Whoever serves me must follow me, and where I am, there will my servant be."

It is stated of this group of women that they served him (διηκόνουν). Rengstorf puts it like this: "... the scene of Peter's mother-in-law, who after being cured set to and served Jesus (Matt. 8:15), as also the presence of women who, as the Gospel states, accompanied Jesus serving him and helping him with their goods (Luke 8:3; cf Matt. 27:55 par.), and then the busyness of Martha ... (Luke 10:40)" indicate "a service [that] is not limited to that of table, though this is particularly envisaged."[7]

In the definition and development of the meaning of the terms, Klaus Hess identifies: the meaning of serving at table, helping one person (he places Luke 8:3 here) and also rendering assistance in the community in the sense of preaching the gospel.[8] Beyer maintains that "the concept of serving is expressed in Greek through several verbs," and that "in διακονέω what is mainly stressed is the idea of service rendered out of love."[9] But if it is true that Jesus, as Beyer writes, "in service ... sees also the attitude that makes a person a disciple of his,"[10] it is nevertheless not clear how he can then conclude that "perhaps the link to service at table is still clearly recognizable, and this is what is meant ... in Luke 8:3."

Some gospel passages referring to service provide useful pointers. "'For I was hungry and you gave me no food, I was thirsty and you gave me nothing to drink, I was a stranger and you did not welcome me, naked and you did not give me clothing, sick and in prison and you did not visit me.' Then they also will answer, 'Lord, when was it that we saw you hungry or thirsty or a stranger or naked or sick or in prison, and did not take care of you?'" (Mat. 25:42-4). It is Jesus who is speaking and the term used at the end to sum up all the

---

[6] Kittel, *art. cit.*, p. 574.

[7] K. H. Rengstorf, "διδάσκω," *TWNT* 2 (1933), p. 157.

[8] K. Hess, "διακονέω," *DCBNT*, pp. 1734-9.

[9] H.W. Beyer, "διακονέω," *TWNT* 2 (1935), pp. 81-94.

[10] *Ibid.*

actions listed ("take care of") is διακονέω, to indicate "true belonging to the circle of Jesus' disciples."[11]

Overturning the concept of authority and greatness, Jesus automatically also revolutionizes the meaning of service:

> A dispute also arose among them as to which one of them was to be regarded as the greatest. But he said to them, "The kings of the Gentiles lord it over them; and those in authority over them are called benefactors. But not so with you; rather the greatest among you must become like the youngest, and the leader like one who serves. For who is greater, the one who is at the table or the one who serves? Is it not the one at the table? But I am among you as one who serves" (Luke 22:24–7).

And in John, as the moment of the passion approaches, we find these words: "Those who love their life lose it, and those who hate their life in this world will keep it for eternal life. Whoever serves me must follow me, and where I am, there will my servant be. Whoever serves me, the Father will honour" (John 12:25–6). Here the term "serve" "indicates ... the following ... proper to disciples."[12]

It is within this revolution of the concept of serving and in the context of the supreme dignity in which Jesus sets it (referring it to himself and his mission of salvation) that we must see the service he accepts from the group of women.

Restoring a Face and Identity to the "Many" Women who followed Jesus

The group of women travelling with Jesus is identified in several ways as far as the number of persons involved is concerned. Two aspects are common to the Synoptics: all report a list of three names, but at the same time speak of πολλαί, "many." I have already made some observations on the significance of the number three in the culture of the time; we now need to restore an identity and a face to the greatest possible number of women in the group, so as to draw them out from the anonymity to which they are consigned by the indefinite πολλαί, "many." While this term expresses the idea of a

---

[11] *Ibid.*
[12] Hess, "διακονέω," p. 1736.

significant number, it also undervalues them. The women formed a consistent part of Jesus' following, in numbers as well as other ways, and so constituted a clearly visible reality.[13]

Perhaps a trace that confirms the *visibility* and consistency of the female presence around Jesus is provided indirectly by a passage from the Gospel of Marcion, which states that Jesus was accused before Pilate of "seducing women and children."[14]

The table below enables us to restore a definite name to the greatest possible number of women.

Synoptics	Mark 15:40	Matt. 27:56	Luke 8:2	Luke 24:10	John 19:25
Mary Magdalene	1. Mary Magdalene	1. Mary Magdalene	1. Mary Magdalene	1. Mary Magdalene	1. Jesus' mother
Mary the mother of James and Joses	2. Mary the mother of James the younger and Joses	2. Mary the mother of James and Joseph			2. His mother's sister
Salome	3. Salome				3. Mary the wife of Clopas
Mother of the sons of Zebedee		3. Mother of the sons of Zebedee			4. Mary Magdalene
Joanna			2. Joanna	2. Joanna	
Susanna			3. Susanna		
				3. Mary the mother of James	

The first thing that stands out is that one name only is common to all the Synoptics and John: Mary Magdalene. Furthermore, in the Synoptics, her name always appears first on the list. These facts too underline the importance of Mary Magdalene as the figure set at the centre of the group of women, around which the others revolve.

---

[13] This idea of a "visible" reality is brought in here because it is also used in our day in reference to the quest to make women more visible in church and theology. Cf. *Concilium* 172 (1985), *Women – Invisible in Church and Theology*.

[14] A. von Harnack, *Marcion. Das Evangelium vom Fremden Gott* (Leipzig, 1924, reprinted 1960), p. 235 (= Epiph. *Pan.* 42, 11, 17 ref. 70: GCS 2, p. 152).

This is said not to give an impression of hierarchy and dependence: the encounters examined earlier between other women and Jesus demonstrate the deep sincerity of direct *rapport* and dialogue– exchange these women, personally, have with Jesus. Mark, after Mary Magdalene, puts:

1. Mary the mother of James the younger and Joses;
2. Salome.

Matthew names the following, besides Mary Magdalene:

1. Mary the mother of James and Joseph;
2. the mother of the sons of Zebedee.

Luke gives, after Mary Magdalene in the list in 8:2:

1. Joanna the wife of Chuza;
2. Susanna;

and in 24:10:

1. (again) Joanna;
2. Mary the mother of James.

John, who does not speak expressly of the women following, names those standing by the cross, besides Jesus' mother and Mary Magdalene:

1. Jesus' mother's sister;
2. Mary the wife of Clopas.

This comparison lends itself to the following considerations and possibilities:

1. Mary Magdalene is the only one on whose presence all four writers agree;
2. Luke's "Mary the mother of James" could be the same person as:

- the Mary mother of James the younger and Joses in Mark 15:40 (whom Mark himself in 15:47 then calls
- Mary the mother of Joses, and in 16:1
- Mary the mother of James),

or as

- Mary the mother of James and Joseph, in Matthew 27:56 (called, in Matthew 27:61 and 28:1, "the other Mary"). James and Joseph or Joses are "brothers" of the Lord according to Matthew 13:55 and Mark 6:3; James was probably the head of the first community in Jerusalem (Acts 12:17).[15]

---

[15] On the figure of James, see H. Conzelmann, *Geschichte des Urchristentums* (Göttingen, 1969): here It. trans. ch. 2, n. 6, pp. 223–5).

3. The "mother of the sons of Zebedee" in Matthew 27:56 can be identified precisely as the mother of the two apostles whose calling while they were with their father in a boat is recounted in Matthew 4:21 and Mark 1:19. And it is she who in Matthew 20:20–23 asks the Lord that her sons may be seated next to him in the Kingdom (in Mark's account the sons themselves make this request of Jesus: 10:35ff). Matthew does not mention her name here.

4. The "Salome" in Mark 15:40 and 16:1 might also be identified with the "mother of the sons of Zebedee, but such an identification is counter-indicated by the custom of identifying a woman by reference to her sons, or, in their absence, her husband.

5. The "Mary the wife of Clopas" in John 19:25 has also sometimes been identified with the "mother of the sons of Zebedee."

6. The "sister of Jesus' mother" has also hazardously been superimposed on "Mary the wife of Clopas," who would then be reduced to a mere amplification of the former's name.

7. We are then left with the two names that appear only in Luke: Joanna and Susanna.

If the possibilities that emerge from a comparison between the three Synoptics can be considered fairly straightforward, those that are translated into parallels in John are far more complex, owing to the very nature of this compilation.[16] The women he names present three possibilities:

1. only two persons are involved: Jesus' mother and her sister, named respectively as Mary of Clopas and Mary Magdalene;

2. three persons: Mary of Clopas would then be the name of Jesus' mother's sister;

3. four persons: the first two indicated by degree of kinship, the other two each given a proper name.

Of these, the first can be ruled out, since there is no textual foundation for maintaining that Mary Magdalene was Jesus' mother's sister: apart from anything else, they would hardly have the same name. This consideration equally rules out the second possibility, leaving us with the third as the most probable; it is also the one supported by most modern exegetes.

---

[16] Cf. R. Schnackenburg, *The Gospel according to St John*, vol III (London and New York, 1982), pp. 300–40, esp. 315.

From this examination what emerges is that, if we take account of the Synoptic Gospels alone, comparison of their lists gives a minimum of five different people: Mary Magdalene (in all the Synoptics), Mary the mother of James the younger and Joses (in Mark, the same person as Matthew calls Mary the mother of James the younger and Joseph, and perhaps the same as Luke identifies as the mother of James – and then one can ask if she is the mother of the sons of Zebedee, James the elder and John, or hold that "Mary of James" does not imply his mother, but his wife, as some would say also applies to Mary of Clopas in John 19:25. . . . In the first case the number of women named does not change, since it is merely replacing another present; in the second, however, another person is added), Salome (in Mark, maybe the same person as Matthew calls the mother of the sons of Zebedee), Joanna and Susanna.

Staying with the Synoptics alone, the variety of possibilities gives a maximum number of seven women named: Mary Magdalene (in all), Mary the mother of James the younger and Joses (in Mark, the same person Matthew calls Mary the mother of James and Joseph), Salome (in Mark), the mother of the sons of Zebedee (in Matthew), Mary the mother of James (in Luke), Joanna and Susanna (both in Luke).

Taking the women John names as standing by the cross into account, and accepting that there are four of these, this adds Jesus' mother's sister and Mary of Clopas. The number of women identified thus varies from a minimum of seven to a maximum of nine.

Now within the framework of the the remaining possibilities, and the fact that putting forward several serves simply to relativize each of them, one can suppose that because Jesus' mother's sister was present at the dramatic events of the passion, this does not have to be taken as an indication that she belonged to the group of those who followed Jesus, and that she was there simply to help and support his mother in these tragic circumstances; this reduces the number of followers identified to eight. It is still possible to look, in the Gospels, for figures of women who had a special link with Jesus; without wanting to force the texts, which do not provide any evidence for claiming that these women then followed Jesus, there are still some questions to be asked.

The woman who was forgiven (Luke 7:36–50), who went through such an extraordinary and intense experience in her meeting with the Master: would she, after experiencing his compassion and the transformation of her life, have lost interest in him? And the woman cured of the hemorrhage that had tormented her for twelve years (Luke 8:40–56): would she not, once healed, have felt a deep tug of gratitude drawing her toward Jesus?

The woman bent over for eighteen years, healed by Jesus on the sabbath (Luke 13:11–13), called by him a daughter of Abraham and accepted by him as a creature of God caught up in his plan of salvation: would she not have responded to his message of liberation? And what could the woman he saved from stoning (John 8:1–11) have thought and felt? And the sisters Martha and Mary (Luke 10:38–42; John 11:1–44; 12:1–11), who welcomed Jesus into their house with such confidence: would they not at some stage have followed their friend-teacher?

So, by adding the first four women over whom there is a question-mark (leaving out Martha and Mary as the text emphasizes their welcoming Jesus in their house) to the eight already identified as followers, we have a total number of twelve women who had very or fairly close dealings with Jesus. One might then be forgiven for thinking that if a first-century compiler had set out to show (not invent) the special part played by twelve women close to Jesus, he would not have found much difficulty in doing so.

The attempt to restore a visage and identity to the "many" women who followed Jesus, through comparing the various lists of names, is also significant in distinguishing the traditions and sources used by the redactors of the gospel texts. Luke in 8:2 is not taking Mark's list, as he includes Joanna and Susanna and does not mention Mary the mother of James the younger and Joseph.[17] We should therefore conclude, as already said, that he is using a source of his own.

---

[17] It is also worth noting that Luke 8:2 and Mark 16:9 are the only passages of the New Testament where it is said of Mary Magdalene, respectively, "from whom seven demons had gone out" and "from whom he had cast out seven demons." On the sources of these two passages, cf. J. Hug, *La finale de l'Evangile de Marc* (Paris, 1978), p. 164: "The variant formulation, while that of Luke 8:2 is typically Lucan, might indicate that this is a borrowing from a tradition on the women of which Luke himself used elements at various points." Cf. also E. Schweizer, *Das Evangelium nach Markus* (Göttingen, 1967); R. Pesch, *Das Markusevangelium* (Freiburg, 2d ed., 1977).

Matthew, in common with Mark, gives Mary the mother of James and Joseph and, as a separate figure, the mother of the sons of Zebedee, who should not be identified with Mark's Salome. If Matthew had in fact used Mark's list, and Salome was the name of the mother of the sons of Zebedee, why should he not have given, as he did for the second woman on his list, either her name or those of her sons? The third name in Matthew must therefore derive either from a source proper to him or from Q. But the comparison between Luke and Matthew, which shows the absence of names that fulfill the double condition of belonging to both and not to Mark, suggests the first alternative.

In short, then, it seems that three different sources gave an identity to more women. The information that women followed Jesus and the identity of some of these is preserved and handed down in the tradition of at least three sources: Mark, one proper to Luke, one proper to Matthew, and perhaps Q.

The difference between Mark, Matthew, and Luke in these passages should be seen as an enrichment; it is not a problem to be resolved at all costs in the pressing interests of canonical harmonization (i.e. the need to harmonize texts that arose in the bosom of the church when the canon was formed), but a valuable lead to dig deeper into the texts and reach as far as possible into the actual situation echoed and remembered in the word handed down.

In this context, what the passages have in common acquires a special and greater value: the importance given to Mary Magdalene is such that the different sources not only all mention her, but all place her first.

The Diaconate

In their specific contribution to the activity of the group, the women are placed within a vision that has service at the centre of the manifestations of brotherly and sisterly love. Christ himself presents himself as one who came to serve.

The verb διακονέω, "to serve," used in Luke 8:3 is not isolated, but linked to the noun ὑπάρχοντα, "goods" or "resources"; the phrase can be translated "provided (or helped or assisted) out of their own resources (or funds)." This indicates something different from and also more complex than serving at table. One can suppose that the women also provided the usual services that would have been expected of them, such as preparing meals, but Luke is not referring to this. When in Acts he speaks of "serv[ing] at tables," the twelve are first named and then "seven men of good standing, full of the Spirit and of wisdom" to be appointed to this task and on whom the "apostles . . . laid their hands" (6:2–6). This service is thus shown as being carried out by men, and such is the importance attached to it that those to whom it is entrusted are "ordained" to it by the laying on of hands. The women, in providing this service for Jesus and the group around him, were carrying out an activity that in the early church became the "prerogative of an 'ordained' person."[18] In relation to carrying out the traditional roles to which women were relegated in the social order of the time, I refer back to what has already been said about Jesus' attitude to such roles, using those *revealing traces* that have emerged from the investigation carried out.

So in the analysis made of the episode of his "true relatives," we saw how Jesus refused to relate to his mother on the basis of simple biological-parental fact and how he suggested she should emerge from her maternal role and projected her into the situation of those who listen to the word of God and act on it. Jesus did not conduct his dealings with others on the basis of blood ties, of the needs these implied, the functions or roles they covered, but established a direct relationship with others, whom he saw as creatures of God, recipients of his proclamation.

This is why the presence of women in his group is absolutely unthinkable if this is confined to their traditional roles. The relationship he established with them, as confirmed by many other passages in the Gospels and the still extant *footprints* we have been able to uncover, needed to have far wider and deeper room for expression than those roles would have allowed.

Luke himself recounts an episode that sheds further light on this. Jesus, welcomed into Martha and Mary's house, sees the former "distracted by her many tasks" (διακονίαν: 10:40) while the latter "sat at the Lord's feet and listened to what he was saying" (10:39). Martha, thinking it right to be concerned with welcoming their guest and do what was needed to prepare and serve food for him,

---

[18] R. Brown, *The Community of the Beloved Disciple* (New York, 1979): here It. trans., p. 222. Cf. R. Petraglio, ". . . e tutti profeterrano," *MO* 9 (1988), pp. 32–7, esp. 34 for the term *diakonos*.

asked him to tell Mary to help her. She failed to understand that her sister was welcoming Jesus in a deeper sense. Mary was not attending to him and caring for him only in relation to the meal, but set herself to listen to him and thereby attend to his deeper reality with which she longed to enter into communication: to welcome and be welcomed. Jesus' reply is unequivocal: "Martha, Martha, you are worried and distracted by many things; there is need of only one thing. Mary has chosen the better part, which will not be taken away from her" (10:41–2). This text can be taken as a *trace* of the position Jesus took against women's traditional *service*, in favour of an integral discipleship.

Women are recipients of the proclamation, and their lives should not be closed and suffocated in domestic roles: not because these are lacking in value, but because roles, all roles, should not be imprisoning structures; for women as well as for men, the full and free essence of their person should always come first.

The women in Luke 8:1–3 are distinguished from others who appear around Jesus and are relatives (wives or mothers) of the disciples or apostles. These autonomous women, who do not *belong* to male leaders of the group, therefore have a direct relationship to Jesus outside the usual ones of clan, parental group or the structure of family relationships dominated by males. From this an important socio-anthropological indication emerges: Jesus had dealings of various kinds with women because these were not governed by the institutional structures of the Judaic world.

Women Disciples

Should the women be regarded as disciples or not? To answer this, we need to distinguish the various elements that make up being a disciple of Jesus, and to see in what ways this differed from other forms of discipleship current at the time.

New Testament research points to two main features of the relationship between discipleship of Christ and rabbinic discipleship or discipleship in general, which was a fairly widespread social phenomenon in Jesus' time:

(a) Discipleship of Jesus should not be understood on the basis of rabbinic Judaism (he was not a "rabbi") but – and here authorities diverge – on the basis either of the Old Testament prophetic tradition or baptist movements or again Galilean charismatic Judaism.

(b) "Its 'outward form' is similar to that of rabbinic Judaism, despite its 'contents' being substantially different."[19]

The most obvious differences compared to rabbinism are:

(a) It is Jesus who calls, not the disciple who seeks a school;

(b) What is taught is not the Torah but the coming of the Kingdom linked to the presence of Jesus himself, in whose being and destiny, including that of suffering, disciples are called to an almost total involvement. However, like the disciples of the rabbinic schools, those of Jesus also live a communal life with their master and are required to serve him.

Calling

An aspect about which the Gospels tell us is the personal call made by Jesus to various disciples. But, as Rengstorf notes, if "... it is less important to know whether among Jesus' [disciples] there were those who joined him without receiving an explicit call," tradition nevertheless agrees "in saying that in the final analysis it was always Jesus who decided who followed him."[20]

Luke 8:26–39 relates the episode of a man who was possessed by demons, who, once cured by Jesus, "begged that he might be with him; but Jesus sent him away, saying, 'Return to your home....'" So it is Jesus alone who decides who is to form part of his following. If the texts do not make clear that the women were called as some of the men are said to have been, apart from the possibility that this has not been handed down, under the great cloak of *silence* that envelops women, it is in any case clear that women were welcomed and chosen by him.

Travelling

Those closest to Jesus followed him on his travels from one place to another. The existence of "sedentary groups of sympathizers" has

---

[19] M. Pesce,, "Discepolato gesuano e discepolato rabbinico. Problemi e prospettive della comparazione," *ANRW* II 25/1 (Berlin, 1982), pp. 351–89, here 356; cf. also K. H. Rengstorf, "μαθητής," *TWNT* 4 (1942), pp. 417–65; D. Muller, "μαθητής," *DCBNT* 1720–26.

[20] Rengstorf, *art. cit.*, pp. 1195, 1196.

then to be considered additional to that of "itinerant charismatics."[21]

Women belong to both to the first sort of group and the second: those in Luke 8:1–3 were "itinerant"; others, such as Martha and Mary, normally stayed in their homes, where they welcomed Jesus.[22]

Separation from the Family Circle and Previous Activities

All those who belong to the itinerant group are asked to leave their family and work, though this does not generally imply a complete break with them. Leaving their work obviously then brings the need to rely on others' help for their sustenance.[23] In this respect, we have already seen that some women in Jesus' entourage were in the same position, sharing with others in the group separation from their previous way of living. This leaving of home and family was clearly more traumatic for the women, for mainly cultural reasons.

Service

The disciples, including the women, were bound to Jesus in a relationship of service. This concept of service, however, is set within the new and rich expectation of the Kingdom and Jesus' words as expressed by John: "I do not call you servants (δοῦλοι) . . . but . . . friends (φίλοι). . . . You did not choose me but I chose you. And I appointed you to go and bear fruit. . ." (15:15–16). Several elements are brought together here: service, the call–choice by Jesus, the invitation to proclaim. There is an interesting reference to the relationship between preaching and service in Acts, where the author describes two of Paul's helpers, sent by him to Macedonia, as "διακονούντων αὐτῷ" (19:22). In the Letter to the Romans the

---

[21] This terminology is that used by G. Theissen, *Sociologie der Jesusbewegung: Ein Beitrag zur Entstehungsgeschichte des Urchristentums* (Munich, 1977).

[22] This observation is perhaps worth following up as supporting the fact that Mary Magdalene and Mary of Bethany were two different people, each belonging to a different kind of group.

[23] Pesce, "Discepolato," p. 371.

term διάκονον is used of a woman, "our sister Phoebe, a deacon of the church at Cenchreae" (16:1).[24]

Ephesians 6:21 has: "... Tychicus will tell you everything. He is a dear brother and a faithful minister (διάκονος) in the Lord," and Colossians 4:7–8: "Tychicus will tell you all the news about me; he is a beloved brother, a faithful minister (διάκονος), and a fellow-servant (σύνδουλος) in the Lord. I have sent him to you...." Even though these are texts deriving from different places and times, so that the reference to service has changed and the word has a different connotation, it is worth noting how this return to the idea of serving, applied to both women and men, underlines its importance in the primitive community.

Recipients of Special Teaching from Jesus

There is a special proclamation reserved to the disciples, and it is interesting that this is expressed in Luke with particular emphasis just after 8:1–3: "To you it has been given to know the secrets of the kingdom of God, but to others I speak in parables ..." (8:10). A clear distinction is here being made between the message destined to all and that, different in mode of expression also, reserved to the disciples. The phrase is used here just after 8:1–3, in the telling of the parable of the sower, which is paradigmatic for the themes *proclamation–word–listening* (8:4–18). The women are sharers in this special message, reserved to the inner group.

A proof that women were present alongside the apostles, even when this fact is not mentioned by the compiler of the gospel story, is to be found in Luke precisely at a moment when Jesus turns to "his own" with another specific and significant teaching: the foretelling of the passion. This brings us up against a line of research to be undertaken backward. This passage provides us with a valuable chance of bringing out a well-defined, precise application of the *exegesis of silence*.

(a) *Recovery of a particular text as a "revealing indication."* In Luke's account of the visit of the women to the empty tomb, they find two men who say to them: "'Why do you look for the living

---

[24] On the presence of woman deacons in the early church, see P. Sorci, "Ministeri liturgici nella chiesa antica," C. Militello (ed.), *Donna e Ministero. Un dibattito ecumenico* (Rome, 1991).

among the dead? He is not here, but has risen. Remember how he told you, while he was still in Galilee, that the Son of Man must be handed over to sinners, and be crucified, and on the third day rise again.' Then they remembered his words" (24:5–8). This is in fact more than a *revealing indication*; it is a clear statement that Jesus told them about this when he was still in Galilee. Those who speak are addressing the women, and them alone: "he told you" means he told these women, and they, the text goes on to say, "remembered his words."

(b) *A simple inquiry into other passages of "indicative" text.* Luke has three passages in which Jesus foretells his pasion: 9:18–22; 9:43–5 and 18:31–4. In the first two of these the announcement is made to the μαθηταί, "disciples," and in the third to the twelve.[25] In the three parallel passages in Mark (8:31; 9:30–32; 10:32–4) and Matthew (16:13–20; 17:22; 20:17–19) (the first two use the word μαθηταί or an indirect reference to the same word used earlier, while the third has δώδεκα).

In Mark and Matthew these occasions are referred specifically to Galilee (Mark 9:30; Matt. 17:22), which is the geographical setting in which the itinerant following by the women is then situated. Neither makes an explicit reference to the presence of women, but the indication of Galilee can still be taken as an element that reveals it.

(c) *A presence hidden in silence.* There are at least two possibilities: the word μαθηταί, as used by the gospel redactors, includes women; in the evangelists' intentions, μαθηταί does not seek explicitly and deliberately to include women, but they are present and this is not mentioned.

In the passages where δώδεκα appears, we need to ask whether this necessarily and definitely excludes the presence of others, and therefore that of women.

---

[25] It is interesting to note how the restricted meaning exegetes and translators tend to give to terms such as μαθηταί and απόστολοι in themselves, and certainly without considering the question of women, is sometimes reflected in translations in a way that leads to imprecision and confusion. So G. Nolli, in Luke 9:18–22, translates μαθηταί "twelve," though this would have required the Greek δώδεκα: *Evangelo secondo Luca*, p. 417. [Modern English translations – JB, NEB, NRSV – all have "disciples" here – Trans.]

The setting for the third prediction of the passion is the journey up to Jerusalem, in all three Synoptics, and we have seen how Mark in 15:40–41 underlines the presence both of the women who have followed Jesus from Galilee and of those "many others" who joined him on the way up to Jerusalem. Must we take it that the redactors, in using the term δώδεκα, meant to assert that it was only to the narrowest group around Jesus that this new prediction of now imminent events was made?[26]

But indicating the presence of the twelve does not mean excluding the presence of others. Furthermore, both Mark and Matthew report precisely a special situation in which the prediction of Jesus' death is made explicitly in the presence of a woman. This is the woman who at Bethany, in the house of Simon the leper, anoints Jesus' head with precious ointment. (In Mark 14:3–9 and Matthew 26:6–13 the incident is told without giving the woman a name, but in the parallel passage in John, 12:1–8, she is identified as Mary of Bethany, the sister of Martha and Lazarus.) "But when the disciples saw it, they were angry and said, 'Why this waste? For this ointment could have been sold for a large sum, and the money given to the poor.' But Jesus, aware of this, said to them, 'Why do you trouble this woman? She has performed a good service for me. For you always have the poor with you, but you will not always have me. By pouring this ointment on my body she has prepared me for burial. Truly I tell you, wherever this good news is proclaimed in the whole world, what she has done will be told in remembrance of her" (Matt. 26:8–13).

This account not only explicitates Jesus' foretelling of his own death, in relation to which he sets the ultimate significance of the woman's gesture, but also shows the male disciples' inability to open their minds to her feminine nature. She does not measure her actions by an aridly and rationalistically calculated economic criterion, but by holding fast to a deeper feeling, following an inner line of thought which meets Jesus' own, perhaps to the point where she has a presentiment of the hidden, precious meaning of what she

---

[26] This wishing (on Jesus' part) to address the narrowest circle is assumed by Nolli to the extent of translating the text "παραλαβὼν δὲ τοὺς δώδεκα," (Luke 18:31: literally: "taking then the twelve") as "and taking the twelve alone." *Ibid.*, p. 86.

is doing. She is a woman who gives rein to her feelings and then to the deep call of her instinctive nature; it is an inner clinging to Jesus that leads her to act as she does and it is the diciples' distance from this mode of being that leads them, as Mark says, to be angry with her and "scold her," prompting Jesus' riposte: "Let her alone; why do you trouble her? ... She has done what she could ..." (Mark 14:5–8). This is a very powerful phrase. The woman has done what "she could" do, what was given to her, and her alone, as a woman and as such willed and created by God, to be possible to do.

These disciples, who in general had so much trouble in understanding the ways and actions of women, would often not have been able to grasp, and at other times would not have bothered to remember, the meaning of what women did, and would therefore not have recorded the fact of their presence.

(d) *Comparison of the Synoptics.* A profitable vein of investigation is opened up when, having found a *revealing trace* hidden in a text, we compare it with parallel passages in the other Synoptics. This shows one of two things: the trace identified in one text either is or is not present in the other writings. When a *revealing trace* disappears in the parallel text, this shows the androcentric attitude of the compiler of this, or at least of his source.

So when Matthew says: "... there were about five thousand men, without counting women and children" (14:21 and similarly 15:38), and we find that Mark merely notes: "Those who had eaten the loaves numbered five thousand men" (6:44),[27] without mentioning women at all, the androcentric mentality of Mark's text is clearly more marked that that of Matthew at this point.

Another example can be found in Mark himself: "You are looking for Jesus of Nazareth.... He has been raised ... But go, tell his disciples and Peter that he is going ahead of you to Galilee; there you will see him, just as he told you" (16:6–7, which parallels Luke 24:5–8 examined earlier). Besides other problems raised by this text, here it is interesting to note that Mark's text is much less explicit

---

[27] In the parallel passage in Luke 9:10–17, he has: "All ate and were filled ...," but before this v. 14 says that "there were about five thousand men." In John 6:1–13, v. 10 reads: "so they sat down, about five thousand in all."

with regard to the women than Luke's.[28] In the message to be taken to the disciples, the expressions "he is going before you" and "as he told you" could also be taken as referring exclusively to the male disciples.[29] In this case, Luke's text, compared to Mark's, stands out for its different attitude to the women, perhaps showing that he is using his own source which he considers more securely based than Mark.

In more general terms, one can say that when a revealing trace concerning women present in one text is shown to have disappeared in a synoptic parallel, what happened was that the compiler of the first text, if he had a choice of several sources, considered the one that mentioned women more secure. It is far less likely to suppose a pure and simple redactional intervention by the author of the text in favour of women when, either because of his own mentality, which would tend to be androcentric, or because of the general and cultural climate in which he was writing, there was absolutely no benefit to be gained from bringing women in except when the sources made the most definite reference to them. (This same patriarchal context suggests that any redactional intervention would more naturally have removed references to women that actually appeared in his sources.)

When, therefore, the second possibility is the case, that comparison of the Synoptics provides confirmation of the *revealing trace*, then the submerged reality of women acquires further consistency.

Going back, after this example of applying an *exegesis of silence*, to consideration of the special teaching Jesus reserved to his disciples and the women with them, we cannot but recall the first announcement of the passion (Luke 9:18–22). Note the following points:

– the context: "Once when Jesus was praying alone with only the disciples near him";

---

[28] For example, Galilee and Jerusalem have specific theological connotations in Luke. Cf *Nouveau Testament T.O.B.* (Paris, 1973), pp. 172, 179, 277; Schweizer, Das Evangelium *nach Markus*: It. trans. pp. 383–95; J. Gnilka, *Marco* (Assisi, 1987), pp. 921–3.

[29] This is the interpretation made by P. Benoît and M. E. Boismard, *Synopse des quatre évangiles en français*, vol II (Paris, 1965), pp. 433–44.

– the subject: "he asked them, 'Who do the crowds say that I am?'";

– the different, more personal question to the disciples: "But who do you say that I am?";

– the answer: "the Christ of God";

– the conditions laid on the disciples: "He sternly ordered and commanded them not to tell anyone";

– a disconcerting announcement reserved to the disciples: "The Son of Man must undergo great suffering ... and be killed, and on the third day be raised."

In this passage, which details a special teaching reserved to the disciples (with its contrast between "the crowd" on one hand and "you" on the other, and the instruction to keep the information to themselves – with a further confirmation that this was special information for the disciples coming in the verse following those just examined, 23: "Then he said to them all ..."), the women are not expressly mentioned, but their presence is confirmed *a posteriori* in the context of the resurrection: both by the words of the two men – "Remember how he told you..." – and the reference to the fact that the women "remembered his words" (24:6–8).

The Call to proclaim

The disciples, after being made recipients of the proclamation, are themselves called to take the *good news*. More particularly, they are *sent out to proclaim*.

Two terminologies are deliberately used: *taking the good news*, which represents the more general concept of being *called to proclaim*, and *sent out to proclaim*, which is one of the ways in which the *call to proclaim* can be put into effect.

Now women are included in the call to take Jesus' message to the extent that proclaiming the good news is also a way of life, according to the Lord's phrase "those who hear the word of God and do it" (Luke 8:21). But the texts also provide many pointers to the fact that Jesus entrusted the specific task of proclamation to women. The Risen Christ tells the women to take the message of salvation to his brothers. These are the texts: "Then Jesus said to them, 'Do not be afraid; go and tell my brothers to go to Galilee, where they will see me'" (Matt. 28:10); "Jesus said to her (Mary Magdalene) ... 'Go to my brothers and say to them: I am ascending to my Father and your Father, to my God and your God" (John

20:17). The "longer ending of Mark" does not mention the fact that Jesus sent Mary Magdalene, but does say that after the Risen Christ had appeared to her, "She went out and told those who had been with him, while they were mourning and weeping" (16:10).

I have already stressed the importance this most exceptional proclamation has for the women; it makes them mediators of the word between Christ and the apostles and also gives them the role of re-forming the group when it had scattered as a result of the dramatic events of Jesus' arrest and crucifixion.[30]

The episode of the Samaritan woman (John 4:1–42) lends itself to particular analysis. The woman personally receives from Jesus the good news that "the hour is coming, and is now here, when the true worshipers will worship the Father in spirit and truth" (v. 23) and, even if it is not explicitly said that he sends her, she goes away to carry the news, with the result that: "Many Samaritans . . . believed in him because of the woman's testimony" (v. 39).[31] The Samaritans themselves "asked him to stay with them; and he stayed there two days" (v. 40). And then "many more believed because of his word. They said to the woman, 'It is no longer because of what you said that we believe, for we have heard for ourselves . . .'" (vv. 41–2), which gives expression to the problem of the lack of credibility attributed to women and their juridical incapacity to act as witnesses at the time.

Rengstorf, analyzing the term ἀπόστολος, specifies that:

> It designates a man who is sent out, more precisely a plenipotentiary. The Greek lexicon therefore provides the New Testament with the word as such, but its content is determined by the šālîăh (= sent) of late Judaism. This can be stated categorically, since the word in the whole of the New Testament is used only of men. In particular circumstances some women could also have borne the name apostle, but this would have been a contradiction in terms, since šālîăh is a

---

[30] Cf. L. Schottroff, "Maria Magdalena und die Frauen am Grabe Jesu," *Evth.* 42 (1982), pp. 3–25.

[31] Cf. A. Valerio, "Jesù e la Samaritana: la donna di fronte al Regno," *Ricerca*, Jan.-Feb. 1987, pp. 31–2 (Acts of the 48th FUCI National Congress). [Cf. also A. Primavesi and J. Henderson, *Our God has No Favourites* (Tunbridge Wells and San José, Ca., 1989), pp. 14–24. – Trans.]

juridical term, and among the Hebrews women not only had limited rights and above all could not act as witnesses ... but juridically came even behind slaves; these in fact, being the property of their master, could represent his will on the juridical level as well (e.g. they could offer the sacrifice of the paschal lamb in his place).[32]

Rengstorf's interesting analysis requires one observation: in the New Testament the term ἀπόστολος is in fact appled to a woman, in Romans 16:7: "Greet Andronicus and Junia [or Julia], my compatriots who were in prison with me; they are prominent among the apostles, and they were in Christ before I was." The title of apostle is not reserved here either to the twelve alone or to men alone.[33]

Perhaps women were not sent out by Jesus to preach in the same manner as the male disciples (though it is not possible to rule this out); furthermore, social conditions and the grave problems that would have been caused by preaching carried out by itinerant women, perhaps women on their own, have to be taken into account. Even though Jesus was not afraid to act freely in relation to cultural conditionings and provisions such as the purity laws, the prohibitions governing the sabbath and the like, he could not have failed to take account of the hostility and even danger to which he would have exposed the women by asking them to undertake preaching missions in a socio-cultural environment in which they would have met with disdain, mistrust and scant consideration. But then he found them adequate when he sent them to proclaim the resurrection. Perhaps in this case he, besides taking account of the innate value of having chosen women, also realized that sending them to the other disciples, among whom they lived, was not exposing them to risk. It is in any case worth noting that their familiarity with the apostles did not spare them the humiliation and pain of not being believed.

---

[32] Rengstorf, "ἀποστέλλω," *TWNT* 1 (1933), pp. 397–448.

[33] On the meaning of "apostle" and more generally on the active presence of women in the early community as evidenced from Romans 16, cf R. Petraglio, "... e tutti profeteranno," *MO* 9 (1988), pp. 32–7.

Witnessing

The disciples lived in close proximity to Jesus, sharing much of his life experience, and bearing witness to him. Women took part in this important activity and, as Luke 8:1–3 tells and the other Synoptics confirm, did so from the beginning of his preaching.

They are privileged witnesses: some of them had personal experience of his healing powers (note that in the Gospels none of the male disciples is said to have been cured). They too, as we have seen, shared the special teaching reserved to the disciples and were witnesses to and depositories of the Master's words. Finally the women, the only ones of his followers to be present at the foot of the cross, were chosen to be the first and privileged witnesses to the ultimate reality of the resurrection.[34]

The first witnessing of the most *humanly absurd* event possible to imagine was reserved to women, to those women whose juridical witnessing was not considered valid. Luke, in his prologue, makes a vital reference to the value of witness: the sources of the information he has about the events of which he intends to write "an orderly account" are "those who from the beginning were eye-witnesses and servants of the word" (1:2–3).

Sharing Jesus' Life and Fate even in Suffering

The radical nature of the call that singles out disciples is shown by the way they are asked to be ready to undergo sufferings, just like Jesus, and even martyrdom. The women bore witness to their faithfulness by standing at the foot of the cross, with the attendant risks this involved for them.[35]

Of all the elements that made up discipleship: call, travelling, separation from previous activities, service, special teaching, being called to proclaim, witnessing, sharing in Jesus' life and fate, perhaps the only one in which things were different for women was the call to proclaim, in the sense of being sent out to preach on an itinerant

---

[34] Cf. M. L. Rigato, "Donne testimoni della risurrezione," S. Spera (ed.), *Uomini e donne nella Chiesa* (Rome, 1988).

[35] Against the possible objection that the women ran no risk through their actions during and after the crucifixion, see Schottroff, "Maria Magdalena und die Frauen," p. 5. The women's "from a distance" (Mark 15:40); Matt. 27:55; Luke 23:49) led to witnessing and the appearance of the Risen Christ, while Peter's "at a distance" (Luke 22:54) led to his denial.

mission over a long period of time. These constituent elements go to define the figure of Jesus' followers in the strictest sense it seems possible to give to the term disciple.

Other connotations are possible, as can be seen from the use the evangelists make of the term, and from the way it was probably used in the early Christian community, as far as can be deduced from an examination of Acts. Luke in particular extends use of the word "disciple" to describe "a broader collection of followers" of Jesus.[36] In Acts the word is also used to indicate people belonging to the community who had not known the Lord.

Used in the feminine gender, the word appears only once in the New Testament, in Acts 9:36: "Now in Joppa there was a disciple whose name was Tabitha...." Karl Rengstorf states: "We need to ask if Tabitha had been a disciple of Jesus ... or was a Christian.... On the basis of the use made of the term μαθητής, the first hypothesis is also possible, particularly as the Gospels speak of women who had set out to follow Jesus (Mark 15:40; ... Luke 8:2ff)...." He then concludes: "But the general linguistic usage of Acts rather suggests the second meaning."[37]

An apocryphal text, the *Gospel of Peter*, describing the visit to the empty tomb, uses the expression, "Mary Magdalene, a disciple of the Lord."[38] In this case, "disciple," being used of a woman who had certainly belonged to the circle of Jesus' close followers, should be understood in the more specific sense that identifies the travelling disciples. This analysis therefore produces variable results and could be continued, were it not that a more general reflection leads beyond the question of establishing the way in which women were disciples and even apostles.

What is the purpose of determining whether women belonged to the categories of disciple or apostle? Is it not enough to discover what sort of relationship they had with Jesus?

We need perhaps to free ourselves from the appeal of trying to show that women had roles and places exactly like the men, and to be on our guard against entering into a competitive-polemical

---

[36] Pesce, "Discepolato gesuano," p. 362.
[37] Rengstorf, "μαθητής," p. 1237.
[38] M. Erbetta, *Gli apocrifi del Nuovo Testamento. Vangeli. Testi giudeo-cristiani e gnostici* (Casale Monferrato, 1975), p. 144.

argument that is a-historical and certainly not evangelical. We have in fact seen that Jesus refused to relate to people by virtue of their established roles and ties of kinship, and when a competitive debate broke out among the disciples over who was to be the greatest, he swept all categories aside, proclaiming that "the greatest among you must become like the youngest, and the leader like one who serves. . . . I am among you as one who serves" (Luke 22:26–7).

For the sake of argument one could maintain that Mary Magdalene is above the apostles because Jesus chooses and sends her to take the news of the resurrection to them, making her *"apostola apostolorum."*[39] But as Jesus did not make so many comparisons and distinctions, is it perhaps still not following his approach to single out the significance contained in his gesture of choosing this woman as mediatrix between him and the apostles, and to seize on this in what we are trying to express? It is to Jesus' actions and words, in that foundational, informal, creative period of his proclamation, that we should look, rather than to later structurings and institutionalizations. Otherwise we run the risk of reading the situation that obtained around Jesus through institutional categories that historically cannot be applied to him, still less in the way he is viewed today.

What belongs to Jesus is primarily the content of his message, not more or less strict, more or less schematic, more or less artificial categories that people might try to place on that content, classifying and ordering it in a rigid, well-constructed framework, all closely defined, closed off, with no room for openings on to growth and life. Whereas Jesus himself proclaimed a course of the Spirit too, opening out beyond his own proclamation: "I still have many things to say to you, but you cannot bear them now. When the Spirit of truth comes, he will guide you into all the truth . . ." (John 16:12–13).

---

[39] Cf. Hipp., In cant. 25, pp. 6–9; CSCO 264, pp. 47–9; Rab. Maur., *De vita beatae Mariae Magdalenae*, 27, PL 112, 1474: "Salvator . . . ascensionis suae eam (= Mariam Magdalenam) ad apostolos instituit apostolam"; Thomas Aquinas, *In Ioannem Evangelistam Expositio*, c. XX, L. III, 6: "Facta est apostolorum Apostola, per hoc quod ei committitur ut resurrectionem dominicam discipulis annuntiet."

Apostle to the Apostles

I have not appeared
to you until I saw your tears and your sorrow [. . .] for me.
Cast aside your sadness and carry out this service,
be my messenger to the [dis]tressed orph[ans].
Hasten to rejoice and go to the eleven.
You will find them gathered on the bank of the Jordan.
The deceiver has persuaded them to be fishermen
as they were at first and to cast aside the nets with which they
    won men to life.
Say to them: Get up, let us go, your brother is calling you.
If they spurn my brotherhood, say to them:
He is your master.
If they pay no heed to my authority, tell them: He is your
    Lord.
Use every art and ruse until you
have brought the flock back to the shepherd.
If you see they are upset by you, take
Simon Peter with you; say to him: Remember what I said, to
    you alone.
Remember what I said, just to you, on the Mount of Olives:
I have something to say but I have no one to say it to![40]

These words are addressed by the Risen Christ to Mary Magdalene
according to an apocryphal Coptic text of the fourth century. Even
allowing for the limitations and problems connected with this sort
of literature, they do provide an illustration, and perhaps a later
deepening, of some of the themes discussed here.

Mary's response is immediate, full and intense;

Rabbi, my master, I shall carry out your commandment in the
    joy of all my heart.
I shall give no rest to my heart, I shall give my eyes no sleep.
    I shall give no rest to my feet until I have brought the flock
    back to the fold.

---

[40] *Manichaean Manuscripts in the Chester Beatty Collection*, C. R. C.
Allberry (ed.), *A Manichaean Psalm-Book* (Stuttgart, 1938), vol II, p.
187.

And the ancient text concludes:

> Glory to Mary because she has obeyed the master.
> She has carried out his commandment in the joy of all her heart.

This *agraphon* can be taken as a sublime expression of the mission entrusted by Christ to Mary Magdalene and, in her, to all the other disciples. Mary's prompt and total acceptance marks the start of a journey and a presence of women, of which traces are to be found in Acts, and which in often obscure and silent ways have determined so much of the history of the early Christian community. "All these were constantly devoting themselves to prayer, together with certain women, including Mary the mother of Jesus, as well as his brothers" (Acts 1:14). The women were present at the time of the descent of the Spirit and were fully involved in the fulfilment of the prophecy of Joel which Peter declared to have come about:

> This is what was throught the prophet Joel:
> In the last days it will be, God declares,
> that I will pour out my Spirit upon all flesh,
> and your sons and your daughters shall prophesy,
> and your young men shall see visions,
> and your old men shall dream dreams.
> Even upon my slaves, both men and women,
> in those days I will pour out my Spirit;
> and they shall prophesy (Acts 2:16–18).[41]

Travelling the hard roads of the *exegesis of the silence*, I have sought, with the *agraphon* given above, to shed a shaft of brighter light on what is related by John: "Mary Magdalene went and announced to the disciples, 'I have seen the Lord'; and she told them that he had said these things to her" (John 20:18).

My desire to give a new sound to the words Jesus addressed to the woman has led me to look into apocryphal literature also for these

---

[41] Acts 18:24–8 and 21:8–9 provide further evidence of the gift of prophecy and the preaching activity of women.

fragments of texts, given here as a significant part of the message of the Risen Christ, but the fullness of Christ's word and of Mary Magdalene's response is given in its full intensity in the words of John's Gospel: "Mary!" . . . "Master!" (20:16).

AFTERWORD TO AN OPEN RESEARCH

Today, after this course of research, I am convinced that it is possible, at least partly, to break down the androcentric barrier put up by the biblical texts and behind which exegetical interpretation has tried to keep them.

Having spent so much time gazing at a particular text, having come back to it time and time again, after long hours of searching in darkness and silence, I can simply apply to the texts I have examined Jesus' words: "Ask, and it will be given you; search, and you will find; knock, and the door will be opened for you. For everyone who asks receives, and everyone who searches finds, and for everyone who knocks, the door will be opened" (Luke 11:9–10).

I know then what it is like to wait expectantly in front of a *closed text*, to have asked, searched, knocked in an effort to find a way, a route, an instrument to *open it*. I also know that the waiting and the route are not finished, that it is not possible to close a course of research that seeks to *open*.

This book is an *open* text. The attempt at *opening* biblical texts that have been largely *closed* to women has, little by little, allowed me to advance on a course that showed a horizon; once reached, that horizon revealed another farther off.

For this reason I am not putting forward conclusions as though they were final destinations and so, necessarily, closures to the reflections, but I am convinced of and propose those that have emerged at times in the course of the book as definitive annotations, in the deep conviction and inner certainty that they are steps along the journey. If then these are at this moment *points of arrival* thanks to the dynamic of research, they are also, in a process of creative projection, *points of departure*, the beginnings of other ways into the interior of an open-ended process which in its course will be able to look at them anew in new contexts of research and analysis.

> *"Se hace camino al andar"*
> ("You make the path by walking")
> – Antonio Machado

APPENDIX

COMPARATIVE TABLE OF REFERENCES TO WOMEN IN THE FOUR GOSPELS IN RELATION TO:
1. physical presence; 2. speeches by Jesus; 3. speeches by others

THE GOSPEL OF MATTHEW

REF.	DESCRIPTION			PARALLELS
	women named	*speeches by Jesus*	*speeches by others*	
1:3			"Judah the father of Perez and Zerah by Tamar"	
1:5			"Boaz the father of Obed by Ruth"	
1:6			"David was the father of Solomon by the wife of Uriah"	
1:16	"Jacob the father of Joseph the husband of Mary"			
1:18–25	Mary the mother of Jesus engaged to Joseph; from Joseph's doubt to the birth of Jesus			Luke 1:35
2:11	"They saw the child with Mary his mother"			
2:13	"take the child and his mother"			
2:14	"[Joseph] took the child and his mother"			

REF.	DESCRIPTION			PARALLELS
	women named	*speeches by Jesus*	*speeches by others*	
2:18			"Rachel weeping for her children"	
2:20	"Take the child and his mother, and go to the land of Israel"			
2:21	"[Joseph] got up, took the child and his mother"			
5:28		"everyone who looks at a woman"		
5:31–2		"whoever divorces his wife... I say to you that anyone who divorces his wife... causes her to commit adultery; and whoever marries a divorced woman..."		Luke 16:18 Mark 10:11–12 Matt. 19:9
8:14–15	"When Jesus entered Peter's house, he saw his mother-in-law"			Mark 1:29–31 Luke 4:38–9
9:18–26	"a leader of the synagogue came in ..." Healing of the woman suffering from a hemorrhage and raising of the leader's daughter			Mark 5:22–43 Luke 8:41–56
10:35		"to set... a daughter against her mother, and a daughter-in-law against her mother-in-law"		Luke 12:53
10:37		"Whoever loves father or mother... whoever loves son or daughter more than me..."		Luke 14:26

REF.	DESCRIPTION			PARALLELS
	women named	*speeches by Jesus*	*speeches by others*	
11:11		"among those born of women" (the Baptist)		Luke 7:28
12:42		"The queen of the South will rise up"		Luke 11:31
12:46–50	"his mother and his brothers were standing outside, wanting to speak to him. Someone told him . . . Jesus replied . . . 'is my . . . sister and mother'"			Mark 3:31–5 Luke 8:19–21
13:33		"yeast that a woman took"		Luke 13:21
13:55–6			"Is not his mother called Mary. . . are not all his sisters with us?" (Jesus')	Mark 6:3 John 6:42
14:3–4	Herodias			Mark 6: 17–18 Luke 3:19
14:6–11	Herodias prompted by her mother to ask for the head of John the Baptist			Mark 6:22–8
14:21			"those who ate were. . . not counting women and children"	
14:4–6		"God said, 'Honor your father and your mother. . . .' But you say. . ."		Mark 7:10–12
15:22–8	Healing of the daughter of a Canaanite woman			Mark 7:25–30
15:38			"Those who had eaten were. . . not counting women and children"	

REF.	DESCRIPTION			PARALLELS
	women named	*speeches by Jesus*	*speeches by others*	
18:25		"his lord ordered him to be sold, ... with his wife"		
19:3–9		"Is it lawful for a man to divorce his wife...? He answered, '... made them male and female... a man shall leave his father and mother and be joined to his wife... whoever divorces his wife...'"		Mark 10:2–12 Luke 16:18
19:10			"If this is the case of a man with his wife, it is better not to marry"	
19:12		"... who have been so from birth"		
19:19		"Honor your father and mother"		Mark 10:19 Luke 18:20
19:29		"Everyone who has left... sisters or father or mother"		Luke 18:29–30 Mark 10: 29–30
20:20–23	The mother of the sons of Zebedee asks a favour			
21:31–2		"... and the prostitutes are going into the kingdom of God ahead of you... and the prostitutes believed him" (John)		
22:23–33		The woman who had seven husbands: whose wife will she be at the resurrection? He answers: "... they neither marry nor are given in marriage"		Mark 12:19–25 Luke 20:27–35

REF.	DESCRIPTION			PARALLELS
	women named	*speeches by Jesus*	*speeches by others*	
24:19		"Woe to those who are pregnant and to those who are nursing infants in those days!"		Mark 13:17 Luke 16:18
24:38		"... in those days before the flood... marrying and giving in marriage"		Luke 17:27
24:41		"Two women will be grinding meal together"		Luke 17:35
25:1–13		"the kingdom of heaven will be like this... ten bridesmaids..."		
26:6–13	A woman anoints Jesus at Bethany			Mark 14:3–9 John 12:3–8
26:69–71	"A servant-girl came to him... Another servant-girl saw this..."			Mark 14:66–70 Luke 22:56–7 John 18:16–17
27:19	"[Pilate's] wife sent word to him"			
27:55–6	"Many women... looking on from a distance..." at the crucifixion. Among them were Mary Magdalene, and Mary the mother of James and Joseph. and the mother of the sons of Zebedee"			Luke 23:49 Mark 15:40–41 John 19:25
27:61	"Mary Magdalene and the other Mary were there, sitting opposite the tomb"			Luke 23:55 Mark 15:47
28:1–8	Mary Magdalene and the other Mary at the tomb; the angel's message			Mark 16:1–9 Luke 24:1–10 John 20; 1–2
28:9–10	Jesus appears to the women			

THE GOSPEL OF MARK

REF.	DESCRIPTION			PARALLELS
	women named	*speeches by Jesus*	*speeches by others*	
1:29–31	Healing of Simon's mother-in-law			Matt 8:14–15 Luke 4:38–9
3:31–5	"Then his mother and his brothers came; and standing outside, they sent to him and called him. . . And he replied, '. . . is my. . . and sister and mother'"			
5:22–43	"one of the leaders. . . named Jairus came . . ." Healing of the woman suffering from a hemorrhage; raising of Jairus' daughter, with her mother present			Matt 9:55–6 Luke 8:41–56
6:3			"Is not this the. . . son of Mary. . . are not his sisters here with us?"	Matt. 13:55–6 John 6:42
6:17–19	Herodias			Matt. 14:3–4 Luke 3:19
6:22–8	Herodias' mother tells her to ask for the head of John the Baptist			Matt. 14:6–11
7:10–12		"Moses said, 'honor your father and your mother,' and, 'Whoever speaks evil of father or mother. . .' But you say. . ."		Matt. 15:4–6
7:25–30	Healing of the Gentile Syrophoenician woman's daughter			Matt. 15:22–8

REF.	DESCRIPTION			PARALLELS
	women named	*speeches by Jesus*	*speeches by others*	
10:2–12		"Is it lawful for a man to divorce his wife?" He. . . said to them, "Because of your hardness of heart. . . But 'God made them male and female,' . . .let no one separate"		Matt. 19:3–9 Luke 16:18
10:19		"You know the commandments. . . honor your father and mother"		Luke 18:20 Matt. 19:19
10:29–30		"Truly I tell you: there is no one who has left. . . sisters or mother. . . who will not receive a hundredfold. . . sisters, mothers. . ."		Matt. 19:29 Luke 18:29–30
12:18–25		"Some Sadducees. . . asked him a question, saying, '. . . in the resurrection whose wife will she be?' Jesus said to them, '. . . when they rise from the dead, they neither marry nor are given in marriage'"		Matt. 22:23–33 Luke 20:27–35
12:38–40		"Beware of the scribes. . . they devour widows' houses"		Luke 21:2–4
12:42–4	"A poor widow came and put in two small copper coins"			Luke 21:2–4
13:17		"Woe to those who are pregnant and to those who are nursing infants in those days"		Matt. 24:19 Luke 21:23

REF.	DESCRIPTION			PARALLELS
	women named	*speeches by Jesus*	*speeches by others*	
14:3–9	A woman anoints Jesus with ointment at Bethany			Matt. 26:6–13 John 12:3–8
14:66–70	"One of the servant-girls came by..." Peter's denial			Matt.26:69–71 Luke 22: 56–7 John 18: 16–17
15:40–41	There were also women looking on from a distance; among them Mary Magdalene, and Mary the mother of James... and of Joses, and Salome"			Matt. 27:55–6 Luke 23:49 John 19:25–7
15:47	"Mary Magdalene and Mary the mother of Joses saw where the body was laid"			Matt. 27:61 Luke 23:55
16:1–8	Mary Magdalene, Mary the mother of James, and Salome at the tomb. The young man's message			Matt. 28:1–8 Luke 24:1–10 John 20: 1–2
16:9–11	"[Jesus] appeared first to Mary Magdalene... She went out..."			John 20:11–18

THE GOSPEL OF LUKE

REF.	DESCRIPTION			PARALLELS
	women named	*speeches by Jesus*	*speeches by others*	
1:5–25	Elizabeth. Announcement of the birth of John the Baptist			
1:26–38	Annunciation to Mary: "you will conceive. . . and bear a son. . . Elizabeth. . . has also conceived a son. . ."			Matt. 1:18
1:39–45	"Mary set out. . . to a. . . town in the hill country. . .". Visitation to Elizabeth			
1:46–56	"And Mary said, 'My soul magnifies the Lord. . .'"			
1:57–8	"Now the time came for Elizabeth to give birth. . ."			
1:59–66	". . . to name him. . . But his mother said, 'No, he is to be called John'"			
2:5–7	Mary goes with Joseph to Bethlehem and there gives birth to Jesus			Matt. 1:25
2:16–19	The shepherds come: "and found Mary and Joseph, and the child"			
2:22–35	Presentation in the Temple; Simeon's prophecy regarding the child's mother			
2:36	"There was also a prophet, Anna. . ."			

REF.	DESCRIPTION			PARALLELS
	women named	*speeches by Jesus*	*speeches by others*	
2:41–50	Jesus and the teachers; Mary's words and Jesus' reply			
2:51	"Then he went down with them and came to Nazareth, and was obedient to them. His mother treasured . . . in her heart"			
3:19–20	". . .because of Herodias. . .": John the Baptist shut up in prison			Matt. 14:3–4 Mark 6:17–19
4:25–6		". . . there were many widows in Israel. . . yet Elijah was sent to none of them, except to a widow at Zarephath in Sidon"		
4:38–9	"he entered Simon's house. . ."; Simon's mother-in-law healed			Matt. 8:14–15 Mark 1; 29–31
7:12–15	"his mother's only son, and she was a widow." Raising of the widow of Nain's son			
7:28		"I tell you, among those born of women. . ."		Matt. 11:11
7:37–50	"And a woman in the city, who was a sinner. . ."; the woman forgiven			

REF.	DESCRIPTION			PARALLELS
	women named	*speeches by Jesus*	*speeches by others*	
8:1–3	"... he went on through cities and villages.... The twelve were with him, as well as some women... Mary, called Magdalene... Joanna... Susannah, and many others, who provided for him out of their resources"			
8:19–21	"Then his mother and his brothers came to him... And he was told... But said to them, 'My mother and my brothers are those...'"			
8:41–56	Healing of the woman suffering from hemorrhages and raising of Jairus' daughter			Matt. 9:18–26 Mark 5:22–43
10:38–42	"... he entered a certain village, where a woman named Martha welcomed him into her home. She had a sister named Mary..."			
11:27–8	"... a woman in the crowd raised her voice and said to him, 'Blessed is the womb that bore you and the breasts that nursed you!'"			
11:31		"The queen of the South will rise at the judgment with the people of this generation..."		Matt. 12:42

REF.	DESCRIPTION			PARALLELS
	women named	*speeches by Jesus*	*speeches by others*	
12:45		". . . and begins to beat the other slaves, men and women. . ."		
12:53		"they will be divided. . . mother against daughter and daughter against mother. . ."		Matt. 10:35
13:11–13	". . . there appeared a woman. . . bent over. . ."			
13:16		"And ought not this woman, a daughter of Abraham. . . be set free. . . on the sabbath day?"		
13:21		"It is like the yeast that a woman took and mixed in. . ."		Matt. 13:33
14:20		"Another said, 'I have just been married and therefore I cannot come'"		
14:26		"Whoever comes to me and does not hate father and mother, wife and children. . ."		Matt. 10:37
15:8–9		"Or what woman having ten silver coins, if she loses one of them. . . When she has found it, she calls together her friends and neighbors. . ."		
15:30		". . . who has devoured your property with prostitutes. . ."		

REF.	DESCRIPTION			PARALLELS
	women named	*speeches by Jesus*	*speeches by others*	
16:18		"Anyone who divorces his wife and marries another... whoever marries a woman divorced..."		Matt. 5:31–2; 19:9 Mark 10:11–12
17:27		"They were... marrying and being given in marriage, until the day Noah..."		Matt. 24:38
17:32		"Remember Lot's wife"		
17:35		"... two women grinding meal together... one will be taken and the other left"		Matt. 24:41
18:3–5		"In that city there was a widow..."		
18:20		"Honor your father and mother"		Matt. 19:19 Mark 10:19
18:29–30		"... there is no one who has left house or wife... who will not get back..."		Matt. 19:29
20:27–35		"... asked him... '... if a man's brother dies, leaving a wife ...' Jesus said, '... marry... neither marry nor are given in marriage'"		Matt. 22:23–33 Mark 12:19–25
20:46–7		"Beware of the scribes... They devour widows' houses..."		Mark 12:38–40
21:2–4	"he also saw a poor widow put in two small copper coins"			Mark 12:42–4

REF.	DESCRIPTION			PARALLELS
	women named	*speeches by Jesus*	*speeches by others*	
21:23		"Woe to those who are pregnant and to those who are nursing infants in those days"		Matt. 24:19 Mark 13:17
22:56–7	"Then a servant-girl... stared at him and said, 'This man also was with him.' But he denied it, saying, 'Woman, I do not know him.'"			Matt. 26:69–71 Mark 14:66–70 John 18:16–17
23:27–31	"... among them were women who were beating their breasts and wailing for him. But Jesus turned to them and said, 'Daughters of Jerusalem...'"			
23:49	"But all his acquaintance including the women who had followed him from Galilee..."			Matt. 27:55–6 Mark 15:40–41 John 19: 25–7
23:55–6	"The women who had come with him from Galilee... and they saw the tomb..."			Matt. 27:61 Mark 15:47
24:1–11	The women at the tomb. The angels' message. "... they told all this to the eleven and to all the rest. Now it was Mary Magdalene, Joanna, Mary the mother of James, and the other women with them who told this... they did not believe them"			Matt. 28:1–8 Mark 16:1–8 John 20:1–2
24:22–4			"Moreover, some women... came back and told us that they had indeed seen a vision..."	

THE GOSPEL OF JOHN

REF.	DESCRIPTION			PARALLELS
	women named	*speeches by Jesus*	*speeches by others*	
2:1–11	"... there was a wedding in Cana of Galilee, and the mother of Jesus was there. Jesus and his disciples had also been invited..."			
2:12	"... he went down to Capernaum with his mother..."			
3:4			"Can one enter a second time into the mother's womb...?" "He who has the bride is the bridegroom"	
4:7–42	The Samaritan woman			
6:42			"... whose father and mother we know"	Matt. 13:55–6 Mark 6:3
11:1–45	Lazarus, Mary and Martha			
12:1–8	Jesus at Bethany in the house of Lazarus, Martha and Mary. Martha serves him. He is anointed by Mary.			
16:21		"When a woman is in labor, she has pain"		
18:16–17	"... spoke to the woman who guarded the gate, and brought Peter in. The woman said to Peter..."			Matt. 26:69–71 Mark 14:66–70 Luke 22:56–7

REF.	DESCRIPTION			PARALLELS
	women named	speeches by Jesus	speeches by others	
19:25–7	Standing near the cross of Jesus were his mother, and his mother's sister, Mary the wife of Clopas, and Mary Magdalene."			Matt. 27:55–6 Mark 15:40–41 Luke 23:49
20:1–2	"Mary Magdalene came to the tomb... So she ran and went to Simon Peter..."			Matt. 28:1–8 Mark 16:1–8 Luke 24:1–10
20:11–18	Two angels and then Jesus appear to Mary Magdalene			Mark 16:9–11

BIBLIOGRAPHY

A – Basic Bibliography on Women and the Gospels

Adinolfi, Marco. *Il femminismo della Bibbia*. Rome: Spicilegium Pontificii Athenaei Antoniani, 1981.

Alcalá, Manuel. *La mujer y los ministerios en la Iglesia*. Salamanca: Sígueme, 1982.

Ambroggi, Pietro De. "Maria Maddalena." EC 8 (1952), pp. 138–41.

André-Vincent, P.-M. *Marie Madeleine et la Sainte-Baume*. Paris: Téqui, 1980 (1st ed., 1950).

——————. *Marie Madeleine et le mystère pascal*. Paris: Téqui, 1983.

Aubert, Jean-Marie. *La femme: antiféminisme et christianisme*. Paris: Cerf-Desclée, 1975.

Avi-Yonah, Michael. "Magdala." *En Ju* 11, p. 685.

Badet, R. P., *Jésus et les femmes dans l'évangile*. Paris-Lyons: Delhomme et Briguet, 1893.

Bartolomei, Maria Cristina. "*La Parola di Dio e le parole delle donne.*" *Le scomode figlie di Eva. Le comunità cristiane di base si interrogano sui percorsi di ricerca delle donne*. Rome, Ed. Com. Nuovi Tempi, 1989, pp. 41–61.

——————. "Il soggetto e la parola dell'altro. A proposito della interpretazione femminista della Bibbia." *Annali di Storia dell'Esegesi 1* (1990), pp. 323–34.

Blank, J. "Frauen in den Jesusüberlieferungen." Various. *Die Frau im Urchristentum*. Freiburg: Herder, 1983, pp. 32ff.

Boff, Leonardo. *O rostro materno de Deus. Ensaio interdisciplinar sobre o feminino e suas formas religiosas*. Petrópolis, RJ: Vozes, 1979. Eng. trans. *The Maternal Face of God*. New York: Harper, 1980.

Bonora, Antonio. "Riflessioni bibliche sulla liberazione e promozione della donna." *Humanitas* 32 (1977), pp. 630–49.

Bovon, François. "Le privilège pascal de Marie-Madeleine." *New Test. Stud.* 30 (1984), pp. 50–62.

Brooten, Bernadette. "Feminist Perspectives on New Testament Exegesis." *Concilium* 138 (1980), pp. 55–61.

Brown, Raymond E. "Die Rolle der Frau im vierten Evangelium." Elisabeth Moltmann-Wendel (ed.). *Frauenbefreiung – Biblische und Theologische Argumente.* Mainz: Grünewald-Kaiser, 1978, pp. 133–47.

—————. *The Community of the Beloved Disciple.* New York: Paulist Press, 1979.

Bruckberger, R. L. *Marie Madeleine.* Paris, 1952.

Burigana, Renato, Roberto Fiorini and Silvano Scarpat. *Dalla Galilea a Gerusalemme. L'itinerario delle donne nel Vangelo di Luca.* Vicenza: Ed. LIEF, 1988.

Buzzetti, Carlo. "Gesù e le donne." *ParVi* 20 (1975), pp. 433–50.

Calmet, Augustin. "Dissertation sur les trois Maries." *Commentaire de l'Evangile de S. Luc.* Paris: Emery, 1726, pp. 403–10.

De Bérulle, Pierre, "Elevation à Jesus-Christ Notre-Seigneur sur la conduite de son Esprit et de sa Grâce vers Sainte Madeleine." J. P. Migne (ed.). *Oeuvres complètes.* Paris, 1856, cc. 531–96.

Di Bari, Nicola. *Il culto di S. Maria Maddalena in Puglia.* Bari: Facultas Theologica "A. S. Nicolao," 1988.

Diez Macho, A. "Magdala." *En Bi* 4, pp. 832–5.

Dolto, Françoise and Gérard Sévérin. *L'évangile au risque de la psychanalyse,* 2 vols. Paris: Delarge, 1977, 1978.

Duperray, Eve (ed.). *Maria Madeleine dans la mystique, les arts et les lettres.* Paris: Beauchesne, 1989.

—————. and Christian Laury (eds). *Marie Madeleine.* Fontaine de Vaucluse, 1988.

Evans, Mary J. *Woman in the Bible.* Exeter: The Paternoster Press, 1983.

Fabris Rinaldo-Gozzini, Vilma. *La donna nell'esperienza della prima chiesa.* Rome: Paoline, 1982.

—————. "Donna: una rilettura biblica." *La donna nella chiesa e nel mondo.* Naples: Dehoniane, 1988, pp. 101–10.

Faillon, E. M. *Monuments inédits sur l'apostolat de sainte Marie-Madeleine en Provence*, 2 vols. Paris: Petit-Montrouge, 1848.

Falk Ze'ev, W. "Women." *Introduction to Jewish Law of the Second Commonwealth*, part 2. Leiden, E. J. Brill, 1978, pp. 261–3.

Feuillet, André. "Les deux onctions faites sur Jésus, et Marie-Madeleine." *Revue Thomiste* 75 (1975), pp. 357–94.

————. "Le récit johannique de l'onction de Béthanie (Jn. 12, 1–8)." *Esprit et Vie* 14 (1985), pp. 193–203.

Flanagan, Neal M. "The Position of Women in The Writings of St Luke." *Marianum* 40 (1978), pp. 288–304.

Florentin-Smyth, Françoise. "Ce que la bible ne dit pas de la femme." *Études théologiques et religieuses* 40 (1965), pp. 76–9.

Fossati, Roberta. *E Dio creò la donna. Chiesa, religione e condizione femminile*. Milan: Mazzotta, 1977.

Garzonio, Marco. *Gesù e le donne*. Milan: Rizzoli, 1990.

Genest, Olivette. "Évangiles et femmes." *Science et Esprit* 37 (1985) pp. 275–95.

Gerstenberger, Erhard S. and Wolfgang Schrage. *Frau und Mann*. Stuttgart: Kohlammer, 1980.

Giavini, Gianni. "La donna nella Bibbia. Appunti per un discorso." *La scuola cattolica* 3 (1981), pp. 258–69.

Gramaglia, Pier Angelo. "La prassi di Gesù." *Tertulliano. De Virginibus Velandis*. Rome: Borla, 1984, esp. pp. 59–81.

Grassi, Joseph and Carolyn. *Mary Magdalene and Women in Jesus' Life*. Kansas City: Sheed & Ward, 1986.

Guillaume, Paul-Marie. "Marie Madeleine (Sainte)." *DSp* 10 (1979) pp. 559–75.

Hébrard, Monique. *Dieu et les femmes*. Paris: Centurion-Cerf, 1982.

Heister, Maria-Sybilla. *Frauen in der biblischen Glaubensgeschichte*. Göttingen: Vandenhoeck & Ruprecht, 1984.

Heinzelmann, Gertrud. *Die geheiligte Diskriminierung: Beiträge zum Kirchlichen Feminismus*. Bonstetten-Zurich: Interfeminas, 1986.

Hengel, Martin. "Maria Magdalena und die Frauen als Zeugen." *Abraham unser Vater. Festschrift O. Michel*. Leiden-Cologne: AGSU 5 (1963), pp. 243–56.

Hölscher, Gustav. "Magdala." *RE* 14, p. 298.

Holzemeister, Urban. "Die Magdalenenfrage in der Kirchlichen Überlieferung." *ZKTH* 46 (1922), pp. 402–22, 556–84.

Kelen, Jacqueline. *Un amour infini. Marie Madeleine, prostituée sacrée.* Paris: Albin Michel, 1982.

Ketter, Peter. *Christus und die Frauen.* Düsseldorf: Verbandsverlag weiblicher Vereine, 1933.

Kipper, Balduino. "Maria Maddalena." *Enciclopedia de la Bibblia* 4 (1964), pp. 1315–8.

Lacordaire, Henri Dominique. *Sainte Marie Madeleine.* Paris: Poussielgue Rusand, 1860.

Lagrange, Marie Joseph. "Jésus a-t-il été oint plusieurs fois et par plusieurs femmes?." *Revue biblique* 9 (1912), pp. 504–32.

Laluque, Bernard. "Quand Marseille fut évangélisée par une femme." *Marseille* 148 (1987), pp. 50–57.

————. "Marie de Nazareth et Marie de Magdala figures de l'Eglise." *Revue Carmel* 35 (1984), pp. 228–38.

Lardner Carmady, Denise. *Biblical Woman. Contemporary Reflections on Scriptural Texts.* New York: Crossroad, 1988.

Laurentin, René. "Jesus and Women: An Underestimated Revolution." *Concilium* 134 (1980), pp. 80–92.

Légasse, Simon. "Jésus et les prostituées." *R.Th.L.* 7 (1976), pp. 137–54.

Legrand, Lucien. "Women's Ministries in the New Testament." *BBIBQ* 2 (1976), pp. 286–99.

Leipoldt, Johannes. *Die Frau in der antiken Welt und im Urchristentum.* Gütersloh: Olms, 1962, pp. 81–98.

Lemonnyer, Antoine, O.P. "Onction de Béthanie. Notes d'exégèse sur Jean XII, 1–8." *Mélanges Grandmaison.* Paris, 1928, pp. 105–17.

Magli, Ida. *Gesù di Nazaret. Tabù e trasgressione.* Milan: Rizzoli, 1982.

Mâle, Emile. *Les Saints compagnons du Christ.* Paris: Beauchesne, 1958, rp. 1988.

Mali, H. Eugene. "Women and the Gospel of Luke." *BThB* 10 (1980), pp. 99–104

Mattioli, Umberto, "Asthéneia e andreìa." *Aspetti della femminilità nella letteratura classica, biblica e cristiana antica.* Rome: Bulzoni, 1983.

Martini, Carlo Maria. *La donna nel suo popolo.* Milan: Ancora, 1984.

Moltmann-Wendel, Elisabeth. *Freiheit-Gleichheit-Schwesterlichkeit. Zur Emanzipation der Frau in Kirche und Gesellschaft.* Munich: Kaiser, 1977.

———. *Ein eigener Mensch werden. Frauen um Jesus.* Gütersloh: Mohn, 1980. Eng. trans. *The Women around Jesus.* New York: Crossroad, 1982.

Monod, Adolphe. "Marie de Magdala." *Encyclopédie des sciences religieuses* 8 (1880), pp. 714–6.

Montagna, Davide. "Rassegna bibliografica sulla teologia della donna," *Servitium* 8 (1975), pp. 245–67.

Mosco, Marilena (ed.). *La Maddalena tra Sacro e Profano.* Milan-Florence: Mondadori–La Casa Usher, 1986.

Oepke, Albrecht. "γυνή." *TWNT* 1 (1935), pp. 775–90.

Parazzoli, Ferruccio. *Gesù e le donne.* Milano: Paoline, 1989.

Parvez, Emmanuel. "Mary Magdalene: Sinner or Saint?" *BToday* 23 (1985), pp. 122–4.

Parvey, Constance F. *Ordination of Women in Ecumenical Perspective: Workbook for the Church's Future.* Geneva: WCC, 1980.

Pesce, Mauro. "Discepolato gesuano e discepolato rabbinico. Problemi e prospettive della comparazione." *ANRW* II 25/1. Berlin: Walter De Gruyter, 1982, pp. 351–89.

Petraglio, Renzo. "Maria figlia e fine del potere del sangue." *Il Tetto* 152–3 (1989), pp. 240–60.

———. " . . . e tutti profetaranno." *MO* 9 (1988), pp. 32–7.

Pirot, Jean. *Trois amies de Jésus de Nazareth.* Paris: Cerf, 1986.

Quéré, France. *Les femmes de l'Evangile.* Paris: Seuil, 1982.

Quesnell, Quentin. "The Women at Luke's Supper." Cassidy Scharper (ed.). *Political Issues in Luke-Acts.* Maryknoll, N.Y.: Orbis Books, 1983, pp. 59–70.

Ricci, Carla. "Maria: dimenticare per ricordare. Frammenti di pensieri per un tentativo di incontro." Various. *Se a parlare di Maria sono le donne*. Milan: In Dialogo, 1988, pp. 5–21.

──────. "Pensare la differenza nell'esegesi." *Progetto donna* 2–3 (1989), pp. 41–5.

──────. "Gesù e le donne." *Famiglia domani* 2 (1990), pp. 41–5.

──────. "Esegesi del silenzio: dall'assenza delle donne nei testi alla presenza delle donne accanto a Gesù." C. Militello (ed.). *Donna e Ministero. Un dibattito ecumenico*. Rome: Dehoniana, 1991, pp. 486–96

Rigato, Maria Luisa. "Donne testimoni della resurrezione." Salvatore Spera (ed.). *Donne e uomini nella chiesa*. Atti VII Primavera di Santa Chiara 1987, Rome: Vivere in, 1988.

──────. "Tradizione e redazione in Mc 1,:29, 31 (e paralleli). La guarigione della suocera di Simon Pietro." *RivBibIt* 17 (1969), pp. 139–74.

Ritt, H. "Die Frauen und die Osterbotschaft." *Die Frau in Urchristentum*. Freiburg: Herder, pp. 117–33.

Russel, Letty. *Feminist Interpretation of the Bible*. Philadelphia, PA: Westminster Press, 1985.

Saxer, Victor. "Maria Maddalena." *Biblioteca Sanctorum* 8 (1966), pp. 1081–104.

──────. "Marie Madeleine." *Catholicisme* 8 (1979), pp. 632–8.

──────. "Santa Maria Maddalena dalla storia evangelica alla leggenda e all'arte." Marilena Mosco (ed.). *La Maddalena tra Sacro e Profano*. Milan–Florence: Mondadori–La Casa Usher, 1986.

──────. "Le culte et la tradition de Sainte Marie Madeleine en Provence." *Mémoire de l'Academie de Vaucluse* 7 (1985), pp. 41–55.

──────. "Le culte de la Madeleine à Vézelay et de Lazare à Autun: un problème d'antériorité et d'origine." *Bulletin de la Société des Fouilles Archéologiques et des Monuments Historiques de L'Yonne* 3 (1986), pp. 1–18.

──────. "Les origines du culte en Occident." Eve Duperray (ed.). *Marie Madeleine dans la mystique, les arts et les lettres*. Paris: Beauchesne, 1989, pp. 33–47.

——————. "Les saintes Marie de Madeleine et Marie de Béthanie dans la tradition liturgique et homilétique d'orient." *Revue des sciences religieuses* 32 (1958), pp. 1–37.

Schlatter, Adolf. "Die beiden Schwerter, Lk 22:35–38." *Beiträge zur Forderung chr. Theologie* 20 (1916), pp. 487ff.

Schottroff, Luise. "Maria Magdalena und die Frauen am Grabe Jesu." *Evth* 42 (1982), pp. 3–25.

Schüssler Fiorenza, Elisabeth. "Il ruolo delle donne nel movimento cristiano primitivo." *Concilium* 111 (1976), pp. 21–36. [No Eng. ed.]

——————. *In Memory of Her. A Feminist Theological Reconstruction of Christian Origins.* New York: Crossroad, 1983.

Sicard, Maximin-Martial. *Sainte Marie-Madeleine*, 3 vols. Paris: A. Savaète, 1904–1910.

Spadafora, Francesco. "Maria di Cleofa." *Bibliotheca Sanctorum* 8 (1967), p. 972.

Swidler, Leonard. "Il Gesù degli Evangeli era femminista." F. V. Joannes (ed.) *Crisi dell'antifemminismo.* Milan: Mondadori, 1973, pp. 135–58.

——————. *Biblical Affirmations of Woman.* Philadelphia, PA: Westminster Press, 1979.

Testori, Giovanni and Gianfranco Ravas. *Maddalena.* Milan: F. M. Ricci, 1989.

Tetlow, Elisabeth Meier. *Women and Ministry in the New Testament: Called to Serve.* Lauham, N.Y.: University Press of America, 1980.

Trémaudan (De), Ernestine. *Jésus Christ et la femme.* Paris: Desclée, 1897.

Tunc, Suzanne. *Brève historie des femmes chrétiennes.* Paris: Cerf, 1989, pp. 23–76.

Valerio, Adriana. "Women in Church History." *Concilium* 182 (1985), pp. 63–71.

——————. "Gesù e la samaritana: la donna di fronte al regno." *Ricerca* Jan.–Feb. 1987, pp. 31–2 (Atti del 48esimo Congresso Nazionale FUCI).

——————. "Femminismo." *Nuovo Dizionario di Teologia Morale.* Milan: Paoline, 1990, pp. 420–9.

Von Speyr, Adrienne, *Drei Frauen und der Herr*. Einsiedeln: Johannes Verlag, 1978.

Walter, Karin (ed.). *Frauen entdecken die Bibel*. Freiburg: Herder, 1986.

Wijngaards, John. *Did Christ rule out Women Priests?* Great Wakering, Essex: Mayhew McCrimmon, 1977.

Witherington, Ben, III. "On the Road with Mary Magdalene, Joanna, Susanna and Other Disciples – Luke 8,1–3." *ZNW* 70 (1979), pp. 243–8.

——————. *Women in the Ministry of Jesus*. Cambridge: Cambridge University Press, 1984.

Wolff, Hanna. *Jesus der Mann: die Gestalt Jesu in tiefenpsychologischer Sicht*. Stuttgart: Radius, 1975.

Zarri, Adriana. "Donna." *Dizionario enciclopedico di teologia morale*. Rome: Paoline, 1973.

——————. *E' più facile che un cammello* . . . . Turin: Gribaudi, 1975.

B – Principal General Works Consulted

Benoît, Pierre and M. E. Boismard. *Synopse des quatre évangiles en français avec parallèles des apocryphes et des Pères*, 2 vols. Paris: Cerf, 1965.

Beyer, Hermann Wolfang. "διακονέω," *TWNT* 2 (1935), pp. 91–4.

——————. "θεραπεύω," *TWNT* III (1938), pp. 128–32.

Blendiger, Christian. "ἀκολουθτεω," *DCBNT* I (1970), p. 1718.

Boman, Thorleif. *Die Jesus Überlieferung im Lichte der neueren Volkskunde*. Göttingen: Vandenhoeck & Ruprecht, 1967.

Bonsirven, Joseph. *Textes rabbiniques des deux premiers siècles chrétiens*. Rome: PIB, 1955.

Bovon, François (ed.). *Analyse structurelle et exégèse biblique*. Neuchâtel: Delachaux et Niestlé, 1971.

——————. *Luc le théologien. Vingt-cinq ans de recherches (1950–1975)*. Paris, 1978.

Brown, Raymond E. *The Gospel According to John*, 2 vols. Garden City, N.Y.: Doubleday, 1966, 1971.

Cantarella, Eva. *L'ambiguo malanno. Condizione e immagine della donna nell'antichità*. Rome: Riuniti, 1981.

Daniel-Rops, Henri. *La vie quotidienne en Palestine au temps de Jésus*. Paris: Hachette, 1961.

Destro, Adriana. *In caso di gelosia. Antropologia del rituale di Satah*. Bologna: Il Mulino, 1989.

Dommershausen, Werner. *Die Umwelt Jesu: Politik und Kultur in Neutestamentlicher Zeit*. Freiburg-Basle-Vienna: Herder, n.d.

Dupont, Jacques. "A che punto è la ricerca sul Gesù storico?" Various. *Conoscenza storica di Gesù. Acquisizioni esegetiche e utilizzazioni nelle cristologie contemporanee*. Brescia: Paideia, 1978, pp. 7–31.

—————. "Le *logion* des douze trônes (Mt.19, 28, Lc.22, 28–30)." *Bib* 45 (1964), pp. 355–92.

—————. "Le douzième apôtre (Actes 1,15–26): à propos d'une explication récente," W. C. Weinrich (ed.). *The New Testament Age. Essay in Honor of Bo Reicke*, vol. I. Macon, GA: Mercer U. P., 1984, pp. 139–45.

Easton Burton, Scott. *The Gospel According to St. Luke. A Critical and Exegetical Commentary*. Edinburgh: T. & T. Clark, 1926.

Ernst, Josef. *Das Evangelium nach Lukas*. Regensburg: Pustet, 1977.

—————. *Lukas. Ein theologisches Portrait*. Düsseldorf: Patmos, 1985.

Fabris, Rinaldo. *Gesù di Nazaret. Storia e interpretazione*. Assisi: Cittadella, 1983.

Fitzmyer, Joseph A. *The Gospel According to Luke*, 2 vols. *The Anchor Bible, 28/28A*. Garden City, N.Y.: Doubleday, 1981–5.

Foerster, Werner. "δαίμων." *TWNT* II (1935), pp. 1–21.

Fusco, Vittorio. "Tre approcci storici a Gesù." *Ra Te* 4 (1982) pp. 311–28.

Gnilka, Joseph. *Marco*. Assisi: Cittadella, 1987.

Godet Fernand. *Commentaire sur l'évangile de Saint Luc*, 2 vols. Paris: Sandoz et Fischbacher, 1872, p. 2.

Graber, Friedrich and Dietrich Müller. "θεραπεύω e ἰάομαι." *DCBNT* I (1970), pp. 1644–50.

Grob, Rudolf. "ἅπτω." *DCBNT* I (1970), pp. 1874–6.

Grundmann, Walter. *Das Evangelium nach Lukas.* Berlin: Evangelische Verlag, 1963.

——————. "La potenza di Cristo." *TWNT* II (1935), pp. 300–19.

Guillaume, Jean Marie. *Luc interprète des anciennes traditions sur la résurrection de Jésus.* Paris: Gabalda, 1979.

Harrington, W. J. *The Gospel according to Luke.* London: Geoffrey Chapman, 1968.

Hess, Klaus, "διακονέω." *DCBNT*, pp. 1734–9.

Hobbs, Herschell H. *An Exposition of The Gospel of Luke.* Grand Rapids, MI: Baker Book House, 1966.

Hug, Joseph, *La finale de l'Évangile de Marc (Mc 16,9–20).* Paris: Gabalda, 1978.

Jacobelli, Maria Caterina. *Sacerdozio-donna-celibato. Alcune considerazioni antropologiche.* Rome: Borla, 1981.

Jeremias, Joachim. *Jerusalem zur Zeit Jesu. Eine kulturgeschichtliche Untersuchung zur neutestamentlichen Zeitgeschichte.* Göttingen: Vandenhoeck & Ruprecht, 1962. Eng. trans. *Jerusalem in the Time of Jesus.* London: SCM Press; New York: Macmillan, 1973.

Kittel, Gerard. "ἀκολουθέω," *TWNT* 1 (1933) pp. 210–16.

Laconi, Mauro. *S. Luca e la sua chiesa.* Turin: Gribaudi, 1986.

Lagrange, Marie Joseph. *Evangile selon Saint Luc.* Paris: Lecoffre, 1921.

Manson, Thomas Walter. *The Sayings of Jesus as recorded in the Gospels according to St. Matthew and St. Luke.* London: SCM Press, 1949.

Martini, Carlo Maria. "Tecniche della ricerca biblica." Giuseppe De Gennaro (ed.). *L'Antropologia biblica.* Naples: Dehoniane, 1981, pp. 205–7.

——————. *L'evangelizzatore in S. Luca.* Milan: Ancora, 1980.

Metzger, Bruce M. *A Textual Commentary on the Greek New Testament.* Stuttgart: United Bible Societies, 1971.

Neusner, Jacob. *Method and Meaning in Ancient Judaism: Second Series, Brown Judaic Studies 15.* Missoula, MA: Scholars Press, 1981.

—————. *Judaism in the Beginning of Christianity.* Philadelphia, PA: Fortress Press, 1984.

Nolli, Gianfranco. *Evangelo secondo Luca.* Vatican City: Ed. Vaticana, 1983.

Paoli, Arturo. *La radice dell'uomo. Meditazioni sul vangelo di Luca.* Brescia: Morcelliana, 1972.

Penna, Renato. *Letture evangeliche. Saggi esegetici sui quattro evangeli.* Rome: Borla, 1989.

Peppe, Leo. *Posizione giuridica e ruolo sociale della donna romana in età repubblicana.* Milan: Giuffrè, 1984.

Pesce, Mauro. "La profezia cristiana come anticipazione del giudizio escatologico in 1 Cor. 14, 24–25." Various. *Testimonium Christi. Scritti in onore di Jacques Dupont.* Brescia: Paideia, 1985, pp. 379–438.

—————. "La trasformazione dei documenti religiosi: dagli scritti protocristiani al Canone neotestamentario." *Ve Chr* 26 (1989), pp. 307–26.

Pesch, Rudolf. *Das Markusevangelium, I Teil.* Freiburg: Herder, 2d ed. 1977.

Petraglio, Renzo. "La Bibbia latina e la morale." *RTM* (1976), pp. 543–68.

Pirenne, Jacques. "Le statut de la femme dans la civilisation hébraïque." *La femme. Recueils de la Société Jean Bodin.* Brussels: Librairie Encyclopédique XI (1959), pp. 107–26.

Plummer, Alfred. "A Critical and Exegetical Commentary on the Gospel According to St. Luke." *The International Critical Commentary* 4. Edinburgh: T. & T. Clark, 1896, p. 5.

Pomeroy, Sarah B. *Goddesses, Whores, Wives, and Slaves.* New York: Schocken Books, 1975.

Prat, Ferdinand. *Jésus Christ, sa vie, sa doctrine, son oeuvre,* 2 vols. Paris: Beauchesne, 1933.

Prete, Benedetto. *Storia e teologia nel vangelo di Luca.* Bologna: Studio teologico Domenicano, 1973.

Radermakers, Jean and Philippe Bossuyt. *Jésus. Parole de la Grâce selon saint Luc.* Brussels: Institut d'études théologiques, 1981.

Rengstorf, Karl Heinrich. *Das Evangelium nach Lukas.* Göttingen: Vandenhoeck & Ruprecht, 1969.

——. "μαθήτρια." *TWNT* 4 (1942), p. 465.

——. "ἀποστέλλω." *TWNT* 1 (1933), pp. 397–448.

——. "δώδεκα." *TWNT* 2 (1935), pp. 321–8.

——. "διδάσκω." *TWNT* 2 (1935), p. 157.

——. "μαθετής." *TWNT* 4 (1942), pp. 417–65.

Romney Wegner, Judith. *Chattel or Person? The Status of Women in the Mishnah.* New York–Oxford: Oxford University Press 1988.

Rouiller, Gregoire and C. Varone. *Evangile selon Saint Luc.* Fribourg: Rouiller, 1980.

Sadler, M. F. *The Gospel According to Luke.* London: Bell, 3d ed. 1889.

Saulnier, Christiane and Bernard Rolland. *La Palestine aux temps de Jésus.* Paris: Cerf, 1978.

Schillebeeckx, Eduard. *Jesus, het verhaal van een levende.* Bloemendal: Nelissen, 1974. Eng. trans. *Jesus: An Experiment in Christology.* London: Collins; New York: Harper & Row, 1979.

Schlatter, Adolf. *Das Evangelium des Lukas aus seinen Quellen erklärt.* Stuttgart: Clawer, 1931.

——. "Die beiden Schwerter. Lk 22, 35–38." *BFchTh* 20 (1916), pp. 487ff.

Schmid, Josef. *Das Evangelium nach Lukas.* Regensburg: Pustet, 1951.

——. *Das Evangelium nach Markus.* Regensburg: Pustet, 1955.

Schnackenburg, Rudolf. *The Gospel according to St John,* vol. 2. London: Burns & Oates; New York: Crossroad, 1974.

Schürmann, Heinz. *Das Lucasevangelium,* vol. 2. Freiburg: Herder, 1969.

Schweizer, Eduard. *Das Evangelium nach Lukas.* Göttingen: Vandenhoeck & Ruprecht, 1982.

Spinetoli, Ortensio da. Luca. *Il vangelo dei poveri.* Assisi: Cittadella, 1982.

Stuhlmüller, Carroll. "The Gospel According to Luke." *JBC* II (1968), pp. 115–64.

Talbert, Charles H. *Luke and the Gnostics: An Examination of the Lucan Purpose.* Nashville–New York: Abingdon Press, 1966.

Tertullian. *Adversus Marcionem.* C. Moreschini (ed.). Milan-Varese: Istit. ed. Cisalpino, 1971.

Theissen, Gerd. *Sociologie der Jesusbewegung: Ein Beitrag zur Entstehungsgeschichte des Urchristentums.* Munich: Kaiser, 1977.

Tostato, Angelo. *Il matrimonio nel giudaismo antico e nel Nuovo Testamento.* Rome: Città Nuova, 1976.

Various. *La parabola degli invitati al banchetto. Dagli evangelisti a Gesù.* Brescia: Paideia, 1978.

NAME INDEX

(Significant persons not given names are described: e.g. "woman forgiven, the.")

BIBLICAL INDEX

OLD TESTAMENT AND APOCRYPHA

NEW TESTAMENT